P9-CBY-946

DWARF RHODODENDRONS

I 'Curlew' (*ludlowii* x *fletcherianum*). Lepidote hybrid

Peter A. Cox

DWARF
RHODODENDRONS

Macmillan Publishing Co., Inc.
New York

Advisory Editor: C. D. Brickell, Director, Royal Horticultural
Society Garden, Wisley

Copyright © 1973 by Peter A. Cox

All rights reserved. No part of this book may be reproduced or
transmitted in any form or by any means, electronic or mechanical,
including photocopying, recording or by any information storage and
retrieval system, without permission in writing from the Publisher.

Macmillan Publishing Co., Inc.
866 Third Avenue, New York, N.Y. 10022

Library of Congress Catalog Card Number: 73–2752

First Printing 1973

Printed in Great Britain

Foreword

For years the urgent need for an up-to-date, authoritative publication on rhododendron species has been discussed at board meetings of the American Rhododendron Society. Much thought has been given to the possibilities for satisfying such a need and some explorations have been carried out. An awareness of the problem is shared by rhododendron lovers around the world.

Large and complex and at times confusing as our present knowledge of the genus has become, it seems unlikely that a single volume covering the entire subject by one qualified writer can be expected in the foreseeable future. It has seemed more realistic to hope for a number of authoritative works, perhaps by specialists in various segments of the genus. These contributions taken together would give the serious rhododendron student the technical references sufficient to satisfy all his needs. *Dwarf Rhododendrons* has fulfilled this concept in one area.

Peter Cox is particularly qualified by background for this work. He is the son of E. H. M. Cox, who as a young man accompanied Farrer into Southeast Asia to explore and collect plant material, and has been throughout his life a student, grower, author and recognized authority in the field of rhododendrons. His son became interested in the subject during his childhood, and later, with Hutchison, made collecting expeditions, notably to Turkey and to Assam in India. He lives in Perth, Scotland, which is fortunately close to Edinburgh, and the immense collection of species in the Royal Botanic Garden. Here there are a number of choice rhododendron gardens and a great variety of dwarf species, and, perhaps most important of all, one of the greatest collections of herbarium material in the world, preserved from many collectors' expeditions over the years.

To cover world rhododendron literature must have required an impressive amount of research time, but to describe the many species as well as hybrids that Cox presents must have taken even longer – a lifetime of dedication.

To some readers the most important part of the book will be the listing of species with descriptions adequate for their identification, cultural characteristics, ratings and other data. Others will value most the information as to where each species came from, who introduced them, and the soil and climatic conditions under which they grew in the wild. Indeed, our success in growing these introductions will be in direct proportion to our ability to create an environment in our gardens at least somewhat similar to that in which they were found in the wild.

Among the large number of species described in the book are the lepidotes, elepidotes, and some Malaysian species and Obtusum azaleas, followed by a list of hybrids suitable for the small garden. Other chapters are devoted to selection of plants, planning the garden, culture, propagation, and hybridizing. The author is to be commended for emphasizing the importance of a definite plan in hybridizing and of discussing with others appropriate goals in breeding. Many have dabbled with pollen for a lifetime and have come up with nothing because of lack of carefully considered objectives.

There is something for everyone here. For the beginner the rhododendron lore and background can be fascinating. The guidance on selection of plants, planting, culture and planning the garden will be of great importance to long-term enjoyment. The advanced student will find in the descriptive list of species just what he has been looking for.

The book could well be the constant companion of the grower from the time he selects his first plant until he has passed through all the phases of rhododendron mania and has finally attained the distinction of being a member of the rhododendron study group. It is ardently to be hoped that in the near future we shall see more of this kind of contribution from the pen of Peter Cox.

Carl H. Phetteplace, M.D.

Eugene, Oregon

Former President,
The American Rhododendron Society

Contents

Acknowledgments

Thanks are due to many people who have helped with information for this book. Firstly, my special gratitude to Mr D. M. Henderson, the Regius Keeper of the Royal Botanic Garden, Edinburgh, for the freedom of the herbarium, library and greenhouses and also to the following members of the staff: Dr D. F. Chamberlain, Mr H. H. Davidian, Mr R. Eudall, Mr Ian Hedge, Mr James Keenan, Mr M. V. Mathew, Mr David Parker, Dr Roy Watling, and Mr P. J. B. Woods.

To Mr Michael Black of Grasmere, Westmorland, Mr John T. Bryan of the Strybing Arboretum, San Francisco and Mr Jack O'Shannassy of Australia for notes on the Malesian species and their culture.

To Lord Aberconway for his Foreword and Dr Carl Phetteplace for his American Foreword and much advice, Dr August Kehr for data on American plant collectors and diseases and also Dr C. J. Gould, Professor H. A. J. Hoitink and Dr R. L. Ticknor on diseases and pests and Mr A. A. Childers on propagating.

To Mr John Bond of Windsor Great Park for assistance over examining the Species Collection, to Mr Chris Brickell, Director of Wisley Gardens, over checking the manuscript, Mr S. F. Christie for material of *R. roxieanum* var. *oreonastes*, and Dr C. North of the Scottish Horticultural Research station for hybridising information.

To Mr Snaebjorn Jonasson of Iceland for a list of successful plants there, Mr Schofield of South Africa about Obtusum Azaleas, Mr N. A. M. van Steekelenburg of the Netherlands for sending Year Books, Mr Tor G. Nitzelius of Sweden for list of species growing well there and Professor and Mrs Philipson of New Zealand for help over the Lapponicum series.

To the Royal Horticultural Society for honouring the book with their joint imprint.

For photographs, the Royal Botanic Gardens, Edinburgh for plates 2, 3, 4, 7, 8, 10, 12–16, 19, 23–6, 28, 29, 30 and 46, Mrs Betty Sherriff and the British Museum, Natural History for plates 1, 11, 20, 32 and 35, J. E. Downward for plates 9, 21, 22, 27, 31, 33, 41 and 43–5 and J. F. Evans for plates 37–40.

Very great thanks are due to Margaret Stones for her gift of the line drawings and for the beautiful coloured plates; also to Mr Peter C. Hutchison, my plant collecting and west coast gardening companion, for the distribution maps.

Last but by no means least, thanks are due to my wife and father who have been full of valuable suggestions and have spent many hours reading and checking drafts and proofs.

The Illustrations

A*

Introduction

This book has been written for those who already have a little knowledge of dwarf rhododendrons and I hope that it will encourage them to delve a little deeper into the subject with the interest and fascination these delightful plants merit.

With the general tendency towards smaller gardens and less hired manual help, these shrubs are proving to be ideal for limited spaces and where the usual annuals, herbaceous plants and roses need too much labour. The minimum of care and maintainance will keep them in good health, the majority are very long lived and all move easily at any age.

I have had a great deal of difficulty in deciding where a dwarf ceases to be a dwarf. So many factors are involved: a plant that reaches 10 feet (3·05 metres) in a sheltered Cornish garden may not exceed 3 feet (·914 metres) at 1,000 feet (304·8 metres) in Perthshire, Scotland. 5 feet (1·52 metres) has been my general limit but in order to include either a whole series or sub-series or a plant that varies in height according to form, this maximum has been stretched in many cases. Any book that only deals with part of a genus causes problems. I know people will say that several I have included are definitely not dwarfs in their own districts.

I have attempted to lay special emphasis on certain points, notably: the correlation of how species grow in the wild and in gardens; a comparison of the various rhododendron-growing areas of the world; encouragement to hybridize with a special purpose in mind; and the easy identification of species.

All the species and varieties that are thought to be in cultivation are described. Unfortunately, for many of the series complete revisions are badly overdue. I have taken the liberty of making a few changes in the classification and naming as printed in the 1967 Royal Horticultural Society's *Rhododendron Species Handbook*, and many of the descriptions have been altered where I find them at fault. It will be noticed that doubt is expressed over some of the details, especially in the relationship of one species to another. This is partly due to the lack of a revision and also because there is always bound to be disagreement about where one species ends and another begins in such a complex genus as *Rhododendron*.

The hybrid lists, apart from the Obtusum azaleas, have been made to include as many cultivars as possible that are in commerce at the present time. Of course a list like this soon becomes partially out of date.

Lastly, a brief description of the climate and conditions at Glendoick, Perthshire, East Scotland, where I base most of my comparisons. I should like to point out that our conditions are far from ideal. The winters are relatively mild, never below 0°F (−17·8°C) and the summers cool, rarely over 80°F (26·75°C). The real bugbear is the frequency of autumn and spring frosts which do appreciable damage to buds, flowers, growth and wood. Rainfall is about 30 inches (76 centimetres), falling throughout the year. Snow only falls some years and rarely lies long. Elevation is between 50 and 200 feet (15·2 to 61 metres) above sea-level. There is fairly good shelter from the north-west, the north and the north-east. Soil is a medium to medium-heavy loam, very short of organic matter. Drainage is generally good.

The following abbreviations have been used in the text:

AMRS–QB   American Rhododendron Society
          Quarterly Bulletin
RHS–RYB   Royal Horticultural Society
          Rhododendron Year Book
RHS–RCYB Royal Horticultural Society
          Rhododendron and Camellia Year Book

1 Rhododendrons in their Natural Habitat

Distribution of Species

Rhododendrons are almost entirely confined to the wetter mountain regions of the northern hemisphere. Their range has never extended naturally to the eminently suitable habitats of parts of New Zealand and Chile, where other ericaceous plants abound, presumably due to geological and evolutionary factors.

Two centres of distribution occur, one in north-west Yunnan and the other in New Guinea. Concerning the former, George Forrest had a theory that the centre of the genus, possibly its place of origin, is in the area where Tibet, Yunnan and Burma meet, around the river divides of Taron–Salween and Mekong–Salween. I shall not go into details of the distribution of the various series and species here, as it will be dealt with in Chapter 5, and also in the maps. Instead, I shall quote various passages from the writings of F. Kingdon Ward and others and also mention areas which have been virtually un-explored botanically.

Kingdon Ward, in *Plant Hunting on the Edge of the World* (*pp.* 312–4), mentioned two distinct alpine communities: (1) on very wet mountain ranges; (2) on drier ranges behind the great peaks. (1) includes the Adung Valley in Upper Burma with at least twelve species of dwarfs. In (2) there is much less variety with enormous areas covered by just two or three species. Kingdon Ward stated (RHS-RYB, 1949): 'Where the rain and mist are everlasting and the snow lies deep and long, there one will seek the greatest concentration and the greatest variety of species. Such a spot is the Doshong La [south-east Tibet].'

In *The Romance of Plant Hunting* (*pp.* 216–7) he said: 'From the Salween in the west to the Min River in the east, and from Kansu in the north to Yunnan in the south, these Lapponicum carpet rhododendrons cover the Alps as heather clothes the Highlands of Scotland.' In *The Riddle of the Tsangpo Gorges* (*p.* 92), he observed that 'it is uncommon to come across a really rare plant'.

Normally, the higher up a mountain one goes, the more dwarf a rhododendron becomes, but Forrest found a most unusual case of the reverse process. In the *Gardeners Chronicle* (LI, 1323, 1912, 291–2), he recorded: 'The pass is a comparatively shallow depression about two miles in length by half a mile in breadth, with open pasture on both sides for some distance up slopes, and from there to the tops of the low hills about 1,000' high is rhododendron forest.' In the foreground he saw a dwarf, probably *R. fastigiatum*, 1–2 feet (30–60 centimetres) high, behind which were masses of *R. yunnanense*, 12 feet (3·66 metres) high; next he came across *R. argyrophyllum* (20 feet; 6·09 metres); and between these and the verge of the alpine pasture on the summits of the hills were thick forests of tree rhododendrons 20–40 feet (6·09–12·2 metres) high, with a dense undergrowth of dwarf bamboo.

Rhododendrons in mainland Asia do not really occur much below the temperate forest belt, but Kingdon Ward wrote in RHS–RYB, 1947: 'The rocks [are] glowing with a bright red crust of *R. simsii*, and this at less than 1,000' above sea level in the midst of tropical jungle. We do not see another rhododendron until we are at least 5,000' above sea level.'

These last two quotations mention exceptions to the general rules and point out how nature sometimes goes a little topsy-turvy in the distribution at various altitudes.

It is sad that the greater part of Asia is now out of bounds to Western plant collectors, as much work remains to be done including the probable discovery of many new species and varieties. Uncollected areas include Saramati Peak, over 12,000 feet (3,657 metres), on the Nagaland–Burma frontier; between the Lohit and the Dihang (Tsangpo), around the Dibang; and many other parts of the North East Frontier Agency (subsequently referred to as NEFA). It is very hard to reach the alpine region because of toothed ridges, a soaking climate and the most resistant and impenetrable barrier it is possible to imagine, a mixture of cane brake and rhododendron scrub. Also large areas of New Guinea, Celebes, Sumatra, etc. remain unbotanized, and other parts of mainland Asia need more thorough exploration.

For a long time the major explorers (especially Kingdon Ward) and botanists claimed that there was no such thing as a natural hybrid, even after years of collecting in the field. Then slowly the light dawned. Farrer discovered two obvious examples in *R. charitopes* × *R. campylogynum* var. *charopoeum* and *R. aperantum* × *R. chaetomallum*. In *Plant Hunter's Paradise* (*p.* 227) Kingdon Ward admitted to having found hybrids of *R. chryseum* and a plum-purple flowered species. Finally in *The Rhododendron Society Notes* (III, 3, 1927, *p.* 149), he climbed down absolutely. 'I am a complete convert to the theory that hybrids occur in nature quite commonly. To my mind, hybrids in nature are as common as species.'

Distribution Maps

The distribution maps on pages 16–19 are largely self-explanatory. It has usually been necessary to include several series per page. When two or more series have a very similar distribution, they are grouped together in the same enclosure. Unfortunately, it is impossible to give more precise details and, in most cases, large parts within the rings will not have any rhododendrons at all. Where numbers are given per ring, these only refer to dwarf species as included in this book, except for the Malesians. The map of the latter gives the total species as recognized by Sleumer in *An Account of Rhododendrons in Malesia*.

NB *R. chrysanthum* (p 1) is also found in Korea and Northern Japan (Ponticum Series).

Ecology

In this second part of Chapter 1, I want to give as vivid a picture as possible of the habitats of wild rhododendrons, to create an interest in how and why they grow where they do. I also wish to show how, in many cases, gardens can be used to simulate these conditions found in nature. To put this across, I cannot do better than quote various collectors writing from their own observations, especially the works of F. Kingdon Ward.

First, we shall consider climate and vegetation. E. H. Wilding, in *The Rhododendron Society Notes* (II, 5, 1923, 200), divided the main Burmese and Chinese rhododendron areas into two climatic regions:

1. Indo-Malayan Region. The basin of the Irrawaddy, tributaries and the Salween from 28°30′ south. Rainfall 80–140 in. (2·03–3·56m) falling throughout the year, but heaviest in summer. Atmosphere

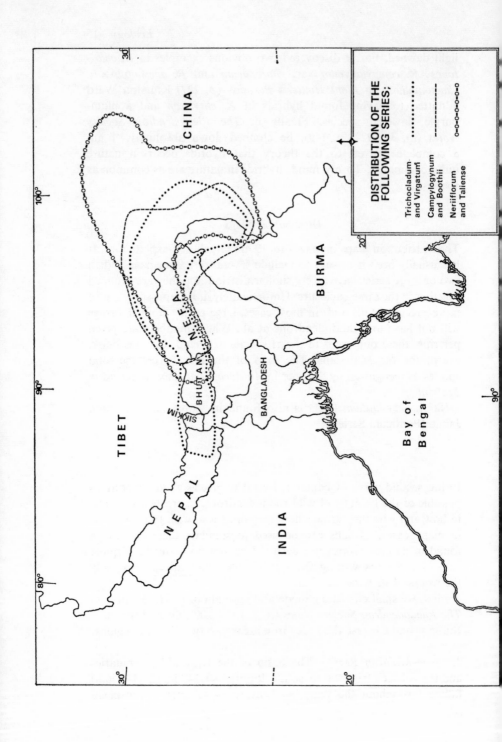

DISTRIBUTION OF THE
FOLLOWING SERIES:

Trichocladum
and Virgatum   ••••••••••

Campylogynum
and Boothii   ——————

Neriiflorum
and Taliense   o-o-o-o-o-o

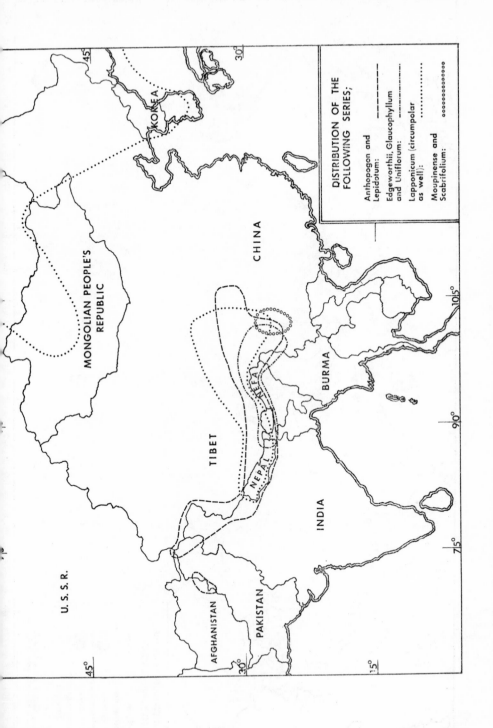

DISTRIBUTION OF THE FOLLOWING SERIES;

Anthopogon and Lepidotum: ————————

Edgeworthii, Glaucophyllum and Uniflorum: —·—·—·—·—·

Lapponicum (circumpolar as well): ·················

Moupinense and Scabrifolium: ०००००००००००००

U.S.S.R.

MONGOLIAN PEOPLE'S REPUBLIC

KOREA

CHINA

TIBET

NEPAL

NEFA

BURMA

INDIA

AFGHANISTAN

PAKISTAN

45°

30°

15°

45°

30°

75°

90°

105°

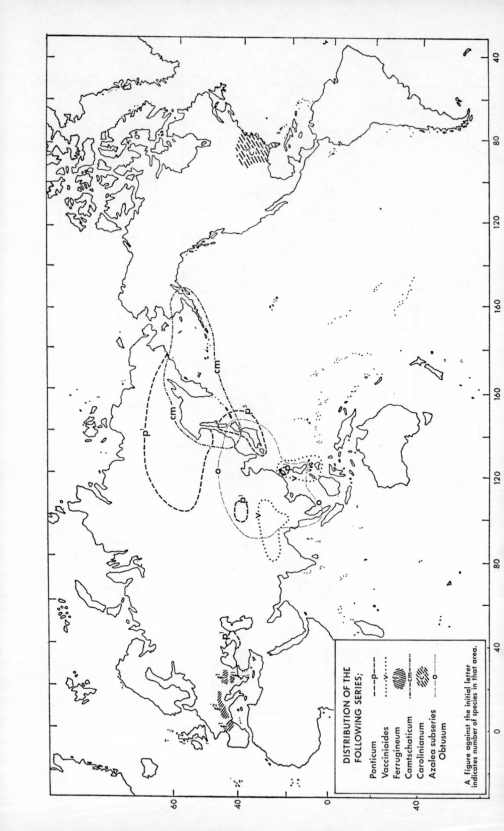

DISTRIBUTION OF THE
FOLLOWING SERIES;

Ponticum ......p......
Vaccinioides .....v.....
Ferrugineum
Camtschaticum ....cm....
Carolinianum
Azalea subseries
Obtusum .....o.....

A figure against the initial letter
indicates number of species in that area.

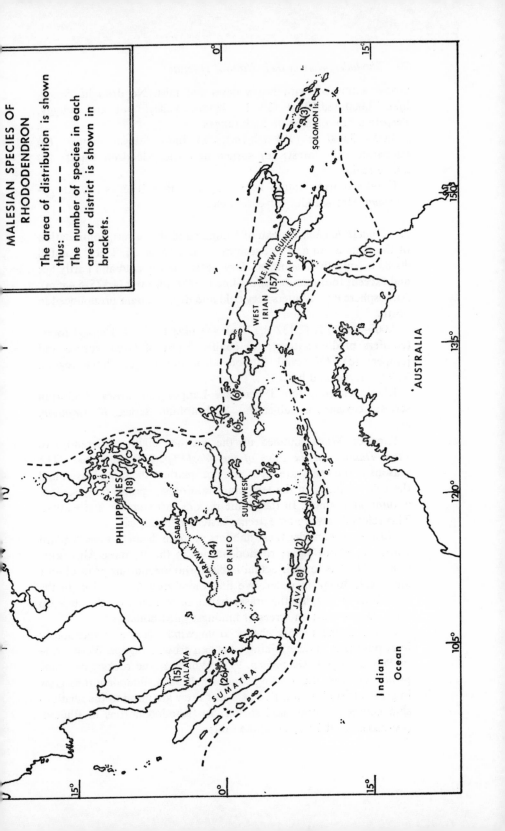

MALESIAN SPECIES OF
RHODODENDRON

The area of distribution is shown
thus: – – – – –

The number of species in each
area or district is shown in
brackets.

always saturated, with heavy dews and mist. No drought. Snow-line 13,000–18,000 ft (3,961–5,486m). Valleys hot and muggy. Perpetual rain or mist on high ranges.

3,000–13,000 ft (914–3,961m): (a) Indo-Malayan jungle; (b) temperate rain forest; (c) spruce and rhododendron forest; (d) alpine region.

Rhododendrons found here are Forrestii sub-series, *R. campylogynum*, Haematodes sub-series, etc.

2. *Chinese Region*. Plateau of Yunnan and the eastern continuation of the Himalayan axis in Szechwan and extreme SE Tibet. Rainfall 40–80 in., mostly in summer. 'Dry' season partly cold and partly hot and exceeds four months. Snow-line 16,000–18,000 ft (4,575–5,486m). Atmosphere dry. Winters very cold and dry. Drought pronounced in north.

7,000–15,000 ft (2,132–4,571m): (a) pine forest; (b) mixed forest (conifers predominating); (c) conifer forest of larch, spruce and juniper; (d) *Abies* and rhododendron scrub; (e) alpine region. Valleys dryish and hot.

Rhododendrons found here are Lapponicum series, Triflorum series; Roxieanum sub-series; Scabrifolium series, *R. virgatum*, etc.

Kingdon Ward summed up the weather slightly differently. In *Plant Hunting on the Edge of the World* (*p*. 275), he stated: 'The seasons in the valley are three, the hot weather, the rainy season and the cold weather. In the temperate rainforest, spring, rainy season, autumn and winter. In the alpine regions just summer and winter.' This refers to the wetter extreme eastern Himalayas.

Now let us consider these habitats in more detail. Kingdon Ward wrote this about alpine rhododendrons in the Burmese Alps (RHS-RYB, 1947): 'As to their actual habitat, rhododendrons grow almost anywhere, except in water. We find them growing on rocks in the river bed; or fringing the grassy banks of torrents; on the cliffs; in bogs; in pastures; on screes or amongst piled boulders.'

In the alpine region, shelter from wind plays a tremendously important part in determining what can grow. Kingdon Ward wrote in *Burma's Icy Mountains* (*p*. 94): 'Wherever the rocks gave some protection from the howling wind, small bush rhododendrons grew in great variety.' Again, R. E. Cooper drew attention to the relationship between altitude and shelter. In 'Rhododendrons in Bhutan' (AM-RSQB, April 1955, 91–2), he said:

Ranging above the sheltered slopes and adorning the rounded tuft-clad crowns of the lower ridges are dwarf bushes of *R. nivale, R. setosum, R. lepidotum,* and *R. anthopogon.* These form continuous stretches in the first low moors, but plants of these species are driven gradually with increasing elevation to seek the hollows, and finally to live their life in the shelter provided between the gaps between big boulders of the moraine. They grow higher up the SE Slopes.

Then he went on to mention the wind and weather.

There is a well-known fact that winds travel up the valley and hillside for most of the day, and blow down from the snows during the night. From May to September on the high slopes there is a succession of blanketing mists, sleet and heavy rain, often with bitterly cold winds.

In 'Rhododendrons in the Wild' (RHS-RYB, 1949, 13), Kingdon Ward stated: 'Shelter in alpine regions is of tremendous importance. An entirely different assemblage of species is found on either side of a valley, like in the Seinghku Valley in North Burma, within 200 yards of each other.'

George Forrest often said that as a rule rhododendrons are social plants, with only the occasional species growing as isolated specimens. Kingdon Ward gave a picture of their social tendencies perfectly when he described rhododendron moorland in West China in *The Romance of Plant Hunting* (*pp.* 211, 216):

They are woven into carpets of queer design and ample pile, or form tuffets or hassocks or mere tangles or mats or brooms. Looking across the dark ocean of moorland you see the billowy hills crested with colour, and where the escarpments break the even roll, the plant growth surges high up on the rocks. It is West Szechwan, the Tibetan Marches, home of the Lapponicum Rhododendrons.

What a gorgeous sight those miles and miles of colour are! For these species grow socially, covering large areas, drifts of purple here, of pink there, broken by patches of bright yellow light sunlight. But in the bogs, the colour is always lavender. Some grow in bogs or marshy meadows, and some in peat and some grow on limestone cliffs. They mostly occur above 12,000 feet (3,657 metres) and are buried under snow for 3 to 4 months a year. Summer rains, of course, they need; but they flower early, quenching their thirst from the melting snow, in a country where spring and autumn droughts are a rule.

This quotation produces several very interesting points which I shall deal with separately.

Bogs and marshes. Several reports from collectors on species growing in these strange conditions have appeared. We are always told, and often prove for ourselves, that all rhododendrons must have perfect drainage. The solution to the problem, I think, is this: we often find heather growing in a similar environment in Britain, forming tussocks in a boggy area. Now, heather too, likes good drainage. These tussocks are slightly raised above the general level of the marsh, and therefore the heather or rhododendrons have their roots above the waterlogged area. Another point is that some of these bogs are only saturated in the monsoon season and by snow-melt, and have a chance to dry out in autumn and early winter.

Limestone. I am no scientist so I shall not attempt to go into the various aspects of rhododendrons and lime here; I shall make some reference to the subject in Chapter 4. George Forrest often reported that he had found rhododendrons growing on bare limestone rock in many parts of Yunnan. He listed these species and it has been proved in cultivation that these are largely the most lime-resistant. Unfortunately, although a rock sample of his was analysed, no careful study was made of the soil overlying the limestone, and no pH ratings and calcium contents were recorded.

A. T. Leiser, in '*Rhododendron occidentale* on Alkaline Soil' (RHS-RCYB, 1957, 47–51), told how the azalea *R. occidentale* was found in California, USA, growing on dry serpentine soil, with little tree-cover and a pH of between 7·2 and 8·5. Little free calcium was found to be present and an experiment in growing other rhododendrons and ericaceous plants in it showed that they all grew perfectly healthily. This more or less proves that in an alkaline soil with low free calcium and other elements, rhododendrons can grow; and that the free calcium, *not* the pH, is the limiting factor. There was little organic matter in the soil, and the azalea roots were right down into the basic serpentine rock.

Drought. It may be thought that in their natural habitat rhododendrons do not suffer from this, one of the commonest hazards in

II *R. trichostomum*. Anthopogon series

cultivation. But this is not so, at least in the drier areas. Drought conditions were noted on several occasions by both Kingdon Ward and Forrest. On the Mekong–Salween Divide, Forrest travelled more than a day's march without seeing a living rhododendron, every plant having been killed in the two previous exceptionally dry seasons. Nothing was left but gaunt sticks of dead wood. I doubt if this ever happens in the wetter regions, for even though the rains may fail partially on occasion, there is sure to be mist. With mist and a highly moisture-retentive soil, they are unlikely to come to much harm.

Let us now move on to the question of soil. We all know that the ideal soil for rhododendrons is one rich in organic matter, and that almost any soil of this type, provided it is well drained, will suit them admirably. So in these soils, in the northern hemisphere in temperate and sub-arctic zones, we may expect to find rhododendrons and their ericaceous cousins growing wild. This layer of organic matter forms because of the combination of high rainfall and fairly low temperature which slow down the breakdown by micro-organisms. Thus cool areas, either near the arctic or increasingly high up in the mountains, approaching the equator, promote the formation of acid soils almost entirely consisting of organic matter. This forms from a build-up from mosses, ferns, leaf-fall, dead wood or dead herbaceous-plant material which breaks down at least as slowly as it accumulates.

These ericaceous shrubs have proved to be a highly successful group of plants, and where conditions are suitable, they manage to colonize and cover the landscape, often to the exclusion of all other vegetation. One of the chief reasons for their success is the enormous abundance of seed they make. As Kingdon Ward stated:

> There can be few genera of plants which produce a higher ratio of viable seed to flower as rhododendrons. In the temperate rain forest, where moss clothes rocks and trees and banks with a soft green dripping sponge, rhododendron seedlings spring up by the million. A new clearing, a path through the forest, a roadside bank, every tree trunk and branch, every rock and cliff, is seized on as a nursery for rhododendrons which often come up in dense masses, to the exclusion of all other plants. Almost any rhododendron including the largest tree species, will grow epiphytically for a year or two. (RHS-RYB, 1947)

In the forest, where there is a tremendous battle for all available light, most of these seedlings die long before reaching maturity and being able to perpetuate their kind. Certain species have surmounted the difficulties of reaching the light in the forest by perching themselves high up in the trees as epiphytes. In places, this has proved so successful that nearly every forest tree, sometimes including the tree rhododendrons themselves, contains epiphytes. These epiphytes obtain no water or plant foods from their host trees. They have to get what they can from the moss that their roots grow in, or from dead bark or a few leaves that gather in the crevices. Epiphytic rhododendrons occur from as low as 4,000 feet (1,219 metres) up to 13,000 feet (3,961 metres). If the forest is cleared or they get a chance to grow on cliffs, or on boulders in a river, most of these species will come down to earth and grow happily there provided the drainage is perfect.

James Keenan made, so far as I can discover, a unique observation on Bumpha Bum, upper Burma, in 1962. One species was epiphytic on itself in the moss forest, even to the extent of reaching flowering size. Another point he noted was that an occasional species was, for example, epiphytic at 7,000 feet (2,132 metres), became terrestrial at 8,000 feet (2,439 metres) where it was most plentiful and created a climax, and then went back to being epiphytic on other rhododendrons at around 9,000 feet (2,743 metres). Like Kingdon Ward and Cox, he told of a solid bamboo brake at about 8,500 feet (2,591 metres) where almost nothing else grew.

Kingdon Ward made some interesting examinations of the different types of rhododendron seeds, and discovered how they separated out into groups, largely depending on the type of habitat they preferred. He actually attempted to classify the species according to their seeds, but this really did not work out in practice. I have changed his divisions slightly and made four groups instead of his three. Some overlapping does occur: 1. small-winged large seeds – forest type; 2. seeds with large or long wings – epiphytic type; 3. wingless seeds – alpine type; 4. tailed seeds – Vireya section of Sleumer–Malesian type, including Vaccinioides series. Thus each type of seed is designed to aid the seedling's survival in its own habitat. The winged and tailed seeds belonging to the mainly epiphytic sections are obviously of practical use for wind dispersal in the tree-tops and for attaching themselves to branches and moss.

In cultivation many species and hybrids have a bad habit of producing odd flowers or even quite a show in the autumn. It is an irritating habit as these flowers are not properly developed because they come from immature buds, and it tends to spoil the display in

1 Mountain peaks in Bhutan, with dwarf rhododendrons in the foreground
(G. Sherriff)

2 Dwarfs under pine trees in north-west China (J. Rock)

the spring. This is not a phenomenon that has appeared only since we started cultivating rhododendrons. Kingdon Ward found many species flowering in the autumn, sometimes almost as well as they do in the spring. He mentioned that certain bushes may continue to flower at the wrong time every year. Examples he saw were *R. hippophaeoides, R. primuliflorum* var. *cephalanthoides, R. megeratum* and *R. glaucophyllum* var. *luteiflorum.* One benefit from this unseasonable flowering to plant collectors is that if the spring flowers are missed, they may be seen in autumn. This happened in the case of *R. glaucophyllum* var. *luteiflorum.* In *Farrer's Last Journey* (*p.* 119), Cox said that he and Farrer saw *R. calostrotum* in the autumn, with fleshy sham flowers coming out of a cluster of terminal leaves. They were almost tubular in shape and quite a vivid scarlet in colour.

In Britain, with our relatively mild winters and unreliable springs and autumns, we cannot produce a climate or other conditions near to those in the alpine rhododendrons' native haunts in the Himalayas and China. Yet most species really grow quite well in cultivation. The most difficult factor to copy is the heavy snowfalls which cover the entire plants for anything up to eight months in the year. Kingdon Ward wrote (RHS-RYB, 1947, 17): '*R. imperator* is, I think, one of the most extraordinary of the pygmy rhododendrons, although some people say it is difficult. It grows in the Seinghku Valley of Upper Burma on a cliff in a rock scupper where the snow lingers late at 9,000 to 10,000 feet (2,743 to 3,048 metres) that is far below the tree line.' Captain Collingwood Ingram (RHS-RCYB, 1969, 33) said: 'Dwarfness is to combat strong winds at high elevations and pressure from a great depth of snow.'

Kingdon Ward observed that tangled species have large cavities left among their twigs which make air spaces under the snow where air temperatures drop little below freezing. In these conditions, he found the leaves uncurled. The Doshong La Pass, famous for the variety of its rhododendrons, is under snow for seven months from about 18 October.

Lastly a mention of diseases and pests in the wild. Kingdon Ward remarked on how seldom rhododendrons are affected by insects and fungus attacks except where large capsules are bug-ridden, and the capsules of Lapponicums may be destroyed by a mildew-like fungus. But he said he had never seen anything in the nature of an epidemic, nor did he fail to collect good seed of any species. He also found blister blight on a few plants.

2 Dwarf Rhododendrons in the Garden

Choice of Site

With spreading urbanization devouring the countryside these days, and with miles and miles of similar streets and houses mushrooming out from towns and cities, each with their own little quarter or eighth of an acre (93 or 46 square metre) plots, most people have little choice of site. Few of the great gardens developed as wild gardens between the wars are being made nowadays, as not many people can afford one private gardener, let alone the several needed to plant and maintain these spacious woodlands. Luckily, there are some people prepared to look after an acre or two of roughish ground in their spare time, sometimes a fair distance away from their permanent house. If only the smaller varieties of rhododendrons are selected, it is surprising what a collection can be gathered together in a comparatively small plot.

As we are dealing here only with dwarf rhododendrons, the large areas of bigger gardens do not concern us. First, let us examine the problems of the small suburban garden where the majority of would-be rhododendron growers live. If the soil is either chalk or heavy clay it is no good planting rhododendrons or azaleas directly into it. With the use of raised beds, a collection of the really dwarf varieties can be grown almost regardless of the existing soil. In a dry part of the country, these beds may need considerable watering in summer. A nice little group of healthy plants can be grown this way in nearly any part of Britain, provided fairly lime-free water is used, but where there is still heavy atmospheric pollution, it is more satisfactory to grow them indoors in an alpine house. Some very exposed coastal districts can suffer from salt spray which can burn the foliage. One should avoid planting in soil too close to concrete which may have an excess of lime in it. Heavy pieces of iron or polythene can be placed between concrete and the planting area.

In a larger garden in the country or outer suburbs, there may be some choice as to where dwarf rhododendrons can be sited. Of course, frost pockets or hollows should be avoided, as they are not only subject to more degrees of frost in winter, but are also much more liable to be affected by late spring or early autumn frosts. North-facing banks are very often excellent for dwarfs, especially in the south of England and warm areas of other countries. Good drainage is always essential for all varieties. Many species and hybrids grow happily on rotten tree-stumps and in very wet districts with high humidity, like parts of western Scotland, it is well worth trying the epiphytes on mossy ledges or boulders, but only if the pile on the moss is deeper than 2 inches (5 centimetres).

Together with two friends, my wife and I have recently started gardening in the west of Scotland in order to be able to grow many rhododendrons which are not hardy in the east where we live. In the wild, partly wooded area chosen, is a large outcrop of rock with oak trees behind it, facing south-east and getting nearly full sun. There are many peaty pockets in it and other crevices where soil can be added. The whole outcrop when fully planted should hold 100–150 real dwarfs, and to my mind we have been extremely lucky in finding the ideal natural site for dwarfs. It may dry out rather in certain summers, but once fully established in the almost pure organic matter present, the plants should be able to withstand this perfectly.

One should not plant rhododendrons below sunny, south-facing walls. This position invariably becomes too hot and dry. A shaded or a north-facing wall is often an ideal situation for planting tender varieties, provided there is no overhang to keep off the rain, and no lime comes off the wall.

Shelter and Shade

I have, in many parts of this book, made a special point of drawing attention to the way dwarf rhododendrons grow in their natural habitat, and where they come from. I have done this for two closely connected reasons. It is undoubtedly more interesting to grow a plant of any kind if something is known of its history, of its wild haunts in the Himalayas and elsewhere. Also, knowing something about the soil, shelter, shade and altitude of its place of origin should at least give some help towards satisfying it in the garden. I agree that it is impossible to lay on monsoons for the summer months, with constant mist; and also a snow covering for between four and eight months in the year. But knowing these factors can give one a guide.

In Britain we can grow most dwarfs surprisingly well if certain measures are taken. We cannot unfortunately grow them as in the wild by planting them on the open moor where heather grows. Maybe not many have tried this, and perhaps a few species might succeed, but the fact is that the climate on our hills is too unreliable. Hard frosts may occur without snow and, together with wind, these cause the rhododendrons to become desiccated.

To return to the garden: because of the winter and early spring drying winds, often with frost, which we get so frequently from the east, some shelter is necessary. When speaking of shelter for dwarfs, what is meant is some break from the full blast. It is rare that reports are heard of winter killings of Lapponicums and Saluenenses in this country, but this can and has happened in north-east England from ferocious frosty winds blowing from Russia. The plants are literally dried out by a combination of wind, frost and sun, and while the ground is frozen stiff, the water cannot be taken up by the roots. This winter desiccation is, of course, a common occurrence in the eastern USA and parts of Europe.

The answer for this country is shelter from the east. In America sun is usually the chief cause of trouble, as it is much more powerful there even in winter and the frost is likewise more severe; so there shade and shelter are necessary, as well as a mulch (see Chapter 4).

No dwarfs need as much shelter as do the larger-leaved species and more tender hybrids. Therefore, providing sufficient shelter to produce good results is not such a difficult problem in most localities. Very often natural configurations of the ground causing, for example, a hollow or valley sloping to the south with fair shelter from west, east and north, will provide all the protection necessary for real alpines and the hardier Obtusum azaleas. Inland gardeners in towns or in broken country with woods and hedges scattered about, again, have adequate protection. But of course not everyone is lucky, and sea-side gardens, those on the exposed sides and tops of hills and on flat bare plains, must provide some shelter for real success. Solid shelters such as walls, buildings and really thick belts of conifers are not really satisfactory, as they only lift or deviate the wind so that it either hits ground-level again farther on, or changes direction and swirls or is funnelled in such a way that certain small areas can be so draughty that plants are literally blown out of the ground. I shall not go into the scientific details of how wind behaves, for lack of space and because every individual case will differ in accordance with the various circumstances involved. Interwoven fencing is quite useful for filling in gaps in the defences, and hessian or plastic mesh will serve as temporary measures. Nothing, though, to my mind, can equal living shelter. What to plant depends very much on what the climate and exposure is like, and how much shelter is desired. On a fairly level site where only low shrubs are to be grown, it would be unnecessary and also unsuitable to plant rows of Sitka spruce, poplars or other tall trees. All that is needed here is a low hedge, low enough to clip from ground-level. In a garden on a sloping hillside, the prevailing wind may sweep up from the bottom. Plant a loose break of deciduous trees such as larch, ash or birch, to filter the wind. If this is too thick, air drainage will be impaired. In a fairly large garden, mixed shrub borders, using shrub roses, escallonias, cotoneasters, etc., will provide ideal interior windbreaks.

SEA-SIDE

Really exposed sea-side gardens require special treatment owing to the velocity of the wind and the salt it may carry. If a high screen is needed the following have proved suitable with the sycamore and Sitka spruce to the windward side: sycamore (very ugly when wind-pruned), Sitka spruce, *Pinus contorta, P. radiata, P. mugo (montana)*, Austrian and Corsican pines, × *Cupressocyparis* 'Leylandii', *Olearia traversii* and *Cupressus macrocarpa* (liable to die off in parts).

Under, amongst and behind these, to provide the very necessary ground-shelter, plant *Escallonia macrantha*, 'C. F. Ball' or other vigorous hybrids, *Griselinia littoralis, Elaeagnus glabra* or *E.* 'Ebbingei', *Olearia albida* or *O. macrodonta*, certain cotoneasters and *Rhododendron ponticum*. *Elaeagnus, Griselinia* and *R. ponticum* are especially suitable for shade. These should all prove fairly hardy around the coast of Britain, except *Olearia traversii* (only for mild areas) and *Pinus radiata* (best in the west).

For lower windbreaks up to 6 to 10 feet (1·83 to 3·05 metres) high in mild areas, use the above ground-shelter plants or the following: *Phormium tenax* (New Zealand flax) and *Senecio* – especially *Senecio rotundifolius* (*reinoldii*).

Cold districts in full exposure are more difficult to cater for with shrubby shelter. Try *Hippophae rhamnoides, Rosa rugosa, Tamarix* species, privet (*Ligustrum*) and the various thorns.

For interior shelter in mild coastal areas where a fair wind can be expected, the above-mentioned plants will do equally well, but will tend to grow taller. Sycamores, Sitka spruce and the big pines are hardly ornamental or small enough for the smallish garden. Others to try would be *Quercus ilex, Arbutus unedo, Phillyrea decora, Tricuspidaria lanceolata* and *Hoheria glabrata.* Beware of planting *R. ponticum* in soils of a peaty or even sandy nature as it can become the worst possible weed, layering and seeding itself everywhere. We are not planting a single specimen of it in our own garden in the west of Scotland. The non-invasive species of bamboo such as *Arundinaria murieliae* and *A. nitida* form good interior screens.

One innovation seen on Innaculin Island, Bantry Bay, Ireland, which was a brainwave of the head gardener, Mr Mackenzie, is to cut out the tops of the sheltering pine trees when they reach about 30 feet (9·14 metres) to avoid their being blown over in the shallow soil. While it seems rather a sacrilegious thing to do, it has paid great dividends in the Atlantic gales experienced there.

Really low shrubs like *Ulex* (whin, gorse, furze), *Atriplex halimus, Genista* species, *Teucrium fruticans,* skimmias, hydrangeas, fuchsias, rosemary, veronicas (*Hebe* species), heaths and *Cistus* species and varieties will grow down near the water's edge, but will only provide the minimum of shelter.

INLAND

For high to medium-sized shelter inland, × *Cupressocyparis* 'Leylandii' is ideal for a narrow semi-hedge where space is restricted. Also good is *Chamaecyparis lawsoniana,* although some clones of this are too narrow in habit; *C.* 'Green Hedger' is very good. If planted in a wide belt of several rows these tend to act as a wall by being too solid, rather than as a wind velocity reducer.

In shade, where tall shelter is needed, plant *Thuja plicata, Tsuga heterophylla,* cherry laurel or hollies (rather slow-growing). For surrounding or breaking up a small garden, nothing is better than a beech hedge, although it too is a trifle slow-growing. Other good formal hedges are hornbeam, *Lonicera nitida,* some cotoneasters, *Chamaecyparis lawsoniana,* and even *R. ponticum,* which clips into quite a tidy hedge in good conditions. Informal hedges can be made out of rhododendrons themselves, using *R.* 'Praecox', *R. racemosum* or *R. kaempferi,* or for a taller hedge, members of the Triflorum or Heliolepsis series, too tall to include in this book.

In all ground, unless it is exceptionally fertile, young shelter trees and shrubs will benefit from a light application of fertilizer to give them a good start. Rock phosphate is very safe to use, but any compound fertilizer with not more than one fifth part ammonium sulphate or the equivalent in other forms of nitrogen should produce good results. Do not apply to trees too often; not more than once every four years.

SHADE

Nearly all dwarfs in the wild live in the full open with no shade-trees, and in the wetter regions they get very little sun at all. Hence, *R. forrestii* and varieties, *R. chamae-thomsonii*, *R. ludlowii* and *R. cephalanthum* var. *crebreflorum* do appreciate some shade, especially in the south of England and north-west USA. Ideally they should be planted to the north side of trees or buildings, and a north-facing bank is very suitable; but not where they can be dripped on. The species and their hybrids from the drier areas such as the Lapponicums, some forms of *R. lepidotum*, *R. racemosum* and several Anthopogons, do have sun and a dryish period before and after, and even sometimes during, the monsoons, so revel in full sun in Britain and much of the Pacific north-west of America. This is only a rough guide. In Scotland, all dwarfs need a fair amount of sun to flower well and grow compactly. In the heavy rainfall and mild climate of western Scotland it is hard to keep dwarfs in bounds. While some shelter is needed, unlimited sun can be given to nearly all varieties. Evergreen (Obtusum) azaleas need full sun in Scotland to flower at all. Unfortunately some varieties with red, orangey or salmon flowers lose their colour in the sun and turn a nasty bleached white. But not every May is sunny in Scotland! In southern England and America where the sun is stronger, dappled shade from high trees preserves the colour in these varieties and in fact suits most of these azaleas well.

Strong sunlight ruins the flowers of many late varieties of rhododendrons even the extent of wilting before opening, so some shade for these is desirable. Shelter also helps to stop wind from damaging the flowers.

What Shade Trees are Best?

The universally best shade tree for rhododendrons is the oak. Usually these do not cast too heavy a shade and their roots do not compete with the plants underneath to the same extent as many other trees. One of the few extensive gardens which has been established in recent years, at great expense, with plenty of gardeners and thousands upon thousands of plants, is Mount Congreve, near Waterford, Ireland. Here, well spaced out, mature oaks pruned well up the trunks give an ideal setting and perfect conditions for rhododendrons. Given every attention they need, I have never seen a healthier collection of plants. Big banks are covered with groups of dwarfs in the more open spaces.

At the famous species collection of Towercourt, Ascot, Berkshire, England (now sold), on heathland, nearly all the shade in the wilder wooded areas was Scots pine and Spanish chestnut. Species from the Forrest, Kingdon Ward and Rock expeditions were planted in batches of fifty to one hundred from many different seed numbers. The late Mrs Harrison (then Mrs Roza Stevenson) told me that, in that light easily-drying soil, it was no use planting any rhododendrons under the drip or within the root area of the pines. No watering could be carried out because of the great area involved, and yet the plants flourished between the pines provided the heather and other undergrowth was kept in check. The rainfall there is only 24 inches (60 centimetres) a year. These two gardens show what good use can be made of existing trees, provided they are thinned out enough to let in plenty of light.

Also, both oaks and pines produce excellent leaves and needles for feeding and mulching the rhododendrons' roots they fall on. Beeches cast a dense shade and little will grow directly underneath them, but their leafmould is the best of all provided they are not growing on lime. They are grand near plantings of bigger varieties, but are hardly suitable near dwarfs as they shut out too much light.

In our own garden at Glendoick we are not so lucky. Nearly all the existing trees are elm and sycamore with some ash, larch, birch and Douglas fir. All are far from ideal: their roots are too shallow, and the first three have leaves which make poor leafmould, usually of a rotten powdery alkaline nature. Elms spread their roots through the soil in an astonishingly large area around themselves, sucking in every grain of moisture and goodness. Sycamores cast far too much shade (when healthy) and drop honeydew from aphids on to leaves underneath, which turn black with sooty moulds. The large leaves smother any dwarfs they fall on, and their weedkiller-resistant seedlings spring up by the million everywhere. Also bad are poplars and Spanish chestnuts, both being too greedy. Douglas firs shed their branches all too readily.

In nature, the true alpine rhododendrons get no leaf-fall near them off broad-leaved trees, and so they are not naturally capable of putting up with soggy leaves falling on top of them. If they are left too long, these leaves may rot out portions of dwarfs. Prostrate plants like *R. forrestii, R. radicans* and *R. nakaharai* are the worst sufferers. If the leaves gather in the heart of the bushes they also cause rotting, so it is well worth picking the worst of them off once or twice a year.

Never associate big-leaved varieties too closely with dwarfs. The former will invariably overshadow and kill out the smaller plants in time. An unhappy example of this has taken place in the vast collection at Muncaster, in north-west England. There, too many big beeches have also taken their toll.

In a small garden where it is planned to have beds and peat banks and walls, a few small trees are desirable. Select some that have a nice shape, foliage, flower or autumn colour. Good examples are the less heavy-leaved smaller maples, cherries, *Cornus* species, *Liquidambar* species, staphyleas, rowans (*Sorbus* species), *Nothofagus* species, hornbeams (*Carpinus* species), cercidiphyllums, *Nyssa sylvatica, Styrax* species and *Halesia* species. Birch and magnolias, which are excellent woodland trees, have too extensive shallow root-systems and the latter have undesirably large leaves and cast heavy shade. So do not plant too close to these. *Eucalyptus* species need open but sheltered situations away from forest trees because they are such heavy light demanders and grow squint if overshadowed, but their interesting foliage and bark look good, well to the background of dwarf rhododendrons. Their roots are also very bad for planting among. Limes cast too heavy a shade, as do horse chestnuts, and the leaves of both make poor leafmould.

In 1920, when the woodland garden at Glendoick was started, the elms and sycamores were left for the shade-trees, and when I started planting in 1950 it was too late to remove these horrors. If I had started from scratch I would have removed the lot, roots and all, and I wish to stress how important it is to have the correct trees with the right balance of shade before undertaking any planting of rhododendrons.

PLANT ASSOCIATIONS

How a rhododendron garden is planted depends largely on whether one's attitude is biased towards that of the collector or the landscape architect. The collector's first thoughts are, where will my rhododendrons grow best? He will plant them here and there haphazardly, with no idea of grouping them to form good colour, foliage or shape associations. The landscape man will place everything purely with an eye for effect, often with little thought for the well-being of the plants involved. Personally I am rather on the side of the collector. I do like to see my plants happy. On the other hand I often regret the fact that, because I have an old-established collection, I have to plant amongst rhododendrons of all ages, shapes and sizes, mixed up with large trees and shrubs and paths which would be beyond my powers to alter much. But in contrast, our virgin west coast site offers much food for thought over the lay-out, and I conclude that a compromise between the two extremes is probably best.

There is a marvellous variety of dwarf rhododendrons and azaleas now available, giving a great variation in plant form, leaf and flower shape and colour. Used on their own with subtle mixtures of foliage and plant habit, a most enchanting effect can be produced. One idea is to group the dwarfest in the form of valleys, making the higher ridges with others of intermediate height, completing the planting with a background of the taller varieties. Or interplanting can be done with groups of lilies, meconopsis, primulas, etc. which enjoy the same type of soil, all being natives of similar mountainous regions. A few upright varieties amongst the dwarf and prostrate ones can some-times improve the effect. Other plants to associate with rhododen-drons are trilliums, dwarf ferns and other ericaceae.

If there is a fairly extensive area to cover, rather than have a general hodge-podge of species and hybrids all mixed up, plant in groups of three or more carefully selected varieties which are likely to grow well together and blend nicely. Dwarf rhododendrons and conifers make a good mixture, their forms producing a good combination. Groups of glaucous-foliaged rhododendron species such as *R. lepidostylum* and *R. calostrotum* look well with the con-trasting dark foliage of *R. campylogynum* or *R. hypenanthum*. Do not mix up dwarf rhododendrons with Obtusum azaleas too much. By all means plant varied groups of each adjacent; but mixed together, the azaleas will out-grow the rhododendrons and swamp them.

Many different flower effects can be thought of which can be very pleasing, although in some places the plants mentioned may not always hit off their flowering together. Here are a number of sugges-tions. Plant blue and purple Lapponicums in front of yellowish hybrids such as 'Cunningham's Sulphur', 'Harvest Moon' or 'Unique'. Try *R. didymum* in a group of *R. calostrotum, R. lepido-*

stylum or *R. viridescens*, to show off the deep crimson flowers. *R. ciliatum* is very effective as a bold edging in front of tall reds which flower at the same time, or with *Erica carnea* 'Vivellii', and try 'Redcap' with *Hoheria glabrata*. The lovely deciduous azalea *R. schlippenbachii* is a good foil for the blue dwarfs. 'Elizabeth' and 'Ethel' can be attractively backed by *Prunus* 'Shirotae'. Pink, white, cream or yellow rhododendrons are excellent with the 'blues'. Species *Narcissus* go nicely with *R. chamae-thomsonii* and *R. forrestii* forms. *R. leucaspis* looks well with *Hepatica nobilis* (*H. triloba*), and *Corylopsis* species with early pinks or mauves like 'Tessa' or 'Praecox'. To fill in between *R. williamsianum* hybrids when they are young try forget-me-not. Plant 'Praecox', 'Emasculum' and 'Tessa' with *Erica* 'Darleyensis' or a late variety of *E. carnea*, or 'Bric-a-Brac' or 'Snow Lady' with *E. carnea* forms.

Do not plant dwarfs in the midst of heaths as the latter dry out and starve the former when their growth and roots close in.

From a landscape point of view it is said that too many colours should not be mixed up at once. The stronger the colour, the more restrained should be its use and the more segregated, in a group or groups with a background of dark evergreens. Paler colours can be used in greater quantities because they tone much better with the local landscape and they can be mixed easily. Good groups are cream and ivory with yellow and some blues; whites and off-whites with pale pinks or some blues or stronger pinks to violets. Try pale salmon and pink Kurume azaleas with an undercover of *Endymion* (*Scilla*) *campanulatus* in a woodland area where it adds much charm. In districts where light woodland is desirable for azaleas, plant drifts among birches, cherries or maples, or on a gentle slope amongst ferns and allied plants such as *Vaccinium* or *Gaultheria* species. Obtusum azaleas are very effective under a Japanese cherry or flanking a flight of steps, and are excellent in a formal garden. In Japan they are often clipped and look well in large flower pots and the larger varieties make a good hedge.

Do not plant the kinds of bulbs such as *Crocus tomasinianus*, *Muscari botryoides*, common snowdrops or *Endymion* (*Scilla*) *nonscriptus* (bluebells) which naturalize themselves easily close to very dwarf rhododendrons. They spread into the root and leaf areas and their coarse foliage is most unsightly; and they can even kill out parts of a species like *R. radicans*.

Rhododendrons for Foliage and Scent

The diversity of foliage in the genus *Rhododendron* is quite staggering. Even among the dwarfs and Obtusum azaleas, the variation is tremendous and when the Malesian types are included, it adds many species totally unlike anything normally imagined as a rhododendron. Unfortunately there is nowhere that I know of where all these species can be grown together satisfactorily. Only in parts of coastal California, Australia and perhaps the north island of New Zealand, can anything like the full range of the genus be grown outside together.

Two most attractive features of their foliage are the silvery glaucous young leaves found in a few species and in the indumentum on the undersides of the leaves of others (occasionally a trace is also present on the upper surface). The finest glaucous-leaved dwarfer species are *R. lepidostylum, R. viridescens, R. campanulatum* var. *aeruginosum, R. calostrotum* and *R. caloxanthum,* and the hybrid 'Intrifast'. These look their best when covered with droplets of water.

Those with the best indumentum are *R. tsariense, R. haematodes, R. beanianum,* certain species of the Sanguineum sub-series, *R. edgeworthii,* many of the Roxieanum sub-series, especially *R. recurvoides, R. wasonii, R. yakusimanum* and some members of the Anthopogon series which have dense reddish-brown scales. The colour of the others varies from fawn to rufous brown. All these make excellent garden plants for foliage, let alone the flowers which are an added bonus.

Other species and some hybrids have delightfully shaped leaves or plant forms. *R. williamsianum* has elliptic-to-rounded leaves and a marvellous plant habit in the open, often making a dome and with closely packed leaves.

Several species and often their hybrids produce charming reddish or bronzy young foliage. The best of these are *R. williamsianum, R. moupinense, R. leucaspis, R. keiskei,* and some clones of *R. chamae-thomsonii.*

A few species and varieties have curious narrow leaves which give a most unusual effect. Notable examples are *R. roxieanum* var. *oreonastes, R. makinoi,* and the Malesian *R. stenophyllum* and *R. hooglandii.* The azalea 'Linearifolium' even has narrow pink flowers to match! *R. pseudochrysanthum* is a most attractive compact shrub with thick stiff leaves.

Some of the Lapponicums, such as *R. dasypetalum* and *R. cham-*

eunum of the Saluenense series, turn a nice shade of brown in winter and these go well with the glaucous species which still retain much of their beauty when dormant.

Many of the Obtusum azaleas give excellent autumn colour on the portion of the leaves which they shed, particularly *R. kaempferi* and its hybrids. Certain deciduous rhododendrons have autumn tints too, but are rarely as good in cultivation as the reports from the wilds indicate.

Unfortunately the species and hybrids with really strongly scented flowers are mostly too large for the scope of this book, but I have included *R. edgeworthii* which has the finest scent of them all. A few others are scented but not strikingly so, such as *R. poukhanense*.

Aromatic foliage in many species gives another attraction. Except in a few cases like *R. brachyanthum* var. *hypolepidotum* which to some is very nasty, all have reasonably pleasant aromas. Most dwarf lepidotes are aromatic to some extent, but the Anthopogon and Glaucophyllum series excel. *R. kongboense* is to me the prince of all and I can never resist rubbing a leaf when I go past it!

Rhododendrons for Pots and Containers
or Greenhouse Borders

Established plants in pots or other containers are a great boon if forced a little and brought out early, to flower indoors in winter or early spring. In the past, the only rhododendrons used this way have been the so called Indian azaleas, which we all know so well, plus a few of the tender-scented varieties.

There appears now to be quite a future in the forcing of the ordinary hybrid rhododendrons as pot plants for the house. A combination of four hours' light at night and the growth regulator B-Nine gives a dwarf plant which will flower from a liner the following winter after a cooling period, according to Ted Van Veen in *Rhododendrons in America*. He recommends the varieties *Anah Kruschke* and *Marinus Koster*.

Obtusum azaleas can now be brought into flower the whole year round by chemical control of growth and flowering, plus the use of different day-lengths and temperatures. This process, though, is at present only for the large commercial grower in a highly specialized trade. They can even be chemically pruned using fatty acid esters.

These azaleas which can be bought in flower are mostly grown in pure peat in Holland and Belgium for exporting to Britain and other parts of Europe. Many are lost the first year through neglect. For those with no greenhouse, keep them well watered until flowering has finished, then re-pot, using a soil-less compost, as an ordinary John Innes potting mixture would be too far removed from the composition of the peat, and the plant would have difficulty in making new roots. Use a peat-sand compost consisting of 75 per cent sphagnum peat and 25 per cent lime-free sharp sand (by volume). The recommended additions to this are per bushel (8 gallons; 36·37 litres): $\frac{1}{2}$ ounce of ammonium nitrate, 1 ounce of potassium nitrate, 2 ounces of superphosphate (18 per cent P_2O_5), 3 ounces of dolomitic or magnesium limestone, $\frac{1}{2}$ ounce of fritted trace elements (No 253.A if possible). Or use 40 per cent oak and beech leafmould (off acid soil), 40 per cent peat and 20 per cent sand. Tease out the surface of the root ball a little and use a pot only a little larger than the previous one. Give plenty of light in a warmish room and keep well watered and apply dilute liquid feeding every fortnight while indoors. Plunge outside in a fairly shady spot when the danger of frost is past, and bring indoors again before the first cold autumn snap. Continue to keep well watered in summer if the weather is dry. I shall not attempt to mention varieties. Nearly all those available are good, and it is more a question of selecting those one likes. Most root well from cuttings, but it is not easy to produce good lush bushy plants oneself.

Most of the tender species and hybrids of the scented Maddenii and Edgeworthii series, and the Boothii series, need greenhouse treatment in all but the western seaboard of Britain, the San Francisco Bay to South Oregon areas of the USA and parts of New Zealand, Australia and Japan.

Unfortunately many of these are naturally straggly plants and are not all easy to grow as good pot plants. Anyway, the taller varieties do not concern us here. Some of the dwarfer early flowering species and hybrids such as *R. leucaspis*, *R. moupinense*, *R. megeratum*, 'Bric-a-Brac', 'Golden Oriole', 'Moth' and 'Snow Lady' can make excellent pot plants and can be kept in bounds as they do not naturally grow very large or straggly. However, they are hard to grow well without a cool greenhouse where they can be kept in a humid atmosphere for the growing season, but like the azaleas, they can be plunged outside during summer in a lath house or shady position. These varieties produce good quality flowers only if they are not over-forced. They can be brought nicely into flower in February–March in a greenhouse where the frost is just kept at bay and no more.

Some of these species are naturally epiphytic and can be grown in hanging baskets like orchids, *Agapetes* species and so on. Francis Hanger suggested growing them on wooden platforms made of seasoned oak or teak, using strips 1 inch (2·5 centimetres) square and ½ inch (1·3 centimetres) apart. He used equal parts of lime-free loam fibre, fresh sphagnum and coarse peat, held in position with wire or string. This would only be a success in a very humid atmosphere where the sphagnum could grow. Osmunda fibre can also be used with coarse sand and sphagnum, but feeding will be needed.

Another good way to grow these tender sorts is in a bed especially prepared for them. Either use a mixture of one part each of sandy lime-free loam, peat, oak or/and beech leafmould and coarse sand or leave out the loam if no good source is available. This mixture *must* be at least 1 foot (30 centimetres) deep and drainage *must* be excellent.

The house should be lightly shaded in summer, by using either blinds made of bamboo, plastic, wooded slats etc., or a proprietary shading compound painted on to the glass. Watering can be done by a hose, an overhead watering fan or perhaps by trickle irrigation.Do *not* use alkaline water. The winter temperature should ideally not be below freezing point, although a degree or two of frost before the buds begin to swell will do little harm. Raise the heat a few degrees above freezing as a minimum by February–March. Certain varieties lose their buds all too easily if the soil dries out too much at any time, the temperature gets too high over a long period, or if frost gets in when the buds start to move. Ventilate well at all times except in frosty weather and damp the house down frequently during the spring and summer months. Other uses of a greenhouse for dwarfs are for the show bench or as an alpine display-house, or because of adverse conditions outside, such as atmospheric pollution or alkaline soil. They may also be grown in frames and taken into the alpine house for exhibition or to a show, or grown through the year in the greenhouse. Square wooden boxes dry out less than pots, and are best made of teak. Leave a space at the top of a pot or box of 1½ to 2 inches (3·8–5 centimetres) to allow for top dressing and re-pot every two years. Prune, if necessary, immediately after flowering; some can be cut back into bare wood. Shade and damp down well in hot weather. Use composts as already suggested or John Innes potting compost without chalk, but with sulphur used instead. If the water is a little hard, try ½ ounce of ferrous sulphate per gallon but if it is very hard and the pH of the compost rises, only use rainwater.

Hardiness

This is a subject on which several volumes could be written. Our climate in Britain is so fickle that every season has an entirely different effect on the more tender rhododendrons. The word hardiness here refers only to the ability to withstand cold and does not mean so-called 'hardiness' as used in Australia, which denotes toughness to survive heat and drought.

Each rhododendron-growing area of the world has a completely different climate and general hardiness problems. This is why I devote the whole of the next chapter to showing a comparison of all the main areas involved.

Through the process of evolution and the survival of the fittest, every rhododendron species, as with other living forms of life, has developed its own characteristics to suit its natural habitat best. When moved into our gardens, usually thousands of miles away and in a completely different climate, each species needs many generations of seedlings to evolve further and adjust itself to the new surroundings. Except where several generations of seedlings have been grown to create hardier strains, or as in the case of *R. ponticum*, which has regenerated itself over many years, no rhododendrons have had a chance to change much from the state they were in when first collected in the wild.

To simplify matters, hardiness will be divided into two sections: first, dormant mid-winter damage; and second, spring and autumn damage. Those with continental climates with hot summers and cold winters are most likely to suffer from the former, and those with coastal temperate conditions, the latter. The parts of California, New Zealand, Australia, north-west Spain and north Portugal which get virtually no frost do not concern us here, except to say that alpine rhododendrons used to cold winters do not like these warm winter areas.

THE CONTINENTAL CLIMATES

These include all of Europe away from any large expanse of water, which means much of Sweden, all Germany, Austria, Switzerland and eastern Europe, and to a lesser extent Holland, Belgium and northern France. In America, eastern USA and Canada, with a few coastal exceptions, the mid-west and some inland areas in the western states where rhododendron culture is just starting. In these places, provided

3 Dwarfs on the lower slopes of mountains in north-west China (J. Rock)

4 Members of the Lapponicum series in the wild, Chungtien plateau, Yunnan (G. Forrest)

5 North peat walls, Royal Botanic Garden, Edinburgh

6 'Blue Diamond' and other dwarf rhododendrons, Glendoick, Perthshire

cultural treatment has been good, there should be little trouble in ripening the young wood, in most years, into a thoroughly dormant state before the hard weather starts. This is a result of plenty of heat and sunshine, and is especially true with the Obtusum azaleas. Likewise, spring comes late and varieties that might flower in Britain in January or February do not come out until April or even May, when winter changes almost straight into summer.

In these areas, the chief problem apart from summer heat and drought is extremely low winter temperatures, and the difficulty is how to minimize the effect of these frosts. Snow is often unreliable and every few years really testing weather strikes. This can come as a combination of no snow covering, sub-zero Fahrenheit temperatures and searing winds, often accompanied by bright sunshine. These conditions literally desiccate the plants if they are not adequately protected. To help prevent this, every available precaution should be taken.

The first essentials are protection against sun and wind, and it is best not to plant on ground facing east, where the early morning sun will strike. Protection from bright winter sunshine by evergreens is necessary for all but cast-iron varieties. This desiccation is caused by ground being frozen throughout the root area so that no moisture can be taken up by the plant, and the wind and sun then drying out the parts above ground or snow level, to below the percentage of moisture level it can stand. This varies considerably from variety to variety. Typical of this type of damage is a faded area of brown or tan at the leaf tip, which is brittle. Sometimes there is a black area between the green part and the dead tissue. In severe cases the whole plant may die. A slightly different type of winter damage is caused by the sun moving on to thawed-out leaves which are then re-frozen with the sun on them, followed by a repeat of the same process. Injury from a really low temperature alone causes blackening of the entire leaf or affected area, without tan or brown outer edges. This too can prove fatal. How can we prepare our plants for winter? In America much argument has gone on for and against late watering in autumn. One faction says that it will keep growth moving, soft and vulnerable; while the others assure us that all rhododendrons must go into winter fully turgid to be at their hardiest. I would agree that enough water should be given to stop permanent wilting, especially with young plants or those newly planted. In severe climates, heavy mulches will minimize the damage caused by constant thawing and freezing, by conserving moisture and preventing the ground from being frozen so deeply. It is even suggested that the mulch should be applied when the ground is moderately frozen so as to keep it in that state as long as possible, thus avoiding fluctuations in soil temperature and helping to retain dormancy longer. One danger of a heavy mulch in autumn and winter is that it prevents the normal modifying effect on the air temperature from warmth escaping from the soil. This can make a difference of about 6°F and therefore can be very dangerous to young plants not properly hardened off.

Fertilizers are dealt with in Chapter 4, but we can mention here their use in connection with wood ripening. Great care must be made of the use of nitrogen on rhododendrons at all times, but especially after June. Nearly every plant in this book is particularly susceptible to over-feeding. Probably the best and easiest way to ripen well and incidentally to encourage the formation of flower buds, is to give applications of potassium and phosphate during summer and autumn. It is hard to suggest a definite amount to apply, Leach says he gave: 0 nitrogen, 25 phosphate, 25 potassium fertilizer, adding 4 per cent magnesium oxide himself at the rate of 35 pounds per 1,000 square feet for specimen stock, and half that for small plants, giving satisfactory results. This mixture is available in America ready mixed.

MARITIME CLIMATES

I suppose we really are much better off here than those poor people with severe continental climates, largely because we can keep alive a great many more species and hybrids. I say 'keep alive' because it has to be admitted that many of us struggle on with plants which look sickly, get frosted back every other year, and generally fail to open any flower buds. Yet we have not the heart to thrown them all out.

In Scotland, we suffer from approximately three times more spring frosts than we do autumn. The worst autumn damage I can remember was in 1955 when after the driest summer in my memory we had sharp frosts in early October, just when many plants were trying to make their *first* growth, after having a little rain. The result was death to several. Mature plants of the larger varieties do, of course, only make one growth flush per year, but more juvenile ones, especially dwarfs, make two or more and may normally carry on growing into September or October. In 1969 and 1971 late growth was excellent, following a moderately dry summer, but as a result frosts in early November did quite appreciable damage. In 1970 when it never stopped raining after June, there was little autumn growth, and no damage when it froze in late November. This lack of growth is due to the rather heavy soil in the nursery beds at Glendoick, which get too consolidated in heavy rain, resulting in poor soil conditions.

The type of damage suffered in autumn is frosted late growth, some bark-split and even flower buds damaged if late warm weather suddenly turns cold. The famous 1955 freeze in the Pacific north-west of America, when temperatures dropped from around 60 °F (15·5 °C) to 10 °F (12·25 °C) overnight, with a searing wind, will never be forgotten by those who experienced it. I saw some of the results in spring 1956 when over there for a brief visit. Many plants were cut right down to the ground or killed, but a surprising number came away again from the roots the following spring.

Alternating mild and relatively cold winter temperatures upset early and even some later varieties, and very often a few pips per truss will be destroyed as a result. It seems that we have to put up with some late spring frosts every year. The main trouble is that there is so often a mild January, February or March, followed by devastating frosts in April or May, or both. The year 1963 was a continental-type winter with no mild spell and a spring which did not return to winter. Although the temperatures were low, quite often around 10 °F, we had one of our best flowering seasons.

In 1968 after a very mild spell and a season a good month in advance, we had ten days of frost ranging from 8 to 12°F below freezing point. All young growth and flowers were blackened and bark-split was widespread (see Chapter 10). Whole plants died, and in others branches collapsed, some not dying back until two years after.

Parts of the south of England have been struck by repeated frosts at two- or three-weekly intervals these last few years, carrying on even into June and causing extensive destruction of flowers and growth. So to those in the eastern USA who think rhododendron growing in Britain is all one glorious holiday, let them have some second thoughts!

Now, what can we do to alleviate frost damage? Frost pockets have already been mentioned briefly at the beginning of this chapter. It may be added here that early varieties depend enormously on their location as to how much they will suffer from spring frost. In 1970 my own hybrid 'Ptarmigan' FCC was frosted in the bud just before flowering in an open position by Glendoick House at 100 feet (30·4 metres) above sea-level. 100 feet higher up with afternoon shade only, it was a full week later and flowered perfectly. Another garden 1,000 feet (304·8 metres) up, 30 miles away, is nearly always about two weeks later than us. Even a few yards can make a difference between complete frosting of flowers and no damage at all, so it is well worth placing the most susceptible varieties in the most frost-free sites. These can only be discovered by trial and error although the use of synchronized thermometers may help.

It is often far from easy to avoid the early morning sun and in any case, if the frost is more severe than about 24 °F (− 4·5 °C), most varieties will be blackened anyway. Other precautions which can be tried are overhead irrigation during frost or 'smudge pots' to raise the temperature above the plants. Both methods are sometimes used for fruit. Glass or perspex cloches over dwarfs do help, but also force flowers to open earlier if not removed during the day.

For winter protection of small plants, cloches can also be used or hessian (burlap) screens. Wire-netting filled with dry straw, bracken or leaves is good, or apply a hat or screen tied around with evergreen foliage. Beware that these do not rot the plants being protected.

Here are some examples of temperatures recorded in the Himalayas by Kingdon Ward. On the dry Nam La Pass, up to 28 °F of frost (4 °F, −16·75 °C) were registered in November where *R. lepidotum*, *R. fragariflorum*, *R. laudandum* and others grew. In January in a valley there were 39 °F of frost (−7 °F, −21·75 °C) and many nights almost as low, with no snow cover.

Lastly, recent research in the USA has found that the percentage of water in the apical stems is closely related to hardiness. One azalea variety with a low percentage of water was more bud hardy and less liable to bark-split than another with a higher percentage. When the stems of the more tender variety were allowed to dry, they could survive at a lower temperature. In future breeding, selection of clones with lower and lower water contents should give increased winter hardiness.

3 *Climates*

In the first part of this chapter, a comparison is made of various places in or near where at least some rhododendrons are grown. These places are thought to be average for the area and are not necessarily important rhododendron-growing places themselves. The second part of the chapter gives brief descriptions of the climates in all the main growing areas in the world.

| | Rainfall | | | Temperatures | | | |
| | | | | Extremes | | Mean | |
	Annual	Summer	Winter	High	Low	July	January
'ain							
w (observatory)	23·8 in. (60·3cm)	11·6 in. (29·5cm)	12·2 in. (31·1cm)	94°F (34·5°C)	9°F (−13°C)	63°F (17·25°C)	41°F (5°C)
mouth	43·6 in. (1·10m)	16·1 in. (40·8cm)	27·5 in. (69·8cm)	85°F (29·5°C)	20°F (−6·75°C)	61°F (16°C)	44°F (6·75°C)
erpool	27·9 in. (70·9cm)	13·8 in. (35cm)	14·1 in. (35·7cm)	89°F (31·75°C)	9°F (−13°C)	60°F (15·5°C)	41°F (5°C)
monell, Ayrshire	44·8 in. (1·14m)	18·1 in. (45·9cm)	26·7 in. (67·9cm)	88°F (31°C)	12°F (−11°C)	58°F (14·5°C)	40°F (4·5°C)
rdeen	29·5 in. (74·9cm)	13·6 in. (34·3cm)	15·9 in. (40·4cm)	86°F (30°C)	4°F (−15·5°C)	57°F (14°C)	39°F (4°C)
ope							
gen, Norway	77 in. (1·96m)	34·8 in. (88·5cm)	42·3 in. (1·73m)	89°F (31·8°C)	8°F (−13·5°C)	59°F (15°C)	34·5°F (1·5°C)
teborg, Sweden	24·3 in. (67cm)	14·7 in. (37·2cm)	11·75 in. (29·8cm)	89·5°F (32°C)	−15°F (−26°C)	62·5°F (17°C)	30°F (−1·1°C)
enhagen, Denmark	23·7 in. (60·1cm)	12·8 in. (32·7cm)	10·8 in. (27·4cm)	91°F (32·7°C)	−15°F (−26°C)	64°F (17·8°C)	31°F (−1°C)
swege, N. Germany	30·5 in. (78cm)				−22°F (−30°C)		
genfurt, Austria	38·7 in. (98·4cm)	24·1 in. (61cm)	14·6 in. (37cm)			65·8°F (19°C)	20·5°F (−7°C)
Bilt, Netherlands	30·2 in. (76·5cm)	15·6 in. (39·5cm)	14·6 in. (27·7cm)	98°F (36·8°C)	−14°F (−24·8°C)	63°F (17°C)	29°F (−1·7°C)
is, France	23 in. (58·5cm)	12·1 in. (30·8cm)	10·9 in. (27·7cm)	103°F (39·6°C)	1°F (−17°C)	66°F (19°C)	26°F (−3·1°C)
e Maggiore, Italy	78 in. (1·98m)				10°F (−11·9°C)		
runna, Spain	38·1 in. (96·9cm)	12·7 in. (32·4cm)	25·5 in. (64·6cm)	92°F (33·6°C)	27°F (−3·0°C)	65°F (18·2°C)	50°F (9·9°C)
stralia							
ney	47·4 in. (1·21m)	23·6 in. (60·1cm)	23·8 in. (60·4cm)	114°F (45·3°C)	36°F (2·1°C)	53°F (11·8°C)	77°F (22°C)
lbourne	27·2 in. (69·1cm)	14 in. (35·4cm)	13·2 in. (33·7cm)	114°F (45·6°C)	27°F (−2·8°C)	49°F (9·6°C)	68°F (19·9°C)
w Zealand							
nedin	31 in. (78·7cm)	16·1 in. (40·8cm)	14·9 in. (37·9cm)	94°F (34·4°C)	23°F (−5°C)	43·5°F (6·4°C)	59°F (14·9°C)
ristchurch	26·2 in. (66·8cm)	12·1 in. (38·8cm)	14·1 in. (36cm)	97°F (36·1°C)	19°F (−7·1°C)	42°F (5·7°C)	62°F (16·4°C)

	Rainfall			Temperatures			
				Extremes		Mean	
	Annual	*Summer*	*Winter*	*High*	*Low*	*July*	*Januar*
Pukeiti (N. Island)	130 in. Evenly distributed (3·30m) throughout the year			80°F (26·75°C)	16°F (−9°C)	60°F (15·5°C)	45–50° (7·25–10
North America							
Boston	44·6 in. (1·13m)	21·7 in. (55·2cm)	22·9 in. (58cm)		−8°F (approx) (−22°C)	71·3°F (22°C)	27·0°F (−3°C
Cleveland Ohio	38·1 in. (96·6cm)	21·1 in. (53·5cm)	17·0 in. (43·2cm)		−9°F (−22·8°C)	71·9°F (22·25°C)	27·1°F (−6·2°c
Washington DC	40·8 in. (1·04m)	22·4 in. (57·0cm)	18·4 in. (46·6cm)			76·8°F (25°C)	32·9°F (0·5°C
San Francisco	22·7 in. (57·6cm)	2·7 in. (6·83cm)	20·0 in. (50·8cm)	97°F (36°C)	27°F (−2·8°F)	57·3°F (14°C)	45°F (7·25°C
Portland Oregon	39·4 in. (1·05m)	8·86 in. (22·5cm)	30·6 in. (77·8cm)	107°F (41·75°C)	−2°F (−19°C)		52°F (11·1°C
Vancouver BC	65·3 in. (1·96cm)	17·4 in. (44·2cm)	47·89 in. (1·22m)	95°F (35°C)	0°F (−17·8°C)		30°F (−1·2°
Atlanta Georgia	47·14 in. (1·19m)	23·04 in. (58·4cm)	24·1 in. (61·0cm)	103°F (39·5°C)	−8°F (−22·25°C)		28°F (−2·2°C
South America							
Valdivia Chile	105 in. (2·67m)	26·7 in. (67·8cm)	78·3 in. (1·98m)			46°F (7·75°C)	59·5°F (59·5°C
Buenos Aires	36·5 in. (92·7cm)	20·4 in. (51·8cm)	16·1 in. (40·7cm)			50·2°F (10°C)	73·6° (23°C)
India							
Darjeeling	122·7 in. (3·12m)	114·2 in. (2·90m)	8·5 in. (21·6cm)		23°F (−5°C)	61·5°F (16°C)	40·1°F (4·5°C
Hong Kong	80·1 in. (2·03m)	67·7 in. (1·72m)	12·4 in. (31·4cm)		29°F (−1·8°C) (approx.)	81·7°F (27·5°C)	59·7°F (15·25°
Japan							
Nagasaki	77 in. (1·96m)	55·7 in. (1·41m)	21·3 in. (54·5cm)	99·5°F (37·5°C)	26°F (−3·2°C)	79·5°F (26·3°C)	43·5°F (6·4°C
Tokyo		Slightly drier			and colder than Nagasaki		
Sapporo Hokkaido	43·8 in. (1·36m)	21·4 in. (54·5cm)	22·4 in. (59cm)	96°F (35·8°C)	−19°F (−28·5°C)	68°F (20°C)	10°F (−11·6°

Regional Climates

BRITAIN

West coastal areas. Plenty of rain falling throughout the year, generally with a high humidity. Rainfall 40–100 in. (1·016–2·54m). Mild winters with temperatures rarely below 15 °F (−9·5 °C). Cool summers, temperatures rarely exceeding 80 °F (26·75 °C). Months of May to October usually free of frost. Little snow.

Central and eastern districts. Occasional droughts but rainfall usually just adequate. Rainfall 20–30 in. (50·8–76·2cm). Moderately cold winters with frosts as severe as 0–+10°F (−17·75–12·25°C). Warmer less humid summers, with temperatures sometimes reaching 90 °F (32·25 °C) or more. Only months of June to September usually free of frost. Some snow most years.

EUROPE

Western and southern Scandinavia. Rainfall throughout the year, plentiful on west coast and just sufficient elsewhere, 20–100 in. (50·8cm–2·54m). Moderate to severe winters down to −22 °F (−30 °C). Cool summers rarely exceeding 90 °F (32·25 °C). Short growing season May to October with fewer warm winter spells to bring on early growth than in Britain. Much snow.

North-western and northern coastal Europe, Belgium to north Gernany. Moderate rainfall throughout the year, around 25–30 in. (63·5–76·2cm). Winters often severe with frosts of 0 °F−−22 °F (−17·75–30 °C). Summers warm, often up to 100 °F (37·75 °C). A moderate amount of snow. Growing season May to October.

South-central Europe around the Alps. Rainfall usually adequate, falling mostly in summer. Few dry periods with little wind and many cloudy or foggy days. Moderate maximum temperatures and few late spring frosts. Little snow at low levels.

North-west Spain and north Portugal. Rainfall mostly in winter necessitating shade and watering in the growing season. Moderate summer and winter temperatures with very little frost. Is proving quite a favourable area for rhododendrons.

AUSTRALIA AND NEW ZEALAND

South-east Australia. Summer rains usually inadequate with severe droughts at times. The best regions for rhododendrons are the mountains such as the Dandenong and Blue Mountains with 50–60 in. (1·27–1·524m) of rain. Winter temperatures rarely fall much below 32 °F (0 °C) with occasional light snowfalls. Summer temperatures can be high, frequently up to 100 °F (37·75 °C). Heavy summer mulches are very beneficial for retaining moisture. Early flowering varieties are often the most satisfactory.

New Zealand. The west coast is wetter and warmer at any given latitude but the majority of people live in the east. The clear atmosphere leads to well-ripened wood and early flowering. The growing season is usually two months longer than in Britain. The extreme north is not cold enough to rest dwarfs sufficiently and pests and diseases are troublesome. Most of the east of the North Island has a rather dry summer with brilliant sunshine, so shade is necessary. The hill country of the South Island is the best, while irrigation is needed in much of the east. Spring frosts can cause damage.

AFRICA

Few rhododendrons have so far been grown on this continent. High regions in East Africa would probably suit the Malesian varieties very well if water is given in the dry seasons.

The escarpment of the Drakensburg Mountains in South Africa, where rainfall is heavy, should be an excellent region. Pietermaritzburg area at 2,000–4,000 feet (609–1,218 metres) is very good for Obtusum azaleas especially *R. indicum* types. Spring and summer rains. Some of the higher coastal areas of Cape Province where heathers grow naturally could be suitable but watering would be needed at times. Obtusum azaleas also successful in Cape when sheltered from south-eastern winds. Rains chiefly in winter.

NORTH AMERICA

There are many different climatic regions in North America. Nearly all have higher summer temperatures than in Britain so some watering is needed in most areas.

North-eastern areas inland. Moderate rainfall, usually falling all the year round. Hot summers and very cold winters as low as $-28\,°F$ ($-33\,°C$) or even lower. Only the very hardiest varieties will survive and these include very few dwarfs.

North-east coastal areas. Moderate rainfall, often falling all the year round. East Long Island has moderate temperatures with $0°F$ ($-17.75\,°C$) minimum and the low 90s F ($32.25\,°C$) maximum in summer.

South-eastern areas inland. Moderate to heavy rainfall falling throughout the year. While the winter temperatures are not unduly severe, northerly blasts alternate with dry south-westerly winds and buds are easily killed. Summers are hot, often reaching over $100\,°F$ ($37.75\,°C$).

Gulf region. Moderate rainfall falling throughout the year. Houston average maximum temperature 108 °F (42·25 °C), minimum 5 °F (−15 °C). Plenty of shade needed. Some Obtusum azaleas succeed. Summers too hot for most dwarfs.

North-west coastal regions: Oregon, Washington and south British Columbia. See Portland for details. Rainfall mostly during winter, needing a considerable amount of watering in summer. Most of the varieties grown in Britain succeed in this area especially in local, micro-climates. A disastrous frost of −12 °F (−24·4 °C) for nearly a week in mid-December 1972, struck parts of this region. Heavy losses are reported. This is the lowest temperature so far recorded in the area.

North-west inland areas: eastern Oregon and Washington over the Cascade Mountains. Rainfall usually inadequate with very dry summers and cold winters.

San Francisco Bay area. Best suited to the larger and tender varieties. Dwarfs are very unreliable owing to the lack of cold winters. Away from the immediate coastal belt where there is less influence from fog, some summers are hotter and winters are cooler. Shade and frequent sprinklings are necessary.

Southern California. Rhododendrons are generally unsuitable south of Carmel although a few are grown in San Diego. Maddeniis and Obtusum azaleas best. Elepidotes not really successful.

SOUTH AMERICA

Southern Chile. Ample rainfall, falling mostly in winter. Winters not very severe and summers not too hot. Probably very suitable conditions for many of the more tender varieties. North Chile too dry.

Argentina: Buenos Aires area. Rainfall all the year round, mostly in summer but the summers are very hot. There is a heavy rainfall near the Chilean frontier. Some varieties do well and the Malesians could be promising.

ASIA

India: Himalayan foothills. Abundant summer rains and no frost. Hardly ideal for dwarfs. Malesians might grow.

D

Hong Kong. Plenty of rain in summer. Sea-level probably too hot but good conditions should be available on the peaks for tender varieties and probably Malesians.

Japan. Lowland districts in central and southern areas are too hot for dwarfs but the hills and Hokkaido will suit hardy varieties. Rain usually abundant mostly falling in summer in central areas. Obtusum azaleas grow well of course.

4 *Planting and Maintenance*

Soil Preparation and Drainage

This is perhaps the most important section of the book, because if rhododendrons are planted in unsuitable soil they will never flourish. Again I want to draw attention to *pp.* 13–25 to show how, why and where they grow naturally, to give an idea of ideal soil conditions and how best to simulate them.

Unfortunately, naturally ideal soil conditions are rarely to be found in one's own garden and there may not even be anything approaching this within hundreds of miles. It might, as I have already mentioned, be possible to beg, borrow or steal a piece of ground where really suitable conditions already exist. Invariably though, something has to be done such as fencing, felling trees or drainage. In natural peat soils, the peat usually forms due to poor drainage, therefore considerable draining will need to be done for rhododendrons to succeed. Laying drainage tiles tends to be unsatisfactory in peat, and in any case, in a woodland area it is just about out of the question. So open ditches are really the only answer and if the peat is thick, they may have to be of considerable depth. Rhododendrons can take a while to establish in pure peat and the addition of a little fertilizer (see *pp.* 56–59), and even some lime (preferably dolomitic or magnesium) or gypsum can help initial growth.

Nearly as good as natural peat, and with few drainage problems, is a really sandy soil such as greensand which sometimes overlies chalk. As long as plenty of organic matter is added (if it does not occur naturally as pine needles, or oak or beech leafmould), which not only helps to feed the plants but also retains moisture and holds nutrients, rhododendrons revel in it. The organic matter added can be peat, oak and beech leafmould, pine or spruce needles. Many other sources of organic matter are used in the USA and these will be studied shortly.

Loams are rather liable to be approaching neutrality on the pH scale and contain a fair percentage of clay and silt which are not really good ingredients in a rhododendron soil. They get sticky and unworkable in wet weather and hard with cracks in a dry summer. The only way to be sure of good growth is to add plenty of peat and leafmould before planting. For really dwarf varieties and Obtusum azaleas, prepare beds by rotovating or forking in an abundance of coarse sand, peat and leafmould, and take care *never* to consolidate these beds too much.

We do not trench our beds. Both the late Lord Aberconway and the late Lionel de Rothschild recommended trenching, but they were rich men with plenty of gardeners. I would agree that rotovating and forking do not go as deep as trenching but the added materials are possibly better mixed at the right level for the shallow root-systems of dwarfs. Larger plants are put in holes well forked over with the above organic matter added, and these are made several times the size of the root ball to be planted. Break into the surrounding soil a little so as not to leave a straight division between worked and unworked soil and fork over the bottom of each hole.

The better clay soils where drainage is fairly good can be improved for rhododendrons to grow in satisfactorily, but not as well as in the light soils. The use of gypsum to floculate the soil often helps considerably, but all manner and means of material to loosen the clay should be added, such as gravel, sand, wood or bark chips and all other kinds of organic matter; only work the soil when it is at its best state for handling. Deep cultivation may help, and under some conditions filling the bottom of the hole with stones, gravel or clinkers is a good idea, but if the drainage is poor, this will only act as a sump. If, when a rhododendron is planted, water will puddle around its roots after heavy rain or hosing, it should be assumed that the drainage is inadequate and the use of a raised bed will be necessary.

Heavy clay needs this special treatment. Large areas of southern England and America suffer from this bugbear. Countless failures have come about by people trying to plant into this stuff, and in the main southern parts of the USA especially, Phytophthora root rot adds another hazard to would-be growers (see Chapter 10).

Many gardeners in these districts have come to the conclusion that all rhododendrons should be grown in raised beds with little or none of the natural soil mixed in. This largely solves the drainage and root rot problems in one. In America, they use virtually any organic matter that they can lay their hands on in each particular locality.

In forested districts, wood chips, sawdust, shredded bark, pine and spruce needles, forest litter, cones, rotten wood, etc., and in others, peat, swamp muck, peanut hulls, crushed corn cobs, etc. can be used. All ingredients should be well mixed and can be surrounded by thick boards, large peat blocks or rocks.

The use of sawdust has caused a tremendous amount of controversy in America. For some reason or another, in the northeastern states it is considered unsatisfactory for mixing into the soil and is hardly ever used. Whether it is to do with the types of tree, climate, soil conditions or what, is not apparently known, but it may be because the sawdust is too fine. In the West, where there is still virgin forest and big second growth to cut, huge saws produce a very coarse sawdust which is found to be excellent for mulching or adding to the soil for raised beds, *provided* plenty of nitrogen is added for its breakdown. If no nitrogen is added, all that is available in the soil is utilized by micro-organisms for the rotting period, which results in terrible chlorosis and frequently death of the rhododendrons. As a rough guide for fresh sawdust, add 12 pounds of ammonium sulphate per 1,000 square feet (93 square metres) for each inch (2·5 centimetres) of sawdust worked into the soil. Old sawdust naturally needs less nitrogen but it decays quicker and looses its property as a soil conditioner more rapidly. Certain sawdusts like alder break down quicker than others. Shredded bark likewise needs nitrogen added in similar quantities. A half soil or sand and half sawdust mixture has given good results where the soil is loam or sand rather than clay.

Some words of warning are needed here. Many dwarfs, notably species of the Neriiflorum series and their hybrids and the Roxieanum sub-series of the Taliense series, are highly allergic to excessive nitrogen, and with them the combination of sawdust and ammonium sulphate should be carefully experimented with in case many valuable plants get severely damaged or killed.

Sometimes even a lighter clay soil can be mixed into a raised bed with good results. One grower from North Carolina on red clay has used the following procedure: raised beds proved to be the only successful method, 10 to 12 inches (25 to 30 centimetres) above normal soil-level. He used 60 per cent *coarse* sawdust, 30 per cent clayey top-soil and 10 per cent sharp sand. Each bushel of sawdust had a quarter of a pint of ammonium sulphate added. 10 to 12 inches (25 to 30 centimetres) of the sawdust-sand and ammonium were mixed with the top 3 to 4 inches (7·5 to 10 centimetres) of existing soil. It was well mixed and all clods pulverized.

In Dallas, Texas, usually considered beyond the suitable area for rhododendron culture in the USA, masses of azaleas were planted in raised beds made of 12-inch (30cm) boards filled with peat moss. Soil was shaped around the beds to blend with the surroundings and the azaleas apparently did well.

For a small area, the soil conditioner Perlite can be used. It is an expanded feather-light (when dry) material of volcanic origin. It holds moisture, largely between its own granules, and facilitates the movement of air in the soil.

One American suggests that a way of getting rid of litter *and* helping rhododendrons is to put it all down large holes on top of which they can be planted. First put in tin cans and other rubbish with a little soil between layers and then add paper and kitchen refuse (taking care there is no grease) and again add a little soil. Trample all down thoroughly and if the soil is poor, add fertilizer to each layer. The paper acts as a reserve for moisture for the first year and the plants apparently do well for year after year with no water-logging experienced.

Rotten wood is excellent mixed generously into planting holes and it has not been found necessary to add fertilizer. (There could be a danger of honey fungus from this.)

One of the most successful ways of growing dwarfs is in peat beds built up in terraces with blocks of peat. It is hard to know what is the best type of peat to use for these walls. Some kinds disintegrate quicker than others. Get the blocks as big as possible and they are better laid when damp or soaked in water as they take a long time to moisten again if laid dry, and distort the line of the wall as they swell again. Slant the blocks inwards and do not build them more than three to four blocks high. If the ground is steep, narrow beds can be made with a wall for each. Pack the soil firmly both behind and under the blocks. These walls usually last a few years but odd blocks may break up quicker than others and can be replaced. Birds are liable to attack them and pull them to bits. Naturally the beds should contain a high percentage of organic matter themselves. Small plants can be placed between the blocks.

A predecessor of the peat wall was the 'rootery' which consisted of old dead tree stumps turned upsidedown with all the root ends sawn off. Such plants as dwarf rhododendrons, primulas, etc., were placed in the corners between the root branches. This method of culture was considered a success for a while but was ousted by the peat wall, because it was more attractive and the danger of honey fungus (*Armillaria*) always hangs over anything connected with dead roots in Britain.

Lastly, be sure to make plenty of paths, and place stepping stones through beds and peat walls, so that all plants can be reached for hand maintenance without having to step on the beds. Rhododendrons cannot abide having their roots trodden on. If the soil becomes solidified they will sicken and die.

Selection of Plants

There are various ways in which a collection of dwarf rhododendrons can be built up. The most usual is to buy plants from a reputable nurseryman. Another is to beg from a friend. In a few cases, occasional species can be collected in the wild, but as most natural rhododendron areas are closed to us at present, we are very limited in this respect. The other way is to propagate from cuttings or seed (see Chapter 9).

Unfortunately, many nurseries send out wrongly named plants with the result that gardens all over the world invariably have many incorrectly labelled. Often this is through ignorance on the nurseryman's part, but sometimes I am afraid he is dishonest and substitutes something else, if sold out of the item asked for. So go to a reputable nursery only.

Likewise, a friend may give a plant which is not what he says it is and even many botanical gardens and other institutions may have plants with the labels mixed up. So it is not always easy to get hold of what is wanted, especially if it is rare.

Self-sown seedlings are also something to beware of. They may be all very well for filling up some odd corner if there is plenty of other room for choice or named varieties. Several people report that their seedlings breed true to type. It is true that some do, especially if a group of the same species grows together, but, by and large, self-sown seedlings, as with open pollinated seed, are an awful gamble (see *pp.* 249, 262) and often produce muddy-coloured flowers of no beauty. The Americans and many others have learned to their cost that open pollinated seed from large collections is hybridized more often than not. Luckily, people are realizing this now and demanding hand pollinated seed. Cuttings of course produce a plant true to type, so it is essential to make sure they come off the clone desired.

So much for the source of plants. While it is tempting to buy large specimens if they can be afforded, they invariably turn out less satisfactory in the long run.

Large specimens of dwarfs often lack vigour and are apt to be somewhat ill-treated in nurseries. But the main drawback of large plants is that the soil at the nursery may be entirely different from the garden they are planted in which can make them hard to re-establish. Rhododendrons from Towercourt, Berkshire, England, had very shallow root-systems in a peculiar light soil lying on a hard pan, and have taken a long time to settle down, if at all, in other districts. Vigorous young stock, on the other hand, readily makes new roots and grows very well, provided the ground is suitably prepared. Container plants require a little extra care over watering if planted in hot dry weather and gently loosen any solid root balls before planting.

Do select the right size of varieties for a given site. All too often, paths disappear after a few years and bigger varieties swamp out the smaller (planting is dealt with later in this Chapter).

No argument will be introduced here on species versus hybrids. All that shall be said is that there should be no discrimination against either. In general, hybrids are the easier to grow and more free flowering, while the species have more interesting flowers and foliage and their beauty is more subtle.

Fertilizers, pH and Lime

FERTILIZERS

Before going into this subject, it should be made clear that a golden rule is – if your soil is naturally suitable for rhododendrons and all are doing well, and if natural mulches are available (this excludes wood by-products like sawdust which needs fertilizer added to it), use them only and do *not* read this part of the book.

The large robust hybrids and deciduous hybrid azaleas, neither of which are dealt with in this book, very much appreciate the use of fertilizers and respond well with additional vigour and flowers. Many dwarfs are rather a different proposition and several words of caution are necessary. The Neriiflorum series and its hybrids and the Roxieanum sub-series of the Taliense series are very sensitive to excessive nitrogen and may suffer from severe leaf-burn or even death from a dose suitable for other varieties.

In the past, only organic fertilizers and manures were recommended for rhododendrons, but now there are slow-acting compounds available which give a gradual release of the elements concerned over a longish period with beneficial results.

The trouble with the use of fertilizers is that few hard and fast rules can be given. So much depends on the state and composition of the soil it is to be added to. The soil itself has a very complex chemical constitution and so many factors are involved with the availability or otherwise of the nutrient present. This all depends on *a*) the pH of the soil (pH for those in doubt is a means of measuring the soil acidity or alkalinity: pH 7 is neutral, 6 is slighty acid and 8 slightly alkaline; pH 5 is ten times more acid than 6 and 4 is a hundred times more acid than 6 and so on; 9 is ten times more alkaline than 8); *b*) the soil composition (i.e. of sand, silt, clay, etc.); and *c*) the quantity of the various elements present. A surfeit of one may tie up others and make them completely unavailable to plants, so unhealthy foliage with chlorosis may occur. This is a common indication of an inbalance of plant nutrients, and may be due to either an excess of one element or an absence or unavailability of another or even several elements.

Rhododendrons grow naturally in soils high in organic matter and relatively low in most essential elements. This is not to say that they can do without any of these.

In Britain, we have grown rhododendrons for many years, and in a large percentage of gardens no fertilizers are ever used and the plants remain in good health.

It is true that in many parts of America, Australia and other countries, conditions are entirely different from here and very often the soil and climate are not as favourable as we enjoy. It must be admitted that British growers, both amateur and professional, are in many ways lagging behind in knowledge and practice of rhododendron culture; but on account of the difficulties in America, much more care over watering, mulching, etc., are needed there. Americans in their enthusiasm over endeavouring to grow perfect rhododendrons have, let there be no doubt, vastly overdone the use of fertilizers and pesticides.

For those varieties that need or appreciate fertilizer, use a balanced mixture of 5 parts nitrogen (N), 10 phosphate (P) and 10 potassium (K), preferably before late April, and not more than one ounce per square yard (0·84 square metres). Commonly, this mixture is available with N as ammonium sulphate, P as superphosphate and K as potassium sulphate. These are quick acting, and for rhododendrons the newer slow-release compounds are better. Urea is a good form of N but may encourage late growth. Organic based fertilizer 12N 6P 6K promotes excellent growth if applied in early spring.

Ripening of wood in the autumn can be improved by the use of a combined P and K fertilizer (see *p.* 42). It has now been discovered that P alone can increase the set of flower buds and the quality of the flowers. This should be applied in late autumn or early spring. Dig some little holes into the root area with a broom or trowel handle, three or four per established specimen of any size, one or two for a smaller plant. Insert a lump of super or triple phosphate, about 1–1½ inches (2·5–3·8 centimetres) across, into each hole and then plug it up with soil or just spread a handful over the root area.

Nurserymen in America now use very heavy doses of phosphate to induce bud set, but this tends to check growth so it is not to be recommended for the amateur. Also, it can produce an iron deficiency if this is locked up by the phosphate.

Various organic fertilizers are used for rhododendrons. Hoof and horn, dried blood, cotton-seed meal and soyabean meal (the last two are available in the USA only). All contain N and break down into the desirable ammonium form. But they are more expensive than inorganic compounds and do not contain enough organic matter to be of any significance. Bonemeal contains a little lime but the amount is rather small.

Magnesium deficiency frequently shows up in rhododendrons. Either magnesium sulphate (Epsom salts) can be applied (rather a low availability normally); or use a modern compound which has Mg added.

Trace elements are also very important and while these do generally occur in sufficient quantities, if chlorosis shows widely, it can be worth while applying these in fritted form (now available in the USA and Britain). Be careful not to overdose with these, and before spreading on the soil, mix with some sand or peat to make an even distribution easier.

For the use of bulky manures, see mulches, *pp.* 66–9. Liquid fertilizers can be watered on foliage as a foliar, or used as a general feed. Many different products are made for this purpose. They can be applied with a syringe, watering-can, or by way of a watering system whether overhead or trickle. Once a fortnight in the growing season is quite sufficient.

pH AND LIME

A great deal has been written in the past about rhododendrons and their pH and lime tolerance or otherwise and many contradictory statements have been made. Most people know that rhododendrons are said to be calcifuge plants and this is by and large true. If excessive free calcium is present in the soil, they are all too ready to take up too much of this and not enough of other elements, resulting in chlorosis and a gradual loss of health. It is probably this ability to assimilate calcium which enables rhododendrons to flourish on soils which contain very little calcium indeed, and they have not the power to avoid taking in a surplus if it is present in the soil. This was discovered by Dr Henry Tod of Edinburgh School of Agriculture.

It has been proved that rhododendrons will grow in a soil of a high pH, provided not too much free calcium is available. As mentioned in Chapter 1, many have been found growing naturally on limestone. These soils have rarely been analysed which is a great pity. Calcium and magnesium (Mg) are associated widely in various dolomitic and serpentine-type limestones and this accounts for some of the reported cases of rhododendrons on limestone. As they are tolerant of the Mg which is a related element, this gets assimilated into the plant instead of the calcium.

Very high or low pH's make certain essential elements unavailable to all plants. Naturally ideal rhododendron soils vary from pH 4·0 to 6·0 for most species and if one's own garden lies above this range, improvements can be made, either by adding organic matter or, if far from ideal, chemicals. Most forms of peat and conifer needles naturally lower the pH a little, but if further help is needed, either sulphur or ferrous sulphate can be added.

There are other ways of improving alkaline soils. If just about neutral, with the careful use of fritted trace elements and chelates, some success can be anticipated. Different forms of chelates (sequestrines) are effective on different soils but it is easy to cause burning of the foliage with these. If the soil is very alkaline with a pH of 7·5 or higher, raised beds (see *p.* 52–3) are the only answer.

If the soil is highly acid, below a pH of 4·0, there are likely to be deficiencies of calcium and magnesium and these should be added, preferably in the form of calcium sulphate (gypsum) or dolomitic limestone or both.

Judith Berrisford in *Rhododendrons and Azaleas* wrote extensively on alkaline soil problems with much personal experience, having lived with a pH of 7·5. She explained how she made holes lined with flowers of sulphur, filled with acid peat and rotted bracken which were also mixed with the surrounding soil at the edges of the holes. The plants were then mulched with pine needles and chopped bracken to a depth of 6 inches (15 centimetres), added twice a year. She found that many lepidote dwarfs grew well treated like this and without the use of sequestrine which was liable to cause toxicity symptoms. Dr Tod told her that magnesium and manganese were equally as important as iron. She applied magnesium sulphate (Epsom salts) at the rate of two tablespoons to two gallons of water over the root area of each plant 3 or 4 times a year during the growing season. Manganese sulphate she used as a leaf spray, one ounce to two gallons, applied in the evening of a dull day. Another point she made is that rhododendrons are much more easily grown on limestone areas than pure chalk.

Some species and their hybrids are moderately lime tolerant and these should be used in preference in doubtful soil conditions (see Chapter 11 for list).

Chlorosis is not necessarily brought on by lime. It can be started by so many different causes such as bad drainage and excessive rainfall, the wrong use of weedkillers, as well as deficiencies and toxicities from the soil elements. Books have been written on deficiencies showing photographs of each example, but although helpful, they cannot be fully relied on. Many rhododendrons are very subject to chlorosis if conditions do not fully suit their needs.

Planting

I must apologize for describing such well-known tasks as planting in detail to those who know it all. The trouble is that it is still all too easy to find even quite extensive collections badly planted and looked after. So these points have to be drummed repeatedly into those who fail to observe these rules.

The first essential point to remember is, never plant too deeply. (The only exception to this golden rule is in growing grafted plants. With each transplanting, place a little deeper so as to completely cover the union and let the scion form its own roots.) Space out any loose roots at their proper level and push soil gently underneath them. Only a bare sprinkling of soil should be put on top of the existing root ball. It is usually simple to locate the old soil-level on the stem(s) near the base. Never mound up soil around the stem after planting. Never trample in a rhododendron too firmly, especially in heavy soil, as remember, they like loose, well-aerated conditions. It pays well to water the plants in with a hose or a watering-can with a coarse rose on it, especially in America. Occasional extra firming may be necessary because of wind-shake, and staking may be needed. Only in light, very well drained soils should they be planted in a saucer which can help to conserve moisture and hold a mulch on a steep slope. In really wet areas with a high humidity, it is not always necessary even to plant. Rhododendrons often flourish if laid on top of the prepared ground with a shovel of leafmould thrown around the roots.

Never plant on a mound in dry areas. It will only lead to the roots drying out quicker and it is hard to retain a mulch on a mound. Only in wet districts and imperfectly drained ground does it pay to plant on such a situation.

The distance apart to plant is a matter of choice, depending whether an immediate effect is required, or you are prepared to wait a few years for the gaps to close. As already stated, rhododendrons are sociable plants, and for their own good, I much prefer relatively close planting and subsequent respacing out every few years. Most dwarfs are fairly easily handled even after a few years' growth. Bare soil is not attractive and encourages weeds, so it is better to have it covered quickly. One, two or three feet apart are the usual distances for planting, depending on how dwarf or slow-growing the variety is. Leggy varieties are best in groups planted close together.

Do not transplant in late spring in hot climates, as this only increases the danger of drying out and leaf-burn. In fact, we recommend autumn planting in all districts of Britain, early autumn being the best, because a few new roots will be made before winter and the whole plant has a chance to bed itself down and withstand dry spring weather. With their compact root balls, rhododendrons *can* be transplanted at any time, provided special care is taken over subsequent watering and mulching. Attach permanent labels after planting.

Some people like to plant in spring because they say that their particular spring weather is extremely severe. But to take a plant from a nursery at sea-level to a cold garden at a thousand feet (304 metres) in March or April is only asking for trouble. That plant will be about two weeks in advance of what the normal growth would be at 1,000 feet and is therefore all the more vulnerable to damage from late frosts and wind.

A few dwarfs planted late can be protected in very hot weather by placing inverted flower pots over them. These can stay in place for a week or more. Another recommendation of Captain Collingwood Ingram's for his dry Kent, or a similar climate, is to cover the roots of dwarfs with two to four stones. Place up to the stems. The stones are all the better for being of a porous nature. This helps to give a cool root run for slow growers such as *R. ludlowii* and *R. pumilum*.

Remember that rhododendron roots are seldom completely dormant. Unless the ground is frozen solid, they are always getting on with the job of taking in the necessary amount of water to keep the whole bush turgid.

Aftercare of Plants

All too many people consider that once a tree or shrub is planted it can fend for itself, provided the worst of the weeds are removed. While this may be true with certain forest trees, it is now found that even they benefit from some fertilizers. Many old-established rhododendrons can, especially if well-clothed to the ground, survive several years of almost total neglect. Dwarfs need a little more care but they are really not great labour demanders as are beds of roses, herbaceous borders and annuals. If well-treated in the first place, only a minimum of care and attention is needed to keep them flourishing for a lifetime or more, especially with the bigger varieties.

It can be said that the further removed from an ideal climate and soil conditions the garden is, the more attention the occupants will require.

WATERING

Fortunate are the gardeners who rarely have to water their rhododendrons. In Scotland we fall into this category, with many summers having no drought periods at all. As fruit growers and grain farmers as well as rhododendron nurserymen, we do like the weather to produce a sort of compromise between ideal rhododendron and ideal farming weather. Many parts of England, too, get away with no watering systems laid on, and in the flat ditch-bound land in Boskoop, Holland, all they have to do is to raise or lower the water levels in the ditches.

In America and Australia, watering systems are essential to anyone doing rhododendron husbandry on any scale at all, as severe droughts are sure to happen sooner or later, and many districts have a long, dry summer season anyway. Much can be done by mulching to conserve moisture, but to succeed over a number of years, piped water *is* necessary. If the water is slightly alkaline, an acidifier (the best is ferrous sulphate) can be applied at 5 pounds per 100 square feet (9·29 square metres) twice a year. If very limey, do not use the water at all.

A golden rule is: once watering has started, it must be continued until the drought has finished. If any restrictions on the use of hoses are likely, it can be better not to start watering at all. The use of hoses was banned in south-east Australia in 1967–8. This of course led to many losses. Great care must be taken in warm climates, where drainage is poor, not to over-water.

In some places, routine watering is carried out every day or two, with a thorough soaking every week or so. Combined fertilizing and watering can be done.

Rhododendrons need abundant water, especially when in full growth, and any lack of it at this vital period will lead to poor growth for that season. This particularly applies to the varieties that make only one growth flush a year, such as species of the Neriiflorum and Taliense series. Watering is best done in early morning to soak in before the sun rises, although no harm has been noticed after watering during strong mid-day sunshine. Do not water in the evening in hot humid climates. It only encourages disease.

There are various ways of spreading water to the plants. Ideally, there should be a system of taps or stand pipes in strategic positions. These are easily laid nowadays with plastic pipes. Many choices of different overhead and trickle irrigation systems are now available and which to use depends largely on local conditions.

DEADHEADING

Rhododendrons are never deadheaded in the wild. There is no one to do it except certain bugs that eat the seeds. With the bigger species, the lack of deadheading leads to a reduced rate of growth and flower bud set, as a great deal of energy goes into the production of seed. Forrest and Kingdon Ward reported seeing practically no flowers at all certain years on the bigger species. The majority of varieties covered in this book are rather a different proposition. Once they reach flowering size (which most do very young) the truly alpine lepidotes flower consistently every year. Those with short flower stalks such as the Lapponicum series are next to impossible to dead-head and, provided they keep in good health, do not suffer. Other series such as Campylogynum, Saluenense and Uniflorum have long flower stalks which hold the flowers and capsules out beyond the leaves. These are quite easily deadheaded with a small pair of scissors. Poor growers like *R. ludlowii* and *R. pumilum* are well worth going over and should be done immediately after flowering as the capsules in most dwarfs swell rapidly. It depends on the amount of spare time available and the number of plants in the collection. All will benefit if they can be done. *R. racemosum* sets masses of ugly capsules which should be removed from an aesthetic point of view. Many lepidote hybrids are sterile so set no seed. Elepidote dwarfs are sometimes hard to deadhead too. Either use scissors or finger and thumb, great care being taken not to break the whole shoot off. It is all a question of practice.

PRUNING

If grown in full sun very few rhododendrons ever need pruning, and care should be taken not to spoil the symmetrical shape of a bush by cutting out chunks for show or decorative purposes. It may take years to close the gaps, and can well impair its health. If they get leggy, most dwarf lepidotes will respond well to pruning. They can be cut right back, but it is better to do this in two or three stages and allow young growth to come away from the base before removing all the old wood. If a Lapponicum or Saluenense is moved out of a clump, young growth will very often break away anyway without pruning and, if the shape is not too gawky, it may become quite symmetrical on its own. A good time to prune is during flowering and the prunings can be used for indoor decoration. Another way of dealing with an ugly drawn specimen is to plant it on the side and layer the shoots, resulting in several nice young plants (see *pp*. 260–1).

No rhododendron looks good when full of dead wood. One gardener, strongly in favour of removing all dead branches, says that when the job is completed, people come along and say 'how healthy and happy your rhododendrons look'.

WEEDKILLERS

It is only in the last few years that really suitable, reliably safe weed-killers have come on the market. Rhododendrons hate grass and other weeds growing on top of their shallow root-system. Now, with the use of a knapsack sprayer, it is easy to spray around established bushes.

Weedkillers can be divided into several groups. Firstly, if a piece of ground is to be cleared of all herbage, the most effective killer is still sodium chlorate. Do not plant into the treated area for at least six months after application, or longer in areas with a low rainfall.

There is a group which can be used as total weedkillers, for paths etc., if put on at high strength; but at low, they can be used on clean ground to kill germinating seeds. The best-known of these is Simazine. It is relatively safe to apply under rhododendrons if used very diluted, but all of these substances are rather persistent in the soil.

The so-called 'hormone' weedkillers, once thought to be practically harmless to mammals and birds, are now very suspect and 245T is banned in the USA. This, mixed with 24D, makes the so-called brushwood killer. 245T has not been prohibited here and possibly we use a different, less toxic form. Brushwood killer is very effective on nettles, but needs repeated applications to kill brambles (blackberries) and other shrubby growth. Certain brands are very volatile and the fumes after spraying on a warm, humid day can cause distortion of young rhododendron foliage. So together with the danger from drift, it is advisable not to spray too close to any shrubs. These herbicides are not effective on grasses.

Prefix (Dichlorothio benzamide) and Du Pont Hyvar X Bromacil weedkiller act in a different way through the growing tissues of the roots, and should be used for spot treatment in early spring. Do not apply close to the roots of rhododendrons.

Dalapon (Dowpon) and Aminotriazole are of little use in Scotland as they need high temperatures to act efficiently. These are used almost entirely for couch grass and unfortunately there is at present no good alternative for cold climates. These can be used after most growth is completed but before the temperature drops. They may cause some leaf-tip discoloration in lepidotes which will disappear the following season.

Two new herbicides are selective killers of docks (*Rumex* species) and should be applied twice. They are very slow acting. They are Asulox and Menthoxone No. 2. The former is also proving successful for killing bracken.

Lastly, the most useful weedkiller of them all, Paraquat (trade names Gramoxone, Weedol). This burns off most top growth and is quickly broken down in the soil (except on pure organic matter where it can persist for a while). It is safe to use right up to the trunks of rhododendrons and the odd drop which may get on to the foliage will only cause small brown spots. A little on to the mature

E

bark will do no harm, but do not touch green wood. Applied twice during the growing season, it will keep most non-deep-rooting weeds under excellent control. It will severely check bishop weed (ground elder, *Aegopodium podagraria*) but not nettles (*Urtica dioica*). Moss often forms in place of the weeds.

A word of warning. All prostrate or really low-growing varieties have to be weeded by hand close to them, and do avoid baring the roots by removing too much soil with the weeds.

There is a possibility that certain weedkillers may affect the ease of rooting cuttings if assimilated into the plant. Before applying any of the above, please read carefully all instructions.

MULCHING

A mulch is a layer of organic matter applied over the existing soil and not mixed into it. It is used for the following physical reasons: 1. to retain moisture; 2. to modify surface soil temperatures; 3. to prevent the erosive effect of rain; 4. to reduce the depth to which frost can penetrate the ground; 5. to control weeds; 6. to provide organic matter and nutrients.

In climates with hot dry summers, mulching has become a standard and very necessary method of conserving moisture in the soil. In Britain, with our cool and generally damp summers, these mulches are not essential and when applied, are largely used as a source of organic matter and method of nutrition rather than as a moisture retainer.

The mulch that is used largely depends on local availability. In Britain, the best and most easily obtained materials are oak and beech leafmould, chopped or pulverized bracken fronds, evergreen conifer needles and spent hops. Those to be avoided are peat, which dries out into a hard, water-impervious mat, grass mowings, which may heat and always makes a soggy carpet which spoils soil aeration, and leaves of other broad-leaved trees, which tend to exclude air if matted down and create an alkaline leafmould. British sawdust is usually too fine and likewise mats down too hard, preventing air and water reaching the soil but this is worth further investigation.

Before applying as a mulch, oak and beech leaves may either be chopped or ground into small pieces or stacked for two years to break down into finer particles naturally. If the heap is turned, it will rot quicker. Fresh leaves will blow away unless covered with some other material. If stacked too long, some of the value is lost. A warning: any leaves collected off trees growing on an alkaline soil will produce an undesirable alkaline leafmould.

A mulch has a modifying effect on soil temperatures and helps to stop the frost from reaching the entire root area. On the other hand, air temperatures can be as much as 6°F lower over mulched ground. This is due to the prevention of warmer air escaping from the soil surface. As a result, more damage is apt to be inflicted on immature growth.

The Americans use a large number of different mulches. In the West, wood by-products and waste materials are the most readily come by. The presence of large trees means the use of big saws which produce a very coarse sawdust. Douglas fir is considered the best, alder rots quickly but improves the soil, while the once discarded *Thuja* has now been proved safe to use. As sawdust robs the soil temporarily of nitrogen, due to the fungi and bacteria utilizing what N is present, extra N must be added (see *p.* 53).

As a rough guide for fresh sawdust, add 12 pounds of ammonium sulphate per 1,000 square feet (92·9 square metres) of surface, for every inch (2·5 centimetres) of sawdust applied. Some good gardeners make several lighter applications of fertilizer instead of one heavy one.

Like coarse sawdust, ground bark is excellent, but also needs ammonium sulphate added. Ground bark is in some ways preferable to sawdust, especially in its appearance. Other mulches used in the USA are chopped oak leaves, pine needles, sugar-can bagasse, wood chips and shavings and peanut hulls.

When chosing a mulch, consider cost, availability, appearance, fire hazard, frost protection, weed-seed content, acidity and rodent appeal.

There is little danger of over-mulching, provided there is adequate aeration and foliage is not buried. A big accumulation can lead to the roots becoming too deep unless they have worked their way up near the surface of the mulch itself.

In New Zealand, the late Edgar Stead found sawdust excellent, using *Pinus radiata*. He used it by itself and also on top of a layer of fresh leaves to keep them in place. He found the moisture-retaining properties wonderful. 100 pounds of coarse sawdust with 5 pounds of fish meal or 5 to 10 pounds of hen manure are good mixtures. Leave for 6 to 8 weeks and remix once or twice, adding water.

In the eastern USA entirely different results have been experienced from the use of sawdust. *Pinus strobus* sawdust is reckoned to contain some toxic substance, stunting and even killing plants. Also the smaller trees produce a finer grade. One nurseryman tells of successive applications being mixed with the soil, resulting in a very complicated feeding programme, plus a plague of root weevils and root rot. Some root rot occurred so quickly that the sawdust was a suspected carrier of the pathogen. He considered that sawdust mulching in the eastern states should be confined to permanent plantings.

Wood chips, on the other hand, do not have nearly so many problems. They have a great future as a mulch with no noxious effect if ploughed into the ground. In Britain, with our honey fungus (*Armillaria*) problems, these chips could cause trouble, especially in ground already infected.

According to Dr R. L. Ticknor, President of the American Rhododendron Society, the use of a sawdust or ground bark mulch has beneficial influence on bud and plant size. Mulched plots absorbed rainwater and irrigation much better than bare soil where there was a run-off. A mulch produced better growth than when the sawdust and ground bark was mixed into the soil. Flowers opened 4 or 5 days later on mulched plants than those in bare ground.

Ted Van Veen in *Rhododendrons in America* highly recommended using ground-cover plants over rhododendron roots which he said they do not compete with, and David Leach has said that they do little harm. Van Veen suggests *Ajuga* species, *Epimedium* species, *Euonymous fortunei, Gaultheria procumbens*, dwarf hosta, *Mysotis* (forget-me-not), *Pachistima, Pachysandra, Primula* varieties, *Vinca* (periwinkle), *Ranunculus montanus, Viola* species. *Waldsteinia* and others. Rhododendrons do not naturally have a ground-cover of this nature, and to be quite frank, I consider the use of these plants on the root areas to be harmful. Their roots are bound to compete with the rhododendron root-systems in the vital surface area and also inhibit the use of mulches. I have seen these ground-covers used in this country with very deleterious results. Damage includes smothering the foliage of lower-growing rhododendrons. By all means plant things such as primulas, trilliums and lilies *between* dwarfs, but please do not allow anything to grow on top of any root systems.

Luckily, most well-grown dwarfs are clothed to ground-level, and therefore there is no room for ground-cover to grow *under* their canopy. All rhododendrons are much happier if there is a solid mat of branches and leaves from the highest point of the bush to ground-level. Not only are the roots well shaded, but leaves, both their own and others, get trapped and form a natural mulch. Another way of collecting leaf-fall on a plant whose lower branches are elevated some way above ground-level, is to make a collection of twigs around the root area. This may not look attractive, but it does help the welfare of the plants, with little labour needed. Weeds can be controlled with paraquat amongst the twigs (see *pp.* 65–6).

Moss *is* a natural ground-cover under rhododendrons. Moss species have no normal root-systems like the higher plants mentioned above. They help to keep the rhododendron roots cool and moist, and in certain cases build up organic matter themselves. Obviously moss cannot survive if a heavy mulch of, say, sawdust, is added. Beware of the tall 'hair mosses' (*Polytrichum* species) as they can choke out the dwarfest rhododendrons completely. Many mosses are encouraged by certain weedkillers such as paraquat.

Non-organic mulches, good for retaining moisture and suppressing weeds, are black polythene and aluminium foil. Slits should be cut for each plant. Neither are attractive, and they should only be used temporarily for nursery beds and the like, although either can be hidden by covering with a weed-free substance such as bark fibre. Aluminium foil is said to be a repellant for aphids.

5 Species

The Rhododendron and its Genus

The great genus *Rhododendron*, one of the largest in the plant kingdom with nearly a thousand species, belongs to the order Ericales and the family Ericaceae, in other words the heather family.

I shall not go into the botanical description of a rhododendron although certain extreme species such as members of the Stamineum series and many of the Malesian species would not be generally recognized as rhododendrons, even by people familiar with many of the large-leaved or dwarf smaller-leaved species. I was myself fooled temporarily in India by two species. One was *R. stenaulum* of the Stamineum series, which was many miles west of its known habitat, with white instead of pale lilac flowers. It had reddish-brown peeling bark, shiny leaves and lovely pure white scented flowers which were entirely different from anything I had ever seen before. The other was the new species *R. santapauii* of the Vaccinioides series (see *pp.* 185–6).

In this book I follow the established British and American classification of the genus in *The Species of Rhododendron* edited by J. B. Stevenson which has been partially revised in the Royal Horticultural Society's *Rhododendron Year Books*. Other whole or partial classifications have been made in other countries but these tend to be very misleading and are often based on an insufficient study of the genus.

Unfortunately, several names well known to rhododendron growers are no longer valid, and in some cases practically unknown names have taken their place. In the future this is likely to continue. The reason is that when two or more species are found to be synonymous, the first name published has to take preference, according to the International Rules of Nomenclature.

Azaleas are, of course, included in rhododendrons and have been for many years. The genus is divided into related groups which are called 'series' and these series are often further separated into small sub-series of even more closely related plants. The whole genus is cut in two by one major difference, the presence or absence of scales. These scales are small to minute disc-like dots which occur on many parts of the plants but especially on the undersides of the leaves. Those species with scales are called 'lepidote'. Those without scales, which form the greater part of the genus as a whole, excluding the Malesian species, are called 'elepidote'. Most of the so-called Malesian species, which largely come from Malaya, Sumatra, Java, Borneo, Celebes and New Guinea, are lepidotes, and Dr H. Sleumer of the Netherlands has grouped these plants into the section Vireya, which is again divided into sub-sections. The classification of this Malesian section has not been tackled in Britain so far.

The lepidote series, especially, concern us here because many are partly or entirely dwarfs. Of the elepidotes, only the Neriiflorum series contains a large number of dwarfs.

Rhododendron species do not by any means always have constant characteristics. This often makes positive identification that much more difficult. Those species only collected once or twice like *R. ludlowii* or *R. williamsianum* are quite easily identified but when it comes to variable species like *R. primuliflorum*, *R. sanguineum* and *R. chamae-thomsonii*, with many introductions from widely separated areas, determination becomes decidedly tricky.

In my descriptions, I have tried to give simple, obvious and sound characters with which to identify each species, leaving out those which are either difficult to see without pulling a flower apart or are rather indefinite. I wish to make the point clear that most species can be roughly identified quite easily by a casual glance at them with the naked eye. In many cases, minute botanical details are insignificant and inconsistent factors anyway.

The presence or absence of scales on the corolla, calyx and branchlets rarely hold good. I have tried to avoid the use of petioles (leaf stalks), capsules and calyces any more than is absolutely necessary for identification purposes. Also, I have used as simple a botanical jargon as possible by using the minimum of different terms for hairs, types of scale, etc.

Except when otherwise stated, all leaves are evergreen. Ten stamens and five lobes per corolla are the common numbers. Only exceptions to these will be mentioned.

After the name of the series, (L) = Lepidote and (E) Elepidote.

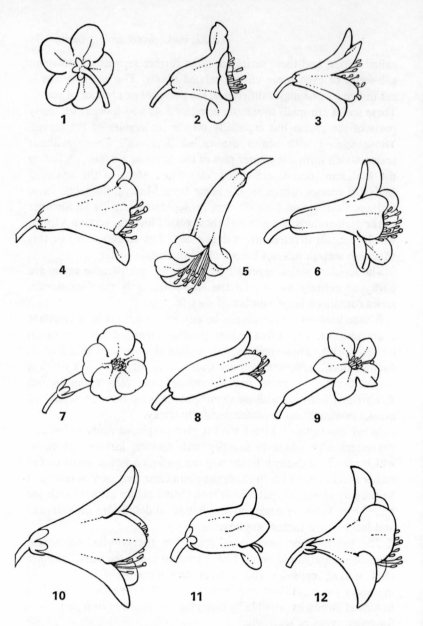

1	Rotate	7	Tubular with spreading
2	Openly Campanulate		lobes or limbs
3	Funnel	8	Tubular
4	Tubular Funnel	9	Salver
5	Tubular hanging	10	Funnel
6	Tubular campanulate	11	Campanulate
		12	Widely funnel

Flower shapes

7 *R. cephalanthum.* Anthopogon series

8 *R. trichostomum.* Anthopogon series in wild (G. Forrest)

9 *R. pseudochrysanthum*. Barbatum series, sub-series Maculiferum

10 *R. leucaspis*. Boothii series,
   sub-series Megeratum

11 *R. megeratum*. Boothii series,
   sub-series Megeratum in wild
   (G. Sherriff)

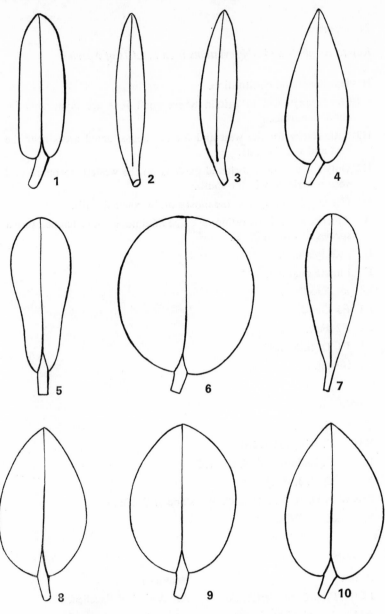

1	Oblong	6 Orbicular
2	Linear	7 Oblanceolate
3	Linear-lanceolate	8 Elliptic
4	Lanceolate	9 Oval
5	Spatulate	10 Ovate

Leaf shapes

Key to Symbols and Abbreviations used in Lists of Species

H Hardiness and constitution.

H4 Hardy anywhere in Britain where conditions are favourable for rhododendrons.

H3 Satisfactory for the west and for the best-situated areas near the east and south coasts.

H2 Only for the most sheltered gardens on the western seaboard and very occasionally in the south.

H1 Greenhouse or against the most suitable shaded walls.

A American hardiness rating: average minimum winter temperature a species can stand in °F.

L Leaf qualities.

F Flower qualities.

L4 F4 Excellent.

L3 F3 Good.

L2 F2 Fair.

L1 F1 Of little merit.

Ht Height.

Plant Collectors

F   G. Forrest

KW   F. Kingdon Ward

L&S   F. Ludlow and G. Sherriff

R   Dr J. J. Rock

SS&W J. D. A. Stainton, W. Sykes and J. Williams

W   E. H. Wilson

AWARDS

British

FCC First Class Certificate

AM   Award of Merit

PC   Certificate of Preliminary Commendation

AGM Award of Garden Merit

American

AE Award of Excellence

PA Preliminary Award

The symbols are those used in the 1963 and 1967 Royal Horticultural Society's *Rhododendron Handbook*, Part One on Species, and the American Rhododendron Society's official hardiness ratings. I have changed a few of the ratings, times of flowering and descriptions used in the 1967 *Handbook* where I find them at fault.

As all species are variable to a certain degree, the ratings are graded, for example, F2–4 or H2–3. This covers not only superior and inferior forms but also the difference in behaviour of species in separate gardens or parts of the country.

When checking on leaf size and shape, pick one or two average typical leaves as they can vary tremendously on one bush.

Species in their Series

ANTHOPOGON SERIES (L)

This is perhaps the most distinctive series amongst the dwarfs. They are all evergreens with small, very highly aromatic leaves, and small narrow tubular flowers, not unlike those of a daphne. There are several flowers to the terminal truss which sometimes forms a tight spherical ball. In many species, the densely scaly leaves are covered underneath with rufous or chocolate scales resembling the indumentum in many species of the Taliense or Neriiflorum series. This series has a unique type of scale called a lacerate scale. The corolla is in five parts with separated petal lobes which are known as spreading limbs. The corolla throat is full of small hairs.

All of the series are hardy in Britain except for some forms of *R. trichostomum*. Unfortunately, five species plus some varieties are not in cultivation, and many of these could make good garden plants. It is hoped that some day it may be possible to introduce at least a few of these.

Those not in cultivation, or doubtfully so, are *R. anthopogon* var. *haemonium*, *R. cephalanthum* var. *nmaiense*, *R. laudandum*, *R. platyphyllum*, *R. pogonophyllum*, *R. primuliflorum* var. *lepidanthum*, *R. radendum* and *R. rufescens*. There is apparently one plant of *R. anthopogonoides* in cultivation.

Points to watch in identification in this series are: 1. whether leaf bud scales are persistent or not; 2. the number of stamens; 3. the size and shape of leaves; 4. to some extent the colour of flowers and 5. the presence or absence of hairs on the outside of the corolla. Some species are very closely related to each other.

In this series are some of the most beautiful, neat and attractive of all dwarf rhododendrons. While all will stand a fair amount of sun, the delicate flowers of some of the species soon shrivel in strong sunlight and heavy rain can bruise them. Many grow better in Scotland than in the south of England.

The majority are true alpines, while some grow wild in light woodlands and nearly all come from the drier ranges away from the full blast of the monsoon. Distribution is from Afghanistan, southern Tibet to Szechwan and Kansu.

R. cephalanthum

R. anthopogon H4 A none L1–2 F2–3

Ht 1–2 ft. (30–60cm). Habit fairly compact, width often more than height. Deciduous leaf-bud scales.

L 1–1½ in. (2·5–3·8cm) long, 1 in. (2·5cm) wide, obovate-elliptic, densely scaly below, often reddish-brown on mature leaves.

F deep pink to cream, sometimes with apricot-coloured buds, ½–¾ in. (1·3–1·9cm) long, narrowly tubular, in an open-topped truss. Flower texture like limp tissue paper. Stamens 5–9.

Attractive in the fine deep pink forms but unusually slow to flower, taking up to ten years. Is inclined to flower in the autumn and is liable to die back, often after it starts flowering.

A good deep pink form is 'Betty Graham'; AM 1969; L&S 1091, KW 7023 is another.

A common species from Nepal, South Tibet to NEFA, at 9,000–16,000 ft (2,743–4,875m), being the dominant plant over extensive areas of moorland and on cliffs and rocks, often flowering in the snow. Found alongside *R. fragariflorum* or *R. setosum*.

April–May

R. cephalanthum (*chamaetortum*) H4 A0 L1–2 F2–3

Ht 1–4 ft. (0·30–1·20m). Habit semi-prostrate to erect and leggy. Leaf-bud scales persistent.
L ½–1½ in. (1·3–3·8cm) long, ⅓–⅗ in. (0·8–1·5cm) wide, oblong-elliptic or broadly oblong, thick and leathery, margins recurved. Densely covered with fawn, reddish or dark brown scales below.
F white or pink flushed yellow, rose or crimson, ½–¾ in. (1·3–2cm) long, narrowly tubular in an open-topped truss. Stamens 5–8.

There are good white and pink forms in cultivation, a low-growing compact pink being especially fine. Most of the whites are of erect habit. Many forms are very closely related to *R. primuliflorum*.

Another widespread species, occurring over huge areas in Yunnan, Szechwan, South East Tibet and upper Burma at 9,000–16,000 ft (2,743–4,875m) on moist moorland, bouldery slopes, screes and dry limestone cliffs, and even as an epiphyte on tree trunks. Farrer described the flowers as 'like melting clots of snow'.

April–May

R. cephalanthum var. *crebreflorum*. F3. Habit dense and compact and generally prostrate. Often stoloniferous. L with margins less recurved. F a most lovely shade of pink. One of the most beautiful of all dwarfs. Grows best in a little shade on a peat bank. Found only in small areas by Kingdon Ward in the Delei and Adung valleys in NEFA and in upper Burma at 11,000–13,000 ft (3,353–3,961m), glued to slabs of rock or on sheltered grassy cliff ledges in wet districts.

April

F*

R. collettianum H4? A none L1–2 F2–3?

Ht about 3 ft. (1m). Habit thicket-forming in the wild.
L up to 3 in. (7·5cm) long, large for the series, broadly lanceolate. Strongly aromatic.
F pinkish in bud, opening to white with pinkish tube, larger than *R. anthopogon*.

This species has recently been re-introduced by Hedge and Wendelbo, having probably died out in cultivation after its original discovery in 1879. Is said to be quite an attractive plant in its habitat of East Afghanistan and the Pakistan–Afghanistan frontier. Of very limited distribution at 10,000–13,000 ft (3,048–3,961m) being locally dominant on north stony limestone slopes with *Juniperus communis,* above the tree-line.

May?

R. hypenanthum H4 A none L1–2 F1–3

Ht 1–2 ft. (30–60cm). Habit usually wider than high. Varies from open growth and large leaves to very dense with smaller leaves. The latter are much superior garden plants. Leaf-bud scales persisting for several years.
L up to 1½ in. (3·8cm) long and ¾ in. (2cm) wide, usually dark green above and often with yellowish edges. Fawn below.
F cream to pale yellow in small very compact trusses. Stamens 5–9.

The dwarf compact forms are excellent garden plants and flower freely from an early age. Seed of SS&W 9090 produced every variation; we have discarded the larger poorer forms. Closely related to *R. anthopogon*. Grows best in full sun but the flowers are susceptible to weather damage. Sometimes flowers in autumn.

Widespread in the west Himalayas, not occurring east of Nepal. Grows on open moorland and occasionally in thin birch woods, often covering large areas from 11,000 ft (3,353m) to the exceptional height of 18,000 ft. (5,486m), about the limit of plant growth. Reported to make a very attractive sight in central Nepal.

April–early May

R. kongboense H4 A none L1–2 F1–3

Ht up to as much as 8 ft. (2·5m) in the wild to as little as 1 ft. (30cm), depending on elevation and shelter. Habit usually fastigiate, but some forms are fairly compact. Leaf-bud scales deciduous.

L up to 1 in. (2·5cm) long, oblong to oblong-lanceolate, with the upper surface greyish-green in some cases.

F pale to bright rose, about $\frac{2}{5}$ in. (1cm) long, narrowly tubular, in a fairly compact truss. Tube densely hairy inside and out. Stamens 5.

The deep-coloured flowers are the most striking, although small. This is probably the most aromatic of all rhododendrons, and of a distinctive perfume which I think quite fascinating. It is not very showy but well worth growing for its other characters. Closely related to *R. primuliflorum* var. *cephalanthoides* which has a longer corolla tube of a paler colour, and it also merges with forms of *R. primuliflorum*.

Somewhat limited in distribution to the province of Kongbo, south-east Tibet, in oak forest, marshy flats and amongst boulders on cliff faces at 11,000–15,000 ft. (3,353–4,571 m).

Early flowering for the series: March–April–early May

R. laudandum It is very doubtful if this is in cultivation.

R. laudandum var. *temoense* H4 A none L1–2 F1–2?

Ht to 3 ft. (1m). Habit fairly compact, with semi-persistent bud scales. L up to $\frac{3}{4}$ in. (2cm) long, oval or oblong-oval. Underside covered with dark red or green scales.

F white or pale lavender-pink, about $\frac{1}{2}$ in. (1·3cm) long, narrowly tubular, 4 per truss. Tube densely hairy inside and out. Stamens 5.

Very rare and little known in cultivation. The only form I have seen, passed as this species, has pale lavender-pink flowers and leaves green underneath, grey–green above, with very few persistent bud scales. Quite pretty.

Found wild in south-east Tibet at 9,500–15,500 ft. (2,896–4,722m) on open hillsides and glacial moraines. Plentiful in limited areas.

March–April

R. primuliflorum (*tsarongense, acraium, adamsii, clivicola, cremnophilum, praeclarum, gymnomiscum*) H4 A none L1–2 F2–3

Ht a few cm up to 6 ft. (2m). Habit often taller than wide, with open fastigiate growth, other forms more compact. Leaf-bud scales drop quickly.

L up to nearly $1\frac{1}{2}$ in. (3·5cm) long, oblong to oblong-elliptic or ovate-oblong. Shiny above, underside fawn, brown or dark greyish-brown. Very aromatic but not so nice a perfume as *R. kongboense*.

F white, tinged yellow, orange or rose; yellow or rose, narrowly tubular, $\frac{1}{2}$–$\frac{3}{4}$ in. (1·3–1·9cm) long, not hairy outside. Stamens 5.

Has never been as popular in cultivation as *R. trichostomum* because it is harder to grow well and is not so free-flowering. A very variable plant.

Common in the wild in south-east Tibet, Yunnan, Szechwan, north to Kansu at 11,000–15,000 ft. (3,353–4,571m). From dryish areas on alpine meadows, screes, cliffs, thickets, mossy banks and boulders, sometimes on limestone.

April–May

R. primuliflorum var. *cephalanthoides*. As *R. primuliflorum* except that the corolla tube is hairy outside. Rare in cultivation. Other species such as *R. trichostomum* are wrongly placed under this variety. Widespread in Szechwan, Yunnan and Tibet up to the Tibetan plateau north of Lhasa. Habitat as above plus spruce forest and swamps.

R. sargentianum H4 A–5 L1–2 F2–3

Ht about 1 ft. (30cm). Habit wider than high, very compact and dense with short annual growth. Persistent leaf-bud scales.

L up to $\frac{3}{4}$ in. (2cm) long, often less, broadly elliptic, thick and leathery.

F lemon-yellow to creamy-white, $\frac{1}{2}$–$\frac{2}{3}$ in. (1·3–1·6cm) long, and about $\frac{1}{2}$ in. (1·3cm) across. Stamens 5.

Easily distinguished by the compact often mounded habit, and wider open flowers. A very neat attractive plant but it does not always flower freely. The creamy-white form 'Whitebait', AM 1966, has larger leaves and flowers which are more freely produced. Not too easy to grow well and needs a little shade in warmer districts. Heat killed in Washington DC. 'Maricee', AE, an American clone, may be a form of this species. Pale yellow form, AM 1923.

Very rare in the wild, only found on one mountain in Szechwan, on exposed rocks and cliffs at 9,000–11,000 ft. (2,743–3,353m) by E. H. Wilson.

Late April–May–early June

R. trichostomum (*sphaeranthum*) H3–4 A–5 L1–2 F2–3

Ht 4 ft. (1·20m) or more. Habit often loose and untidy with occasional compact forms. Leaf-bud scales persistent or deciduous.

L up to 1⅓ in. (3·4cm) long, linear lanceolate to narrowly oblance-olate.

F rose to white, up to ¾ in. (2cm) long, tubular, in a many-flowered globular truss. The flowers are a firmer texture than most of the series and are much longer lasting.

A beautiful species in the best rose or white forms, intermediate colours being less desirable. Very free-flowering and an excellent garden plant. Tender forms which suffer from bark-split should be avoided. Best in full sun in most areas. Separated from *R. primuliflorum* by its narrow leaves and smaller calyx.

Very common in the wild, found over much of Yunnan and Szechwan at 8,000–12,000 ft. (2,439–3,657m), growing in oak and pine forests, thickets and meadows in dry and moist situations. Forest forms are presumably the tender ones.

May into June

R. trichostomum var. *hedyosmum*. Said to have larger flowers.

R. trichostomum var. *ledoides*. Purely a botanical variety with a non-scaly or sparsely scaly corolla. AM 1972.

R. trichostomum var. *radinum*. Corolla either densely or sparsely scaly. In my opinion these two last varieties should be abolished as every variation in the number of scales is found, and in any case it is a poor horticultural or botanical distinction. 'Sweet Bay', AM 1960, AM 1972.

BARBATUM SERIES (E)

Sub-series Maculiferum

R. pseudochrysanthum H4 A none L2–3 F3–4

Ht 3–9 ft. (1–3m) in the taller forms but the recently introduced dwarf alpine forms may be less. Habit slow-growing and compact.

L up to 3 in. (7·6cm) long, 1½ in. (3·8cm) wide, ovate to elliptic to oblong-lanceolate, thick and rigid, dark green above. Underside usually glabrous with indumentum on the raised mid-rib. Leaves densely clothing the plant.

F dark pink in bud opening to paler pink or white, with deeper rose lines outside and spotted within, $1\frac{1}{4}$–$1\frac{1}{2}$ in. (3–4cm) long, $1\frac{3}{4}$ in. (4·5cm) across, campanulate, in trusses of 9 or more. Stamens 10.

This excellent species is only now becoming popular, and seems little known in America to date. Habit and foliage are first rate and very distinct and the beautiful flowers are produced in quantity once the plant reaches a reasonable size. Does best in a fairly sunny position. AM 1956, white flowers flushed pink and spotted crimson.

Endemic to Taiwan at 6,000–13,072 ft. (1,828–3,980m). Often grows mixed with *R. morii* as undergrowth in forests of fir, spruce and juniper, covering large areas. Extends to the summit of Mount Morrison with juniper, 1 ft. (30cm) high.

April

Other species in this series are too tall for inclusion here.

BOOTHII SERIES (L)

A rather diverse series divided into three sub-series. All the species are tender or marginally so, and are of little use to those in cold districts. This series is most closely akin to the Glaucophyllum series. They vary in height from 1–9 ft. (30cm–3m) with evergreen leaves, usually thick, oblanceolate to ovate or obovate, and a terminal inflorescence. Corolla usually campanulate, 5-lobed, $\frac{2}{3}$–$1\frac{3}{5}$ in. (1·5–4 cm) long, yellow, white, pink or rose. Stamens 10, unequal. Ovary 5-celled. *R. chrysodoron*, 6-celled. Many are in nature epiphytic at times. They are mostly good garden plants where they can be grown satisfactorily.

Distribution NEFA, upper Burma, south-east Tibet and Yunnan, usually from wet regions.

Sub-series Boothii

Ht small to medium, often epiphytic, 1–9 ft. (30cm–3m) high. Branchlets often densely bristly and scaly. Leaves often hairy and leaf stalks usually bristly. Flowers yellow, 3–10 per truss. Style short, stout and sharply bent.

R. boothii H1 possibly 2 A none L1–2 F2–3

Ht up to 6 ft. (2m) or more. Habit straggly, usually epiphytic. L 4–5 in. (10–13cm) long, ovate to broadly elliptic, glaucous below. F bright lemon-yellow, unspotted, about $1\frac{1}{4}$ in. (3cm) long, broadly bell-shaped with 5 spreading lobes, in trusses of 7–10.

R. sulfureum

A fine yellow-flowered species, closely related to *R. mishmiense*. It is only likely to be hardy in extreme west coastal districts of Britain, California, southern Oregon, Australia and New Zealand. Unfortunately it may be lost to cultivation in Britain although it is said to be grown in western America.

Collected by Booth in NEFA and not Bhutan as generally stated. Kingdon Ward reported it to be a common epiphyte on the Poshing La Pass in NEFA, north-east India, and Booth probably found it nearby.

April–May

R. chrysodoron H2–3 A none L1–2 F2–3

Ht 8 in.–5 ft. (20cm–1·50m). Habit bushy with peeling red papery bark.

L 2–3 in. (4·5–8cm) long, $\frac{3}{4}$–1$\frac{2}{3}$ in. (2–4cm) wide, elliptic to oblong-elliptic, glaucous and densely scaly below.

F bright canary-yellow, unspotted, up to 1$\frac{1}{2}$ in. (3–4cm) long, widely bell-shaped. Calyx small, fringed with white hairs.

A lovely low-growing yellow, hardy enough for sheltered gardens on the western seaboard of Britain. AM 1934.

Plants in cultivation are from two parts of north-east upper Burma and possibly west Yunnan. These are the only places it has been found wild, growing as an epiphyte, high on the boughs of trees and on rocks, sometimes at the water's edge, at 6,500–8,500 ft. (1,980–2,591m).

March–April

R. mishmiense H3 A none L1–2 F2–3

Ht up to 4ft. (1·22m). Habit a straggly epiphyte with shortly haired branchlets.

L up to $3\frac{1}{2}$ in. (11cm) long and 2 in. (4·5cm) wide, elliptic to oblong-elliptic, ciliate at margins and on mid-rib above, glaucous and densely scaly below.

F. bright lemon-yellow, usually spotted, about $1\frac{1}{4}$ in. (3·2cm) long, broadly bell-shaped with spreading lobes. Calyx $\frac{1}{2}$in. (1–1·3cm) long, fringed with hairs.

Like the closely related *R. boothii*, this species is probably lost from cultivation in Britain so it may occur nowhere outside its native habitat. It was undoubtedly a fine plant and there were never more than a handful in gardens. Kingdon Ward thought quite highly of it. AM 1940, pale yellow flowers.

Only found in the Mishmi Hills, NEFA, and the Tsangpo Gorge, south-east Tibet, by Kingdon Ward at 7,000–9,000 ft. (2,132–2,743m). Epiphytic on *Abies* and in scrub growth along exposed ridges and rock faces. Fairly common in a limited area.

April–May

R. sulfureum (*cerinum, commodum, theiochroum.*) H2–3 A none L1–2 F2–3

Ht quite dwarf, up to 4 ft. (1·20m) or more. Habit neat and compact to straggly, depending on form. Bark smooth brown.

L 1–$3\frac{1}{2}$ in. (2·6–8·6cm) long, $\frac{1}{2}$–$1\frac{1}{2}$ in. (1·3–4·2cm) wide, extremely variable in shape, oblanceolate to ovate, rounded at apex, rounded or narrowed at base, glaucous and scaly below.

F bright or deep sulphur-yellow, rarely greenish-orange, about $\frac{3}{4}$ in. (1·5–2cm) long and about $1\frac{1}{4}$ in. (3cm) wide, campanulate, sometimes reflexed, in trusses of 4 to 8. Scentless.

A very variable plant of which some forms should be hardy enough to grow in most parts of Britain. Most forms in cultivation are only fit for mild sheltered areas. Attractive in the better forms. AM 1937.

Has a very wide distribution in the wild, in south-east Tibet, Yunnan and north-east upper Burma, at 7,000–13,000 ft. (2,132–3,961m). Grows occasionally as an epiphyte in moss on *Abies* but more often on overhanging cliffs, dense wet forest, open rocky pastures and on boulders and ledges.

March–April

Sub-series *Megeratum*

This small sub-series consists of two fairly closely related and very distinct species of dwarfs, 1–3 ft. (30–90cm) high, often spreading much wider than their height, with compact habits. Branchlets densely bristly and scaly. Leaves elliptic, obovate-elliptic or obovate with the upper surface and/or margins hairy. Undersurface glaucous and densely scaly. Flowers only 1 or 2 or rarely 3. Style short, stout and sharply bent. Two good garden plants, on the borderline of hardiness.

R. leucaspis

R. leucaspis H3 and occasionally to 4 A0 L2–3 F3–4

Ht 2 ft. (60 cm) or less. Habit bushy, usually wider than high. Branchlets hairy and scaly.

L up to $2\frac{1}{2}$ in. (6cm) long and $1\frac{1}{4}$ in. (3cm) wide, elliptic to obovate, dark green and hairy above, glaucous and scaly below, ciliate at margins.

F milky white with chocolate-brown stamens, about 2 in. (5cm) across, rotate, solitary or up to 3, usually in pairs.

A beautiful species, worth trying in most gardens, and now very well known. Unfortunately the flowers open early and are very easily frosted. Also, it is susceptible to bark-split from late frosts and we have actually had plants killed by this. Makes a fine pot plant and flowers quickly from seed. Loses some of its character if planted in a wood. Not hardy in eastern USA. AM 1929; FCC 1944.

Very rare in the wild, only found in the Tsangpo and other nearby river gorges in south-east Tibet, on cliff faces and grassy banks in limited numbers at 8,000–10,000 ft. (2,439–3,048m). My guess and Kingdon Ward's is that it may occur more commonly as an epiphyte. Only found by KW and L&S and introduced by KW.

March–April

R. megeratum H3–4 A+10 (seems rather pessimistic) L1–2 F2–3

Ht 1–3 ft. (30–90cm). Habit bushy and often compact and spreading. L $\frac{3}{5}$–$1\frac{1}{2}$ in. (1·5–4cm) long, $\frac{2}{5}$–$\frac{3}{4}$ in. (1–2cm) wide, elliptic to oval, very glaucous and scaly below, ciliate at margins.

F pale to deep yellow, sometimes referred to as 'brassy' and one report of honey-coloured in the wild; $\frac{4}{5}$–$1\frac{1}{5}$ in. (2–3cm) long, campanulate or rotate-campanulate, solitary or up to 3 in a truss.

At its best, it is a beautiful little species but it has the reputation for being tricky which may partly account for its being rated so tender. In suitable localities, I would suggest planting it on rotten tree stumps, damp mossy rocks or on peat walls in a fairly sunny situation. Some forms are shy-flowering but may bloom better in pure peat. Variable in habit and leaf shape. AM 1970.

Quite a common and widespread species in the wild, coming from Yunnan, south-east Tibet, Mishmi country NEFA, and north-east upper Burma at 8,000–13,500 ft. (2,439–4,113m). The forms from the highest elevations should be perfectly hardy in Britain, if in cultivation. Grows wild mostly on rock faces and on mossy rocks, and more rarely epiphytically in moss on fir and other trees in great bunches like mistletoe. Usually on non-calcareous rocks. The Mishmi and Burmese forms are said to be superior to the Chinese.

March–April

Sub-series Tephropeplum

Ht 1–5 ft. (30cm–1·50m) or more high, not bristly. Leaves lanceolate to oblong-obovate, 1–5 in. (2·5–13cm) long, $\frac{2}{5}$–$1\frac{1}{2}$ in. (1–3·8cm) wide, usually glaucous and densely scaly below. Inflorescence 3–9 flowered, corolla tubular-campanulate, 5-lobed, bright yellow, pink, rose or creamy-white tinged pink. Style long, straight and slender.

Good garden plants, but again all are barely hardy or definitely tender in most of Britain.

R. tephropeplum

R. auritum H2–3 A+10 L1–2 F2

Ht to about 10 ft. (3m). Habit erect and rather ungainly with fine coppery-red peeling bark. Rather tall to be termed a dwarf.

L 1–2$\frac{1}{2}$ in. (2·5–6·6cm) long, $\frac{2}{5}$–1$\frac{1}{12}$ in. (1–2·7cm) wide, elliptic to lanceolate, covered with brown scales underneath.

F very pale yellow slightly touched with pink on the lobes, about 1 in. (2–2·5cm) long, tubular-campanulate, in trusses of 4–7. Calyx lobes reflexed, about $\frac{1}{6}$ in. (4–6mm) long.

Closely related to *R. xanthostephanum*. Surprisingly plentiful in cultivation, as it was only collected twice. To me, the flowers are rather dull but the attractive bark makes it worthy of a large collection. Just survives at Glendoick but the flower buds never open. AM 1931.

Only found wild in the Tsangpo Gorge, south-east Tibet at 7,000–8,500 ft. (2,132–2,591m) on open stony banks, cliffs and by the river. Very rare.

April

R. chrysolepis H2 A none L1–2 F2–3?

Ht small epiphyte. Habit long branches with deep red-brown peeling bark.

L 2$\frac{1}{2}$–5 in. (6·3–13cm) long, $\frac{3}{4}$–1$\frac{1}{4}$ in. (2–3cm) wide, oblong-lanceolate, glabrous above, glaucous with large golden-yellow scales below.

F bright canary-yellow with bands of scales outside, 1$\frac{1}{4}$–1$\frac{1}{2}$ in. (3–3·4cm) long, campanulate, 4–6 per truss. Calyx with short undulating rim, style longer than corolla.

Very doubtful if this is in cultivation, which is sad as it is said to be a good plant with excellent flowers, freely produced.

Found only in the Seinghku Valley, upper Burma at 7,000–8,000 ft. (2,132–2,439m) where it grows as a epiphyte and in moss forest in shade.

Flowering time not known.

R. tephropeplum (*deleiense*) H3–4 A+10 but hardier forms probably +5 or 0 L1–2 F2–3

Ht 2$\frac{1}{2}$–5 ft. (60cm–1·50m). Habit bushy and fairly compact to upright and leggy.

L 1$\frac{1}{4}$–5 in. (3–13cm) long, $\frac{1}{3}$–1$\frac{1}{2}$ in. (1–3·8cm) wide, lanceolate to oblong-obovate, very variable, usually dark green and shiny above, glaucous and with black or brown scales below. The widest-leaved form was formerly called *R. deleiense*.

F pale pink, pink, rose, carmine-rose, purplish or rarely white, $\frac{7}{8}$–

1¼ in. (2·2–3·2cm) long, tubular-campanulate, 3–9 per truss, occasionally more.

A very variable species in habit, leaf shape, height, flower size and colour and hardiness. It is always free-flowering but unfortunately many forms are rather bud tender, especially after they have swelled a little after a mild spell. As there are many forms in cultivation, it should be possible with careful selection, to find clones suitable for most parts of Britain. It is a lovely plant at its best, and should be placed on the edge of woodland with a little shelter. In too much shade it becomes leggy. The *deleiense* form has fine large dark-coloured flowers. AM 1929, pale pink flowers.

Found wild over large areas of north-east upper Burma, Yunnan, south-east Tibet and eastern NEFA at 8,000–14,000 ft. (2,439–4,265m). Grows abundantly on crags, rocks, cliffs, cliffs amongst cane brakes, screes and meadows; the rocks are sometimes limestone.

Late April–May

R. xanthostephanum (*aureum*) H3 A+15 L1–2 F2–3

Ht 1–9 ft. (30cm–3m). Habit usually upright and rather leggy, sometimes flopping in the wild.

L 2–4 in. (5–10cm) long, ½–1¼ in. (2–2·5cm) wide, lanceolate to oblong-lanceolate, glaucous below.

F bright yellow to creamy-yellow, ¾–1 in. (2–2·5cm) long, fleshy, tubular-campanulate. Calyx deeply lobed, 3–6mm long. Style longer than corolla.

The taller forms are beyond the size limit for this book but dwarfer ones do occur. A very pretty floriferous plant which does well in mild areas along the western seaboard of Britain. Best grown in thin woodland. Prune back if necessary. It would be imagined that it should be hardy from 13,000 ft. A good clone is 'Yellow Garland', AM.

Found wild in south-east Tibet, Yunnan and upper Burma at 7,000–13,500 ft. (2,132–4,113m), on overhanging granite cliffs, cane and rhododendron scrub, dense wet forest, rocky slopes, pastures and edges of pine forests. Quite a widespread species but scarce in some areas.

April–May

CAMPANULATUM SERIES (E)

This is a very interesting series. Excluding *R. sherriffii*, the species fit into three distinct groups: 1. *R. campanulatum* and var. *aeruginosum*, and *R. wallichii*; 2. *R. fulgens*, *R. succothii* and *R. miniatum*; 3. *R. lanatum* and *R. tsariense*. *R. sherriffii* is rather an odd man out with glandular branchlets and in the structure of the indumental hairs. Groups 1 and 2 both have species with and without (or nearly so) indumentum on the leaf undersides. For many botanical reasons, I propose to move *R. lopsangianum* from the Thomsonii series and include it along with the aberrant *R. sherriffii* which is found in the wild growing in the same area. Perhaps *R. sherriffii* could be moved to the Thomsonii series. The fact is that the only apparent differences between *R. sherriffii* and *R. lopsangianum* are the presence or near absence of indumentum (which has not stopped *R. fulgens* and *R. succothii* being grouped together), a slight difference in leaf and flower shapes, and the fact that *R. sherriffii* is sometimes a little taller. Therefore in this book, I am including *R. lopsangianum* tentatively in the Campanulatum series. Unfortunately, all except *R. campanulatum* var. *aeruginosum*, *R. lopsangianum* and *R. tsariense* are too tall to include here.

R. tsariense

R. campanulatum var. *aeruginosum* H4 A0 L4 F1

Ht up to 8 ft. (2·44m) but usually 4–6 ft. (1·22–1·83m). Habit very dense, compact and rounded, fairly slow-growing.

L 2–4½ in. (5–11cm) long, 1¼–2 in. (3–5·5cm) wide, margins sharply recurved, upper surface with a metallic glaucous bloom, especially when young, deepening to a striking soft blue.

F a dirty lilac-magenta, often spotted, about 1⅔ in. (4cm) long, campanulate, in a fairly dense truss of 10–12. Calyx minute.

A magnificent foliage plant which luckily rarely produces its nasty flowers. It should be grown on the edge of woodland or a rhododendron border. Hard to root from cuttings. It is in my mind distinct enough for specific status.

A rare plant in the wild, occurring at 13,000–14,000 ft. (3,961–4,265m) in Sikkim and Bhutan on stony hillsides and ledges. Probably only found by Hooker and L&S and introduced by Hooker.

April–May

R. lopsangianum H3–4 A none L2–3 F1–3

Ht up to 6 ft. (1·80m) but forms were found in the wild not over 2 ft. (60cm) or less. Habit usually low and compact, branchlets glandular.

L 1¼–2½ in. (2·7–6cm) long, ⅔–1½ in. (1·6–4cm) wide, elliptic or oblong-elliptic or oval, underside with very thin, hardly noticeable, indumentum.

F crimson, 1¼–1¾ in. (3–4·2cm) long, tubular-campanulate or funnel-campanulate, in loose trusses of 3–5. Stamens 10, unequal; calyx lobes 5, small, 2–3mm long; style 1¼–1½ in. (3–4cm) long.

A recently introduced species which is still rare in cultivation. Interesting but not all that showy.

Fairly common in a restricted area of south-east Tibet, to the north of western NEFA, at 8,500–14,000 ft. (2,591–4,265m), on rocky hillsides, beside cascades, hanging over cliffs and in *Abies* and rhododendron forest, often in wet zone. Only found and introduced by L&S.

April

R. tsariense H4 A none L2–4 F2–3

Ht 2–12 ft. (60cm–3·60m) but probably under 6 ft. (2m) in cultivation. Habit rigid and twiggy, fairly compact without being dense. Branchlets densely woolly.

L $\frac{7}{8}$–2$\frac{1}{2}$ in. (2·3–6·2cm) long, $\frac{1}{3}$–1$\frac{1}{4}$ in. (1–3cm) wide, dark green above, clad below with dense fawn to rust-coloured indumentum, more or less woolly. Some forms have a thin veil of indumentum on the upper surface.

F pink or white, often delicately spotted, 1–1$\frac{2}{3}$ in. (2·6–4cm) long, campanulate, in loose trusses of 2–6.

The fairy-like flowers look charming set off against the dark foliage. One of the finest foliage plants among the dwarfer species in certain forms, although all are nice. While it is hardy and can be grown in fairly open situations, it is very bud tender once these begin to swell. Rather slow to reach flowering size and unfortunately hard to propagate. Closely related to and merges with *R. lanatum* which usually has bigger leaves and yellowish flowers. 'Yum-Yum', AM 1964, white flushed pink flowers.

Found wild in south-east Tibet around the Bhutan–west NEFA frontier and east Bhutan, at 9,500–14,500 ft. (2,896–4,417m) in rhododendron and *Abies* forest, at the edge of forest, in bamboo jungle, on rock faces, ledges and open hillsides, sometimes flowering beside snow. Fairly common over a limited distribution. Found only by KW and L&S.

March–May

CAMPYLOGYNUM SERIES (L)

This is now classed by most authorities as one very variable species, containing several horticulturally distinct varieties which are in fact largely connected by intermediate forms. For the descriptions here we can largely discount these intermediates and concentrate on the types of each variety. This species is a beautiful little plant in most forms, usually having dark shiny leaves and nodding campanulate flowers with a glaucous bloom, held above the leaves by long flower stalks. At its best it is amongst the finest of dwarf rhododendrons, excellent for rock or peat gardens or the front of a border. It appreciates a fair amount of sun and is reasonably hardy throughout most of Britain except one dark form of var. *myrtilloides* which can be frost tender. Fairly closely related to the Glaucophyllum series but all parts in the latter series are larger except occasionally the flowers. Has not proved reliably hardy in eastern USA being liable to die-back. Some forms have a yellow edging to the leaf. Foliage aromatic.

R. campylogynum

R. campylogynum H4 rarely 3 A0 L2–3 F2–3

Ht 2 in. (5cm) (rarely as low as this in cultivation) to 1½ ft. (45cm) or a little more. Habit somewhat spreading, usually flat-topped and with dense growth. Leaf-bud scales often persistent.

L ⅓–1 in. (0·7–2·5cm) long, ⅙–⅔ in. (0·3–1·8cm) wide, obovate or oblanceolate, undersurface glaucous (except in var. *cremastum*), upper surface usually dark and shiny. Margin recurved.

F very variable in colour, from black-purple to claret, salmon-pink to creamy-white, not more than ¾ in. (1·8cm) long. Calyx variable in size and colour. Stamens 10, rarely 8, unequal. Style thick and bent.

The claret and pink forms are the most attractive and the rare creamy-white form, var. *leucanthum* Ingram (perhaps only a clone) is well worth growing. All flower at a reasonably young age, that is 2–5 years from a cutting.

A widespread and often common species in the wild, being found in north-east upper Burma, south-east Tibet and a large part of Yunnan at 8,000–15,500 ft. (2,439–4,722m), most commonly at 11,000–14,000 ft. (3,353–4,265m). Grows on moorland, often moist, open rocky hillsides, on mossy boulders and ledges and in clefts of cliffs, usually granite. Often forms mats mixed with other rhododendrons and shrubs or covers yards of cushioned turf in var. *myrtilloides*, or even grows on slatey rocks in an open river-bed. 'Thimble', AM 1966, has salmon-pink flowers; var. *myrtilloides*, AM 1925, FCC 1943.

May–June

R. campylogynum var. *celsum*. A little taller than the type with a more erect habit, 1½–4 ft. (45cm–1·22m) high. Flowers and leaves average size. Up to 6 ft. (2m) in the wild, growing in open situations among bamboo or other scrub, east flank of the Tali Range, Yunnan, at 9,000–12,000 ft. (2,743–3,657m).

R. campylogynum var. *charopoeum*. Of fairly dwarf habit, not more than 1½ ft. (45cm) high, leaves often slightly bigger than type and flowers larger, up to 1 in. (1·9–2·4cm) long. Our form flowers a little earlier than average for the species. Widespread, from south-east Tibet, north-east upper Burma to Yunnan in similar situations to type.

R. campylogynum var. *cremastum* (*amphichlorum* Ingram). More erect habit to 2 ft. (70cm) in height, and larger leaves than type in the red form, up to 1½ in. (3·7cm) long. The really distinctive feature is that the leaves are pale green on both surfaces. Flowers of medium size. We grow two forms, one, the dwarfer, has plum-purple flowers, the other, which has very unusual pale yellow-green leaves, has red flowers.

R. campylogynum var. *myrtilloides*. Typically, this is the dwarfest form with the smallest plant, leaves and flowers. The last are ⅓–⅔ in. (0·8–1·8cm) long. Habit is usually very dense with dark green leaves. The flowers vary from black-crimson (really too dark unless the sun shines through them) and dusky plum to bright wine-red or pink. Usually forms tight cushions in the wild and has been found occasionally on limestone. Has the greatest range of altitude, from 8,000–15,500 ft. (2,439–4,722m) hence the reason some forms are tender. Quite widespread in north-east upper Burma, south-east Tibet and Yunnan. AM 1925.

CAMTSCHATICUM SERIES (E)

This small series is unique among rhododendrons in that the flowers are produced on the current year's young growth and not from resting over-wintering buds as in the rest of the genus (some of Malesian species flower quite soon after making their new growth). Another distinctive factor is the unilaterally split corolla tube. Some botanists have regarded it as a separate genus called *Therorhodion* and may well be correct in doing so. *R. camtschaticum* is said to have been crossed with other rhododendrons such as *R. glaucophyllum* but I have never seen these hybrids.

The other two members of the series, *R. glandulosum* and *R. redowskianum*, are little known and are probably referable to the type species.

R. camtschaticum

R. camtschaticum H4 A—25 L1–2 F2–3

Ht up to 1 ft. (30cm), but usually less. Habit prostrate, flowing with the contours and rooting as it goes, with upright twiggy little branchlets.
L$\frac{3}{4}$–2 in. (2–5cm) long, $\frac{1}{2}$–1 in. (1–2·5cm) wide, obovate to spathulate-obovate, margin clad with setose hairs. No scales present. Deciduous.
F reddish-purple to rose, spotted within, about 1$\frac{1}{2}$ in. (4cm) across, rotate, tube split to base or nearly so. Singly or in pairs at ends of the current year's branchlets. Very rare white forms have been found and

would be well worth introducing. They are reported from Kodiac Island, Alaska. Seed from one source has just been collected.

A most unusual dwarf rhododendron for the reasons described above. It does not seem to like conditions in the south of England and north-west America, possibly owing to the high summer temperatures, but it flourishes in east Scotland in full sun and exposure and also in Scandinavia. A well-flowered mat is most attractive and sometimes the autumn colour is good. Here, the young growth occasionally gets frosted and no flowers are produced. Seeds sometimes germinate badly but can be bloomed in under 12 months.

Comes from a wide area of north-east Asia from north Japan, Sakhalin, northwards on the mainland, to the Aleutian Islands and into Alaska. Has been collected growing in a gravelly loam and in rock crevices, often on the tops of hills.

May–June

CAROLINIANUM SERIES (L)

This is a small, purely American series of three closely related species which bear some resemblance to the taller Heliolepis series. They grow from 4–9 ft. (1·20–2·74m) high and a little more, with relatively large leaves for lepidotes, 1–4½ in. (2·5–11·5cm) long, densely scaly underneath. The flowers are pink to rose to pinkish-purple with the occasional white form. Stamens 10. These are exceptionally useful plants in America for hybridising with the more tender Asiatic species, and are beginning to be grown as garden plants themselves. Not widely grown in Britain and inclined to be unhappy, often with chlorotic foliage. They need perfect drainage but moisture in the growing season.

R. carolinianum H4 A—25 L1–2 F2–3

Ht up to 6 ft. (1·83m). Habit shapely in the open but leggy in any shade.

L 2–3¼ in. (5–8cm) long, 1–1½ in. (2·5–3·9cm) wide, obovate-elliptic to elliptic, densely scaly below and bronzy on the deeper-flowered forms.

F mauve to salmon-pink to white, 1 in. (2·5cm) long, widely campanulate, of fair substance, in compact rounded trusses of 4–8.

The hardiest species in the series and the best for most purposes. Should be grown more often in Britain. There are several white forms

12 *R. campylogynum*, var. *myrtilloides*. Campylogynum series

13 *R. tsangpoense*. Glaucophyllum series, sub-series Glaucophyllum

14 (*right*) *R. edgeworthii*.
Edgeworthii series in wild
East Flank, Tali Divide,
Yunnan (G. Forrest)

15 (*below*) *R. pendulum*.
Edgeworthii series

R. carolinianum

(var. *album*). All have paler foliage than the type. While these are pretty, I have not seen a really pure white. A tetraploid strain has recently been raised in the USA which has a great future for hybridizing. AM 1968. A so-called yellow form is probably a hybrid.

Found wild in eastern USA in the mountains of Tennessee and the Carolinas and into Georgia where it merges with *R. minus*. Grows in woodland and on open slopes.

May–June

R. chapmanii H3–4 A0 L1–2 F2–3

Ht up to 6 ft. (1·83m). Habit erect shoots but the older branches are apt to sprawl.
L $\frac{3}{4}$–2$\frac{1}{2}$ in. (2–6·3cm) long, $\frac{1}{2}$–1$\frac{1}{2}$ in. (1·3–3·8cm) wide, broadly elliptic to orbicular, usually bullate above, olive or bright green.
F pink to rose, about 2 in. (5cm) long, 1$\frac{1}{2}$ in. (3·8cm) across, widely funnel-shaped in a dense truss of about 7.

An interesting species of a most unusual appearance. I have only grown it for a short time and have found the tips of the shoots liable to be frosted back. Could be useful in hybridizing for heat resistance.

Some plants grown under this name are wrongly labelled in Britain, being *R. carolinianum* or *R. minus.*

Only found on sand dunes in Florida gulf country on thin sandy peat in full sun. Nearly extinct in the wild due to civilization, fires and vandalism.

April–May?

R. minus H4 A—15 L1–2 F1–3

Ht rarely up to 30 ft. (10m) in the wild but usually not over 6 ft. (2m) in cultivation. Habit similar to *R. carolinianum.*

L up to 4½ in. (11·4cm) long and up to 2½ in. (6·3cm) wide, ovate-elliptic to elliptic, rusty beneath.

F pinkish-purple to rose or pink or occasionally white, 1½ in. (3·8cm) long and the same wide, funnel-shaped, 6–12 per truss, sometimes with multiple terminal buds.

Very closely related to *R. carolinianum*, just tending to be larger in all parts although the flowers are not much bigger. Leaves more pointed than *R. carolinianum* and foliage often better. Leach says that the good forms are of excellent value and not yet appreciated.

Found in the lower mountains and the plains from Carolina to Alabama, in woodlands.

May–June

EDGEWORTHII SERIES (L)

A small series of rather tender plants, generally only suitable for mild gardens or greenhouses. Related to the Maddenii series. Height from 1–11 ft. (30cm–3·35m), often epiphytic. Leaves ovate or elliptic to oblong-lanceolate or oblong, scaly and also densely woolly below, a most unusual feature only met with in this series. Flowers 1–4 (rarely up to 6) per truss, corolla 5-lobed, flower stalks, ovary and capsules all woolly. Stamens 10.

Distribution, east Nepal to south-east Tibet, Burma and Yunnan in wet regions.

R. edgeworthii (*bullatum, sciaphilum*) H2–3 (occasionally bordering on 4) A+15 L2–4 F2–4

Ht 1–11 ft. (30cm–3·35m). Habit usually leggy, but certain forms are spreading in an open situation. Branchlets densely woolly, rust-coloured or whitish.

L 1–6 in. (2·5–15cm) long, ¾–2½ in. (2–6cm) wide, ovate-elliptic, oblong-elliptic, ovate-lanceolate or oblong-lanceolate. Upper surface strongly or moderately bullate with mid-rib deeply grooved and primary veins impressed. Undersurface with brown, rust-coloured or fawn wool.

F white, white tinged pink or rose, with or without a yellow blotch, 1½–3¼ in. (3·2–7·6cm) long and up to 4 in. (9cm) across, campanulate or funnel-shaped, very fragrant. Calyx deeply lobed, red or tinged red. Style long and straight.

One of the finest species for mild gardens although occasional relatively hardy forms will survive in colder districts in a well-sheltered position. Absolutely intolerant of anything but perfect drainage and dislikes heavy soil. In wet areas, it is worth trying it on cliffs, rocks or tree-trunks covered in deep moss and tree stumps which will retain moisture even in dry seasons. The scent is about the finest in the genus and the foliage is most outstanding. Some forms will outgrow our 5 ft. (1·52m) limit. The flower colour tends to be much deeper on those naturally coloured, out of doors. Now includes the eastern form *R. bullatum*.

A very widespread and often common species which has adapted itself to grow in many different situations. Comes from Sikkim, Bhutan, NEFA, north-east upper Burma, south-east Tibet and Yunnan at 6,000–13,000 ft. (1,828–3,961m). Often occurs epiphytically on oaks and other trees, sometimes so plentifully that it grows on the tops of every tree. Also found on rocks, steep hillsides, ledges of cliffs, and mossy boulders. As *R. bullatum*, FCC 1937, white form; AM 1923, white form Farrer 842; AM 1946, blush-pink flushed with rose. As *R. edgeworthii*, FCC 1933.

April–May

R. pendulum H3 A none L1–2 F1–2

Ht 1–4 ft. (30cm–1·20m). Habit often sprawling but in an open position can be kept quite tidy. Branchlets densely clothed with brown or fawn wool.

L 1–2 in. (2·3–5cm) long, ½–1¼ in. (1·2–3·2cm) wide, oblong to elliptic, or rarely oval, upper surface convex, slightly bullate, densely woolly below with brown or fawn wool.

F white or white tinged pink or pale yellow, ⅔–1 in. (1·5–2·2cm) long, and about 1½ in. (3·5cm) across, rotate-campanulate, 2–3 per truss, rarely single. Style short, sharply bent. Calyx red or tinged red.

An unusual little plant, interesting but not strikingly beautiful. Worth growing in mild areas and can even be attempted in cold districts. A fine specimen grows in a sheltered nook in the rock garden of the Royal Botanic Garden, Edinburgh, but I have so far failed to establish it at Glendoick. Does well in a few gardens in the west of Scotland. Try planting it on tree stumps, mossy rocks or in sandy soil or a raised bed. Strongly resents poor drainage.

Only common locally in a few places in east Nepal, Sikkim, Bhutan and south-east Tibet. Grows epiphytically on conifers, other trees and other rhododendrons and on steep slopes, cliffs, river-bed rocks and rhododendron forest, sometimes pendulous, at 7,500–12,000 ft. (2,284–3,657m).

April–May

R. seinghkuense H? probably 2–3 A none L1–2 F2–3

Ht 1–3 ft. (30–90cm). Habit small more or less erect, slow-growing plant.

L $1\frac{1}{4}$–$3\frac{1}{4}$ in. (3–8cm) long, $\frac{2}{3}$–$1\frac{2}{3}$ in. (1·6–4cm) wide, ovate to oblong-elliptic. Upper surface bullate, with dense brown wool below.

F sulphur-yellow, about 1 in. (2cm) long, and $1\frac{1}{2}$ in. (4cm) across, rotate-campanulate. Style short and sharply bent. Calyx pale green, with brown wool.

A pretty little plant, now exceedingly rare in cultivation and in danger of being lost.

A somewhat rare species in the wild, only being found so far in two valleys in upper Burma by KW and one in Yunnan. Grows in scarred tops of *Abies*, *Tsuga* and *Juniperus*, or on steep rocky slopes, tree stumps and on rocks, sometimes in river-beds, at 6,000–10,000 ft. (1,737–3,048m). A plant, most probably of this species, was found by James Keenan on Bumpha Bum, North Burma, growing epiphytically on itself. AM 1953.

April

FERRUGINEUM SERIES (L)

A small series confined to Europe, the only rhododendrons found in the Alps. They alo grow in the Pyrenees and the mountains between the Alps and the Black Sea. Leaves oblanceolate and densely scaly below. Several flowers to the truss, tubular with 5 distinct lobes. Style short, not longer than the tube. Not closely related to any other series.

E.M.S.

R. ferrugineum

R. ferrugineum (The Alpenrose) H4 A—15 L1–2 F1–2

Ht up to 4 ft. (1·20m). Habit branches often a bit straggly, sometimes trailing along the ground.

L 1–1½ in. (2·4–3·6cm) long, ¼–½ in. (0·8–1·2cm) wide, oblanceolate, densely scaly below, scales reddish-brown, overlapping. Upper surface dark green.

F rosy-crimson or white, about ¾ in. (1·8cm) long, tubular, not hairy outside, several flowers per truss. Very small calyx. Style slightly longer than ovary.

This well-known species makes quite a good garden plant but does not always flower all that freely. Useful for the lateness of its flowers which I have never seen frosted. Has never been a popular landscape species in America, does not like the hot summers of eastern USA and needs some shade in Pennsylvania.

Common in the Pyrenees and the Alps as far east as Austria at 3,000–7,000 ft. (914–2,132m), on alpine moorland, open forest glades or sub-alpine scrub or forest. Sometimes leggy in shade. Flower colour varies considerably in the wild. Hybrids between this species and *R. hirsutum* often occur where the two meet, the former on non-calcareous rock and the latter on limestone. The hybrids are said to be easier to grow. White forms are occasionally found. *R. ferrugineum album*, AM 1969.

June

R. hirsutum H4 A—5 L1–2 F1–2

Ht rarely up to 5 ft. (1·50m), usually less. Habit similar to above.
L ½–1 in. (1·2–2·4cm) long, and about ⅓ in. (0·8cm) wide, usually paler than *R. ferrugineum* above, oblanceolate or elliptic-oblanceolate with margins minutely toothed and fringed with hairs. Scales not as dense on underside as in *R. ferrugineum*, being 2–3 times their own diameter apart.
F rose-pink to nearly scarlet or white, about ½ in. (1·2cm) long, tubular, lobes fringed with short hairs in a several-flowered truss. Style 1½ times as long as ovary.

One of the few species which is sometimes found growing wild on a near neutral soil which overlies limestone or chalk. A pH of 6·6 has been recorded. We are inclined to lose this plant at Glendoick after a few years. Nice where it grows well and the best forms are a glowing rosy-scarlet. The mid-way cross with *R. ferrugineum* is called *R.* 'Intermedium' and these hybrids together with *R. hirsutum* itself are worth trying on alkaline soils. There is a pretty double form. Common on the limestone ranges of the Dolomites and others in central Europe into Yugoslavia, at 1,200–6,000 ft. (365–1,828m) in similar situations to *R. ferrugineum* especially amongst dwarf pine. The rare white form is said to be commoner than the white *R. ferrugineum* in the wild and of a pure colour. A few plants I saw growing out of solid rock in Yugoslavia were chlorotic which perhaps shows that even this species has a limited tolerance of alkalinity.

June–July

R. kotschyi H3–4 A—15 L1–2 F2–3

Ht up to 2 ft. (60cm) usually less. Habit spreading, broader than tall.
L up to 1 in. (2·5cm) long, and ¼ in. (6mm) wide, oblanceolate, margins minutely toothed. Width between scales lies between *R. ferrugineum* and *R. hirsutum*, being about half their own diameter apart or subcontiguous.
F rosy-pink or rarely white, about ½ in. (1·3cm) long, tubular with spreading lobes, softly pubescent on both sides, in trusses of 4–8. Style shorter than ovary.

A nice little plant, somewhat dwarfer than the other two members of the series. I have lost the odd plant here from bark-split in a shady position. Quite often flowers in the autumn. The white forms are said to be attractive but are rare in the wild and doubtfully in cultivation.

Comes from similar habitats to *R. ferrugineum* in the mountains of south-east Europe at 5,000–7,500 ft. (1,522–2,284m).

May or later

GLAUCOPHYLLUM SERIES (L)

This series consists of two sub-series rather remotely related. In any case the Genestierianum sub-series does not concern us here as its two members are too tall to include.

The Glaucophyllum sub-series consists of semi-dwarfs of 1–5 ft. (30cm–1·50m) high. They are a closely-related group of generally hardy, very free-flowering rhododendrons with strongly aromatic leaves, unpleasant in certain forms of *R. brachyanthum* var. *hypolepidotum*. Many are liable to autumn frost damage. The leaves are moderate-sized, lanceolate to obovate, 1–4 in. (2–9cm) long, and $\frac{2}{5}$–1 in. (1–2·6cm) wide, usually very glaucous below; the scales are of two kinds, smaller pale yellow and larger brown ones. Flowers in trusses of 3–10, with a longish flower stalk of $\frac{2}{5}$–1$\frac{3}{5}$ in. (1–4cm). Corolla campanulate, 5-lobed, style stout and sharply bent or deflexed. They are nice garden plants but in some cases the flowers are rather small for the leaves and the bush. Distribution east Nepal to south-east Tibet, upper Burma and Yunnan.

R. brachyanthum H4 A—5 L1–2 F1–3

Ht 1–5 ft. (0·30–1·50m). Habit usually wider than tall, forming a dense bush in the open.

L $\frac{4}{5}$–2$\frac{1}{2}$ in. (2–6·5cm) long, $\frac{2}{5}$–1 in. (1–2·6cm) wide, oblong-lanceolate or oblong-elliptic to obovate, usually very glaucous below.

F yellow, pale yellow or greenish-yellow, $\frac{1}{2}$–$\frac{3}{4}$ in. (1·2–1·9cm) long, broadly campanulate, 3–10 per truss, with a long slender flower stalk, 1–1$\frac{3}{5}$ in. (2·5–4cm) long, calyx large, leafy. Stamens occasionally red. Style bent or deflexed. In the poorer forms, the flowers hang down beneath the leaves.

This is a fairly hardy plant, useful for its late flowering. Unfortunately the rather small flowers can be somewhat insignificant, especially in the greenish-yellow forms. Pinkish-yellow forms occur; these either show hybridity or merge with the closely related *R.*

E.M.S.

R. charitopes

tsangpoense var. *pruniflorum*. 'Jaunce', AM 1966, primrose-yellow flowers.

R. brachyanthum itself is a much scarcer plant in the wild than its variety *hypolepidotum*, being found in small areas in Yunnan and south-east Tibet at 9,000–10,000 ft. (2,743–3,048m), on steep rocky hillsides, often amongst scrub or near bamboo.

R. brachyanthum var. *hypolepidotum* (*charitostreptum*). The only difference between this and *R. brachyanthum* is the density of the scales on the leaf undersides. In *R. brachyanthum* the pale yellow scales are 4–10 times their own diameter apart. This is much more common, both in cultivation and in the wild. It is variable in garden value and in the more or less unpleasant smell from the aromatic leaves. The young growth is occasionally frosted in autumn. 'Blue Light', AM 1951. Comes from Yunnan, south-east Tibet and north-east upper Burma at 10,000–14,500 ft. (3,048–4,417m) in dense mixed forest and thickets, alpine meadows, rocky slopes and on boulders and cliffs. Farrer found an interesting epiphytic form.

May–July for both

R. charitopes H3–4 A0 L2–3 F2–3

Ht 1–5 ft. (30–1·50m). Habit dense in the open but gets leggy in some shade.
L 1–2½ in. (2·6–7cm) long, ½–1 in. (1·3–2·6cm) wide, obovate, dark green above, usually very glaucous below.
F clear apple-blossom pink, usually speckled with crimson, widely campanulate, about 1 in. (2–2·6cm) long, about 1⅕ in. (3cm) wide, 2–6 per truss, usually 3–4. Stamens conspicuous. Style bent or deflexed. Sometimes flowers in autumn.

A very pretty plant, well worth growing. Unfortunately, the flower buds are susceptible to frost once they begin to swell. Best in a large rock or peat garden or the very edge of woodland.

Found wild in north-east upper Burma and just into Yunnan. Common in limited areas. Farrer saw it covering hillsides with colour and remarked on what a fine plant it was; he also saw pure albinos, unfortunately never introduced. Grows on alpine moorland rocky hillsides, thickets, cliff ledges, on boulders and on banks above streams at 10,500–14,000 ft. (3,200–4,265m).

April–May

R. glaucophyllum (*glaucum*) H4 occasionally 3 A−10 L1–2 F2–3

Ht 1–4 ft. (30cm–1·20m). Habit usually raher loose and spreading with nice brownish peeling bark.
L 1½–3½ in. (3·8–9cm) long, showing considerable variation in size and shape and the way the leaves are held. The shape is lanceolate to oblanceolate or elliptic-lanceolate, edges sometimes reflexed, very glaucous below.
F pink, pale rose, pinkish-purple or rarely white, ⅔–1 in. (1·4–2·6cm) long and up to 1½ in. (3·6cm) wide, campanulate to tubular-campanulate, 4–10 per truss. Calyx large and leafy. Style stout and sharply bent or almost straight. Flower stalk slender, ½–1¼ in. (1–2·7cm) long.

Fairly hardy and usually flowers late enough to escape frost. An attractive free-flowering species which has long been in cultivation. Best on the edge of woodland or shrub border. Most effective in clumps on a bank, but not for a really exposed site. Old specimens can spread over a large area.

Found only in extreme east Nepal, Sikkim, Bhutan, the west end of NEFA and a small part of south-east Tibet at 9,000–12,000 ft.

(2,743–3,657m). Grows in clearings in pine and rhododendron forest and along rocks, sometimes beside waterfalls.
Late April–May

R. glaucophyllum var. *tubiforme*. Flower more tubular, 1–1½ in. (2·3–3·2cm) long, on rather a stiff bush; a good shade of rose-pink. Very free-flowering and pretty but more easily frosted than *R. glaucophyllum* as the buds swell earlier. The corollas shed rather quickly after opening. From south Tibet, Bhutan and NEFA at 9,000–10,000 ft. (2,743–3,048m) in open rhododendron, bamboo and mixed forest.
April–May

R. glaucophyllum var. *luteiflorum* H3–4 A none L1–2 F3

Horticulturally, this is absolutely distinct from *R. glaucophyllum* and well worth specific status in my view. Also well separated geographically in nature. Starts dwarf and compact but grows erect and rather leggy on maturity.
F lemon-yellow. A lovely plant well worth any amount of trouble. Only has a chance to flower well in mild districts most seasons as the flower buds often swell in February or March and are very easily frosted. It is also inclined to die suddenly. Surprisingly, reports from Kent tell of a failure to set flower buds so far. It is more closely related in its flowering habits to *R. tsangpoense* and geographically to var. *pruniflorum*. 'Glencloy', FCC 1966; AM 1960.
Only discovered in 1953 by KW in the Triangle, upper Burma, growing about the tree-line on crags at 9,000–10,000 ft. (2,743–3,048m).
March–April, occasionally odd flowers into May

R. shweliense H4 A none L1–2 F1–2

Ht 1–2½ ft. (30–75cm). Habit compact, often wider than high.
L ½–2 in. (1·3–4·7cm) long, ¼–¾ in. (0·6–1·8cm) wide, oblong-obovate to obovate, often not as glaucous below as the rest of the series, with prominent widely-spaced brown scales.
F pale pink tinged yellow with upper lobes spotted pink, ½–⅔ in. (1·3–1·5cm) long, campanulate, 2–4 per truss. Calyx large and leafy.
Not too easy to grow well, as it is liable to languish or die for no apparent reason. Quite nice in full flower and tends to be rather

dwarfer than the rest of the series. Fairly closely related to *R. brachyanthum*. Has a very limited distribution on the Shweli–Salween divide, west Yunnan, at 10,000–11,000 ft. (3,048–3,353m). Grows on open ledges of cliffs and rocky slopes. Only collected by F.

May–June

R. tsangpoense H4 but bud tender in type A none L1–2 F1–3

Ht 1–3 ft. (30–90cm) or a little more. Habit compact to fairly erect. L ½–2¼ in. (1·4–5·2cm) long, ⅓–1 in. (0·8–2·6cm) wide, obovate-elliptic to oblong-elliptic, very glaucous below, pale yellow scales 1–6 (usually 3–6) times their own diameter apart.

F pink or pinkish-purple and may be occasionally deep cerise or violet, ½–1 in. (1·3–2·6cm) long, campanulate, in trusses of 2–6. Calyx smaller than *R. glaucophyllum*. Flower stalks slender, ½–1¼ in. (1·3–3cm) long.

Quite nice in flower but once the flower buds begin to swell, they are very susceptible to frost, so *R. glaucophyllum* or var. *pruniflorum* are better for cold areas. For the front of borders or the edge of woodland.

Found in a limited area of south-east Tibet only, at 12,000–13,500 ft. (3,657–4,113m) on open rocky hillsides with other rhododendron species. Only collected by KW and L&S. AM 1972.

April–May

R. tsangpoense var. *curvistylum*. Only found on the Doshong La Pass in south-east Tibet by KW. He discovered it growing next to *R. tsangpoense* and *R. campylogynum* and, in my opinion, this plant is definitely a natural hybrid between these two species. Having studied the type specimen, dried specimens from cultivation and growing plants, these show the typical variation expected in a hybrid swarm. The type is nearer *R. tsangpoense*, while those cultivated show more of the *R. campylogynum* influence. It is not a plant of great garden merit, with a twiggy, rather open habit and dusky reddish-purple flowers. Rather hard to propagate but not much loss!

May

R. tsangpoense var. *pruniflorum*. This is the most common variety and is a better garden plant because it flowers late and is therefore rarely frosted. The pale yellow scales on the leaf underside are slightly overlapping, to their own diameter apart.

F are a dusky violet or can be dull plum-purple to crushed strawberry or crimson. While the flowers may not be particularly exciting, they are of unusual colours and often attract attention. Habit similar to *R. tsangpoense*. Lionel de Rothschild liked its plum-purple flowers.

Found wild over a wide area of south-east Tibet, NEFA, and north-east upper Burma from 8,000–13,000 ft. (2,439–3,941m) in *Abies* forest, rhododendron thickets, often dense; rocky hillsides, ridges or screes. More lanky in forests.

May–June

LAPPONICUM SERIES (L)

This series contains the largest natural group of truly dwarf alpine species. Except for the aberrant *R. cuneatum* and *R. ravum* (probably conspecific) all are normally under 5 ft. (1·50m) high. They have aromatic, evergreen, densely scaly leaves on both surfaces and early deciduous leaf-bud scales. The flowers are usually in small terminal trusses or are solitary, are openly funnel-shaped or rarely tubular and of a somewhat thin texture. The colours are mostly mauve, purple, bluish or pink with a few yellows. No normally white-flowered species is known to exist but several albino forms have been seen in the wild. The flower stalks are short and the calyx is usually small. Stamens 5–10. The capsule is very short and scaly.

The distribution mainly extends over the mountains of western China, especially Yunnan and Szechwan and also more rarely south-east Tibet and the eastern Himalayas. The type species, *R lapponicum* is circumpolar and the closely related *R. parvifolium* comes from north-east Asia. Many cover vast areas at high altitudes.

R. cuneatum and *R. ravum* bear some resemblance to the Triflorum series and *R. setosum* to *R. fragariflorum* of the Saluenense series.

There are many excellent garden plants in the series, several of which are hardy, free-flowering from a very early age and easily grown. Several have been hybridized with other series, the best known of which are the so-called blues, mostly containing the blood of *R. augustinii* of the Triflorum series.

As this series contains so many similar species, I have shortened the descriptions and only include the most important characteristics.

In the main area of distribution the majority of species grow in a very similar habitat. Unless otherwise stated, the following cover all the various types: open rocky hillsides, grassy pastures, peaty moorland, limestone screes and cliffs, on or amongst boulders, by streams or waterfalls, dry slopes, moist meadows and margins of thickets. All are Hardiness 4 and the American rating will only be included if there is one.

Some species have relatively frost-resistant flowers. Many can be pruned with shears. For the best effect, plant in large groups.

Two revisions of the series are being made, one by Professor and Mrs W. R. Philipson of New Zealand and the other by Mr H. H. Davidian of the Royal Botanic Garden, Edinburgh.

The main points to watch for identification are shape, size and colour of leaves and habit.

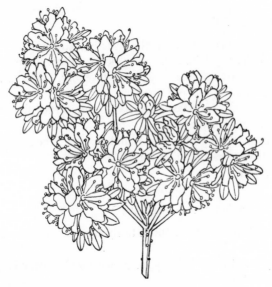

R. scintillans

R. achroanthum L1 F2

Ht to 3 ft. (91·4cm). Habit fairly compact.
L mostly $\frac{2}{3}$–$\frac{3}{4}$ in. (1·6–1·9cm) long, oblong-elliptic.
F deep magenta-red, purple, plum-purple to deep violet-purple, about $\frac{1}{2}$ in. (1·3cm) long, widely funnel-shaped, 3–5 per truss.

Very closely related to *R. rupicola* and possibly conspecific. The flowers are of quite a striking colour in the darkest forms. Some cultivated plants have narrow leaves.

Comes from Yunnan and north-east upper Burma at 12,000–15,000 ft. (3,657–4,571m). Exceedingly common and widespread. April–May

R. alpicola

Small-leaved. Probably of little interest, perhaps close to *R. ramosissimum* and *R. thymifolium*.

R. blepharocalyx

Similar to *R. intricatum*.

R. capitatum L1–2 F1–2

Ht to 3 ft. (91·4cm) or more. Habit usually fastigiate.
L variable in size, ¼–1 in. (0·6–2·5cm) long, elliptic, shiny above.
F deep purplish-red, purple, to purplish-lavender, ½–¾ in. (1·3–1·9cm) long, funnel-shaped, 4–5 per truss.

Unusual for its very fastigiate habit and earlier flowering and growth than most of the series.

Common in Kansu and also found in east Tibet, growing like heather. Also grows in conifer forest.
March–April

R. chryseum (*muliense*) A—10 L1–2 F2–3

Ht to 2 ft. (60cm) or more. Habit fairly compact to more open, not erect.
L about ½ in. (1·3cm) long, ⅓ in. (0·8cm) wide, ovate-elliptic, not shiny above.
F cream through pale yellow to *yellow*, about ½ in. (1·3cm) long and up to 1 in. (2·5cm) across, widely funnel-shaped 4–5 per truss.

Makes an excellent foil for the purple to blue members of the series as, along with *R. flavidum*, it is the only yellow. Although introduced many times, it is generally scarce because cuttings are hard to root. Variable in size of leaves and flowers. Good in southern Sweden. Sensitive to heat and poor drainage in Pennsylvania.

Common in Yunnan, Szechwan and south-east Tibet at 11,000–15,500 ft. (3,353–4,722m). Also grows in and on margins of conifer forest.
April–May

R. complexum L1–2 F1–2

Ht to 2 ft. (60cm). Habit matted shrub, slow-growing.
L $\frac{1}{3}$ in. (0·8cm) or less long, broadly elliptic.
F very pale to deep rosy-purple, $\frac{1}{2}$ in. (1·3cm) long and up to $\frac{2}{3}$ in. (1·6cm) across, tubular with lobes, 3–5 per truss.

Rare in cultivation, one of the smallest and neatest of the series.

Found in Yunnan at 11,000–15,000 ft. (3,353–4,471m).

April–May

R. cuneatum A0 L1–2 F2–3

Ht 4–6 ft. or rarely to 10 ft. (1·22–1·83–3·05m). Habit usually erect.
L $\frac{1}{2}$–2$\frac{2}{3}$ in. (1·3–6·6cm) long, and up to 1 in. (2·5cm) wide, elliptic to obovate-lanceolate. No scent to slightly aromatic.
F the largest in the series, rose-lavender, deep rose-pink to deep rose-purple, about 1 in. (2·5cm) long, widely funnel-shaped, 3–6 per truss. Calyx well-developed.

An aberrant species and in every way the *largest* of the series. Might be better placed in the Triflorum series. Quite pretty in the best selections and good as a background for other dwarfs. Very variable. Good in southern Sweden.

Found from Yunnan into Szechwan at 9,000–13,000 ft. (2,743–3,961m). Also grows on margins of pine forest and in shady oak forest. Common and widespread.

March–May

R. dasypetalum L2–3 F1–2

Ht 1–3 ft. (30–90cm). Habit usually neat and compact.
L about $\frac{2}{3}$ in. (1·6cm) long, oblong-elliptic, often *shiny* above and with light brown scales below.
F rose-purple to deep blue-purple, about $\frac{3}{4}$ in. (1·9cm) long, open funnel-shaped, 1–4 per truss. Corolla hairy outside.

In the shiny-leaved forms it is one of the best of the series for foliage. Good in southern Sweden.

From Yunnan and Szechwan at 11,000–14,000 ft. (3,353–4,265m).

April–May

R. diacritum L1–2 F1–2

Ht to 2 ft. (60cm). Habit matted with thin twigs.
L about ¼ in. (0·6cm) long, *broadly* elliptic.
F deep rose-purple with white throat.

Similar to *R. telmateium* but with wider leaves and a dwarfer habit.
Seems to be rare in cultivation.

From Yunnan at 13,000–15,000 ft. (3,961–4,570m).

April

R. drumonium A0 L1–2 F1–2

Ht to 2 ft. (60cm). Habit tufted and compact.
L about ¼ in. (0·6cm) long, elliptic.
F purplish-blue, deep rosy-purple or mauve, nearly ½ in. (1.3cm)
long, solitary or in pairs.

Probably closely related to *R. telmateium* or *R. diacritum*.

From Yunnan at 10,000–12,000 ft. (3,048–3,657m). Also from
pine woods and oak forest.

April

R. edgarianum L1–2 F1–3

Ht to 3 ft. (90cm). Habit fairly compact or upright.
L about ⅓ in. (0·8cm) long, broadly elliptic, with brown scales below.
F blue-purple or rose-purple, about ½ in. (1·3cm) long, open funnel-
shaped, solitary or up to 3 per truss.

Attractive in the best bluish-coloured forms. Is probably closely
related to *R. tapetiforme* and *R. ramosissimum* with rather undistinguished foliage. Later flowering than most of the series. Good in
southern Sweden.

From Szechwan, Yunnan and south-east Tibet at 12,000–15,000
ft. (3,657–4,571m).

May–June

R. fastigiatum A—10 L2–3 F2–3

Ht to 3 ft. (90cm). Habit not fastigiate as the name implies, but very
compact, though not usually quite so dense as *R. impeditum*.
L about ⅔ in. (1·6cm) long, elliptic-oblanceolate, *glaucous* above.
Scales *rimmed* and *opaque*.

F light purple to deep purple-blue, about ½ in. (1·3cm) long, widely funnel-shaped, 4–5 per truss.

Has amongst the best foliage and habit in the series with fine glaucous blue leaves. An excellent species in the best clones. Closely related to *R. impeditum* but with different scales. Good in southern Sweden. Borderline in eastern USA. AM 1914, blue-lilac flowers.

More or less confined to Yunnan at 11,000–16,000 ft. (3,353–4,875m).

April–May

R. fimbriatum L1–2 F1–2

Ht to 4 ft. (1·22m). Habit fairly open and erect.
L to about 1 in. (2·5cm) long, ⅓ in. (0·8cm) wide, lanceolate to oblanceolate, *pale* and slightly glaucous green above, paler below.
F mauve-purple to pale mauve, about ⅓ in. (0·8cm) long, campanulate, about 8 per truss.

Very closely related to and possibly conspecific with *R. hippophaeoides* but often inferior in flower colour.

From Szechwan at 12,000 ft. (3,657m).

April–May

R. flavidum A—5 L1–2 F2–3

Ht to 3 ft. (90cm). Habit erect.
L about ½ in. (1·3cm) long and ¼ in. (0·6cm) wide, elliptic to oblong, dark green and *shiny* above, with prominent reddish-brown scales below.
F *pale yellow*, ⅔ in. (1·6cm) long, open funnel-shaped, 3–5 per truss. Often flowers in autumn.

Differs from *R. chryseum* chiefly in its shiny leaves and erect habit. Quite pretty in a delicate-looking way. The so-called white forms with longer leaves are hybrids.

From western Szechwan at 10,000–13,000 ft. (3,048–3,961m). Evidently rare in the wild.

April–May

R. glomerulatum

Named from a cultivated plant at Headfort, Ireland. Has an erect habit and pale mauve flowers. Possibly close to *R. yungningense*.

H

R. hippophaeoides A—10 L2–3 F2–3

Ht up to 5 ft. (1·52m). Habit erect.

L up to 1½ in. (3·8cm) long, and ⅓ in. (0·8cm) wide, oblanceolate to elliptic, *pale slightly glaucous green above*, paler fawnish-green below.

F *lavender-blue*, pale lilac to rose, nearly 1 in. (2·5cm) across, flat funnel-shaped, 6–8 per truss.

One of the best known of the series and a good garden plant. Most forms in cultivation are surprisingly uniform for such a wide-spread species in the wild. The Bei-ma-shan form is reckoned to be the finest. Several very narrow-leaved variants were found but do not appear to be in cultivation. Hardy in eastern USA and has flowered successfully in Iceland. AM 1927, lavender-blue flowers; AGM 1925.

From Yunnan and Szechwan at 9,000–14,000 ft. (2,743–4,265m) where it is often common. One of the few species frequently found in bogs, also in and on margins of forests.

April–May, occasionally March

R. idoneum

A rare species, probably similar to *R. diacritum*. Compact with small leaves.

R. impeditum A—10 L1–2 F3–4

Ht usually under 1 ft. (30cm). Habit dense and compact.

L about ½ in. (1·3cm) long and ¼ in. (0·6cm) wide, broadly elliptic, *not shiny or glaucous* above. Scales at first pale translucent and colourless, *golden with jagged edges* when mature.

F mauve to purplish-blue, about ⅔ in. (1·6cm) long, open funnel-shaped, solitary or in pairs.

This well-known dwarf is rightly considered among the best. Some forms in the trade are *R. fastigiatum*. While it is always compact, different clones vary in vigour and the size and height to which they grow. Excellent for the front of a border. Borderline in eastern USA. AM 1944, R 59263; AGM 1968.

Comes from Yunnan and Szechwan at 9,000–16,000 ft. (2,743–4,875m), also in forest and cane brakes. Very widespread and common.

April–May

R. intricatum A—10 L1–2 F2–3

Ht up to 3 ft. (90cm). Habit fairly dense and twiggy.
L about ⅓ in. (0·8cm) long, oblong-elliptic, *glaucous* green above.
F usually pale lavender-blue, sometimes mauve, ⅓ in. (0·8cm) long,
tubular with spreading lobes in a compact truss.

One of the most distinctive of the series with very pretty flowers
which are very frost-resistant for a rhododendron. Earlier flowering
than most of the series. Closely related to *R. blepharocalyx* and *R.
peramabile*. The latter is more vigorous than the usual *R. intricatum*.
Winter killed in Washington DC.

Comes from Szechwan and Yunnan at 11,000–15,000 ft. (3,353–
4,571m), also from margins of conifer forests and is often marsh-
loving, sometimes surrounding pools. FCC 1907.

March–May

R. lapponicum L1 F1

Ht to 3 ft. (90cm). Habit dwarf, spreading and knarled to more
upright.
L ⅓–½ in. (0·8–1·3cm) long, obovate-lanceolate.
F purple, about ⅓ in. (0·8cm) long, funnel-shaped, about 3 per truss.

Plants of this species from most wild locations have proved very
difficult to grow. Those from Mount Washington, north-east USA
are said to be the easiest. A collection has recently been made of an
erect growing variant from along the shores of the Great Slave Lake,
Canada, which apparently poses no cultural problems. Closely
related to *R. parvifolium*.

Is found in the Arctic, circumpolar, often growing on soil overlying
perma-frost. Is also located on a few mountain tops in North
America at up to 5,500 ft. (1,674 m), in peat, clay and moss on limestone, serpentine or igneous rocks. In the Canadian Arctic it sometimes grows in alkaline soil with a pH of up to 8·5.

January–February

R. litangense L1–2 F1–2

Ht to 3½ ft. (1·07m). Habit usually erect.
L about ½ in. (1·3cm) long, oblong-elliptic.
F lavender to plum-purple, about ½ in. (1·3cm) long, widely funnel-
shaped. Not of great garden value. Has sub-persistent flower-bud
scales.

Found in Szechwan and Yunnan at 11,000–14,000 ft. (3,353–4,265m), sometimes in oak forest.
April–May

R. *lysolepis* L1–2 F2–3

Ht to 4 ft. (1·22m). Habit fairly erect.
L up to ¾ in. (1·9cm) long, and ½ in. (1·3cm) wide, oblong-elliptic, *shiny* above.
F purple, deep violet or pinkish-violet, nearly 1 in. (2·5cm) across, widely funnel-shaped, 2–3 per truss. Style short.
  Quite attractive in foliage and flower. Rather similar to *R. stictophyllum* and *R. nigropunctatum* which both have longer styles.
  From Szechwan at 12,000 ft. (3,657m).
  April–May

R. *microleucum* see *R. scintillans*

R. *nigropunctatum* L1–2 F1–2

Ht to 2 ft. (60cm). Habit bushy and fairly compact.
L about ¼ in. (0·6cm) long, narrowly elliptic. Some forms are shiny above, others are not.
F pale purple, about ⅓ in. (0·8cm) long, open funnel-shaped, solitary or in pairs.
  Has neat little leaves but otherwise lacks interest.
  From Szechwan at 10,000–15,000 ft. (3,048–4,571m).
  April–June

R. *nitidulum* L1–2 F1–2

Ht to 4 ft. (1·22m).
L about ½ in. (1·3cm) long and ¾ in. (0·6cm) wide, broadly elliptic.
F violet-purple, ½ in. (1·3cm) long, widely funnel-shaped.
  From Szechwan at 10,000–15,000 ft. (3,048–4,571m).
  April

R. *nivale* L1 F1

Ht to 1½ ft. (45cm) rarely to 5 ft. (1·52cm) in the wild. Habit usually with very short growth and thickish branchlets, making a fairly dense bush.

L often less than ¼ in. (0·6cm) long, elliptic with *prominent dark scales* on both surfaces.

F purple, reddish-purple, bright mauve to violet or pink, about ½ in. (1·3cm) long, widely funnel-shaped, solitary or in pairs.

Comes from the highest elevation of all rhododendrons and has proved difficult to grow in cultivation. Is interesting but not of much garden value.

Found over large areas of the eastern Himalayas and Tibet around Lhasa, at 10,000–19,000 ft. (3,048–5,789m); sometimes grows in a swamp.

April–May

R. orthocladum A—5 L1–2 F1–2

Ht to 4 ft. (1·22m). Habit usually fairly upright but quite compact.

L about ½ in. (1·3cm) long, oblanceolate, very slightly glaucous above.

F lavender-blue, pale mauve to purplish-blue, about ½ in. (1·3cm) long, widely funnel-shaped, solitary or up to 4 per truss. Style *shorter* than stamens.

Quite pretty in the bluer forms. Similar to *R. scintillans* but the latter has a style longer than the stamens.

From Yunnan and Szechwan at 11,000–14,000 ft. (3,353–4,265m) where it is fairly common and widespread and reasonably uniform.

April–May

R. paludosum L1–2 F1–2

Ht to 2½ ft. (76cm). Habit dwarf and compact to more erect and open.

L up to ½ in. (1·3cm) long, often less, elliptic.

F mauve to violet, shortly and openly tubular, usually solitary.

The smaller-leaved types merge with *R. nivale* where the distribution overlaps. Not of much horticultural value.

From Yunnan and Tibet at 12,000–14,000 ft. (3,657–4,265m).

April–May

R. parvifolium L1–2 F1–3

Ht to 2½ ft. (76cm). Habit often erect but fairly compact.

L to ¾ in. (1·9cm) long, ⅓ in. (0·8cm) wide oblong-lanceolate.

F pale magenta-rose, about $\frac{2}{3}$ in. (1·6cm) long, funnel-shaped, up to 5 per truss.

Attractive in full flower in February when there is not much else out. Merges with *R. lapponicum* in central Asia. A white form is known as var. *albiflorum* which does not appear to be in cultivation.

Comes from north-east Asia, Siberia, Korea and Japan.

January–April

R. peramabile. A strong growing *R. intricatum.*

R. polifolium. L1–2 F1–2. Another small-leaved species of no particular distinction.

R. ramosissimum. L1–2 F1–2. Shows some relationship with *R. nivale* and is not of much merit.

R. ravum. Similar to and probably conspecific with *R. cuneatum,* but is possibly more glaucous with narrower, smaller leaves.

R. rupicola A0 L1–2 F2–3

Ht to 2 ft. (60cm). Habit bushy and fairly compact.

L about $\frac{1}{2}$ in. (1·3cm) long, usually broadly elliptic, with prominent dark scales on both sides.

F pale puce to *deep purple or deep plum crimson,* sometimes with a white throat, about $\frac{1}{2}$ in. (1·3cm) long, widely funnel-shaped, 2–5 per truss.

Closely related to and possibly conspecific with *R. achroanthum.* The dark-flowered forms are well worth growing, and are most attractive with the sun shining through them. Good in southern Sweden.

Very common and widespread in Yunnan and Szechwan at 10,000–15,000 ft. (3,048–4,571m).

April–May

R. russatum (*osmerum, cantabile*) A—10 L1–2 F3–4

Ht 1–6 ft. (30cm–1·83m). Habit dwarf and compact to upright and leggy.

L usually $\frac{2}{3}$–$\frac{3}{4}$ in. (1·6–1·9cm) long but occasionally up to 2$\frac{1}{2}$ in. (8·6 cm) long, and 1¼ in. (3·2cm) wide, narrowly elliptic to oblong-elliptic to broadly-elliptic. Scales below rusty brown, fairly prominent. F *bright deep reddish to blue-purple*, sometimes with a white throat, up to ¾ in. (1·9cm) long, open funnel-shaped, 4–6 per truss.

The finest species of this colour in the genus. All are good but the more compact clones are the most desirable. Very variable. Fairly successful in eastern USA and good in southern Sweden. There is an off-white form. FCC 1933, intense blue flowers; AM 1927, intense violet blue; AGM 1938.

Comes from north-west Yunnan and Szechwan at 11,000–14,000 ft. (3,353–4,265m). Also grows in cane brakes and margins of pine forests.

April–May

R. scintillans L1–2 F2–4

Ht to 3 ft. (90cm). Habit rather upright but spreading, loose in shade. L about ½ in. (1·3cm) long and ⅙ in. (0·4cm) wide, oblanceolate, dark green.
F lavender blue and purplish-rose to almost a royal blue, ½ in. (1·3cm) long, about 3 per truss. Style *longer* than stamens.

The best blue forms, FCC and Wisley, are very fine indeed and extremely free-flowering. A must for every dwarf collection. Best in a fairly open situation to avoid a leggy habit. Can be pruned with shears. Fairly successful in east USA. Good in southern Sweden. FCC 1934, lavender-blue; AM 1924, purplish-rose; AGM 1968.

From Yunnan at 10,000–14,500 ft. (3,048–4,417m).
April–May

R. microleucum A—5 L2 F3

Ht to 2 ft. (60cm). Habit compact, forming a mound, foliage dense. F pure white, up to ¾ in. (1·9cm) across, widely funnel-shaped, 2–3 per truss.

This was thought to be a clone, coming from one seedling of *R. scintillans*, F 22108, but at least two different clones exist. One of the very few albino Lapponicums yet introduced. Makes a most attractive little plant with surprisingly frost-resistant flowers. FCC 1939.

April–May

R. setosum L1–3 F1–3

Ht to 4 ft. (1·22m) but usually less. Habit low but shoots usually not densely packed. Branchlets *bristly*.
L up to ¾ in. (1·9cm) long and ¼ in. (0·6cm) wide, oblong-elliptic to oblong, hairy margins, underside and leaf stalks.
F bright purplish-pink or bright rose-purple, up to 1 in. (2·5cm) long, widely funnel-shaped, 3–8 per truss. Stamens prominent.

Very distinct with hairy leaves and branchlets and bright-coloured flowers which are quite striking and showy in the best forms. Closely related to *R. fragariflorum* of the Saluenense series. Often flowers in the autumn.

Comes from Nepal, Sikkim, Bhutan and south Tibet at 9,000–16,000 ft. (2,743–4,875m). Wine-red and pink forms are reported in the wild. Quite common and widespread.
May

R. spilanthum L1–2 F1–2

Ht to 3 ft. (90cm). Habit fairly erect and sparse.
L to ⅓ in. (0·8cm) long, *narrowly* elliptic.
F purplish-blue to pale lavender-blue, ⅔ in. (1·6cm) across, widely funnel-shaped.

Probably close to *R. thymifolium*. The clone we grow is pretty but slow-growing. Rare.
From Szechwan, also in spruce forest.
May

R. stictophyllum L1–2 F1–2

Ht to 2½ ft. (76cm). Habit bushy but fairly erect.
L up to ½ in. (1·3cm) long, narrowly-elliptic, shiny above.
F rose, purple to bright mauve, ⅓ in. (0·8cm) long, open funnel-shaped, solitary to 4 per truss.

Very free-flowering and showy when full out. Good in southern Sweden.
From west Szechwan.
April–May

R. tapetiforme L1–2 F1–2

Ht to 2½ ft. (76cm). Habit low and carpet-forming to more erect.

16 *R. impeditum*. Lapponicum series in wild (G. Forrest)

17 *R. microleucum*. Lapponicum series

18 (*right*) *R. lowndesii.*
Lepidotum series

19–20 (*below*) *R. ciliatum.*
Maddenii series: (*top*)
cultivated; (*bottom*) in wild
(G. Sherriff)

L up to $\frac{1}{2}$ in. (1·3cm) long, often less, broadly elliptic.
F pink or pale rose-purple to deep blue-purple, about $\frac{1}{2}$ in. (1·3cm) long, widely funnel-shaped, 2–4 per truss.

Rather variable in habit and flowers. No special merit. Heat killed in Washington DC. Successful in southern Sweden.

April

R. telmateium L1–2 F1–2

Ht to 3 ft. (90cm). Habit upright, densely branched with very *thin* shoots.
L $\frac{1}{4}$–$\frac{1}{3}$ in. (0·6–0·8cm) long, $\frac{1}{8}$ in. (0·3cm) wide, oblanceolate.
F lavender-purple to deep rose-purple to bright magenta, about $\frac{1}{2}$ in. (1·3cm) long, openly funnel-shaped, 2–3 per truss.

Interesting for the very small leaves and thin branchlets but not much merit otherwise. Closely related to or may include some forms of *R. drumonium*.

From Szechwan and Yunnan at 9,500–14,000 ft. (2,896–4,265m), also in boggy forest margins, in oak forest and on dry pine-clad slopes. Some forms are said to be attractive. Up to 5 ft. (1·50m) high in the wild.

April–May

R. thymifolium L1–2 F1–2

Ht to 4 ft. (1·22m). Habit often erect with thin shoots.
L about $\frac{1}{3}$ in. (0·8cm) long, *narrowly* oblanceolate, slightly glaucous above.
F purple, lavender-blue, mauve or purplish-blue, about $\frac{1}{3}$ in. (0·8cm) long, widely funnel-shaped, solitary or in pairs.

Closely related to *R. spilanthum*. Quite a neat little plant, distinctive for the very narrow leaves.

From Szechwan and Kansu at 10,000–15,000 ft. (3,048–4,571m), abundant.

April

R. verruculosum L1–2 F2–3

Ht to 3 ft. (90cm). Habit compact.
L about $\frac{1}{2}$ in. (1·3cm) long, and $\frac{1}{4}$ in. (0·6cm) wide, broadly elliptic, *pale, slightly glaucous green* above.

I

F purple, pink or purplish-blue, about ½ in. (1·3cm) long, widely funnel-shaped, usually solitary.

Close to *R. impeditum* but slightly later flowering. The blue-purple forms are attractive in foliage and flower. AM 1932, purple flowers.

Late May

R. violaceum L1–2 F1–2

Ht to 4 ft. (1·22m).
L ⅓ in. (0·8cm) long, narrowly oblong-elliptic.
F violet-purple, nearly ½ in. (1·3cm) long, openly funnel-shaped, solitary or to 3 per truss.

From west Szechwan and abundant in Kansu.

April–May

R. websterianum L1–2 F1–2

Ht to 3 ft. (90cm).
L ⅓ in. (0·8cm) long, narrowly elliptic.
F rosy-purple or pale blue, about ¾ in. (1·9cm) long, funnel-shaped, usually solitary.

Leaves rather like a narrow-leaved *R. intricatum*.

From Szechwan at 10,000–15,000 ft. (3,048–4,722m).

April

R. yungningense L1–2 F1–2

Ht to 3 ft. (90cm). Habit rather erect.
L up to ¾ in. (1·9cm) long, oblong-lanceolate, scales rusty-coloured below.
F deep purple, deep purplish-blue or pale rose-purple, about ⅓ in. (0·8cm) long, widely funnel-shaped, solitary or in pairs.

Resembles a small-leaved *R. hippophaeoides*.

From Szechwan and Yunnan at 11,000–14,000 ft. (3,353–4,265m).

April–May

LEPIDOTUM SERIES (L)

A small series of three species, evergreen, semi- or completely deciduous. Leaves densely scaly below, overlapping or close together.

The flowers are pink, purple, crimson, rose, yellow or white, rotate, and the flower stalks are slender, longer than the corolla. Style short, stout and sharply bent. Stamens 8 or 10. Calyx well-developed.

Closest relations are in the Glaucophyllum series but the Lepidotum series generally have sparser or deciduous leaves in winter and are usually less glaucous below, with one type of scale only. The rotate flat corolla contrasts with the campanulate one in the Glaucophyllum series. All have pretty but rather small flowers.

Distribution from the north-west Himalayas eastwards to Szechwan, over a wide area.

Sub-series Baileyi

R. baileyi (*thyodocum*) H3–4 A none L1 F2–3

Ht up to 6 ft. (1·80m) or even more in shade. Habit often scraggy and leggy, taller than broad.
L ¾–2¾ in. (2·2–7cm) long, ⅓–1⅓ in. (0·8–3·3cm) wide, elliptic to obovate, cinnamon, rust-coloured or rarely greenish-brown below, and densely scaly. Old leaves may turn yellow in autumn.
F purple, deep purple or almost red, with or without darker spots, up to 1¼ in. (3cm) across, rotate or sub-rotate, 5–9 rarely to 18 per truss. Flower stalks slender, ½–1½ in. (1·2–3·5cm) long, longer than corolla.

Often an untidy grower. The taller forms are best planted in light woodland or at the back of a bed of dwarfs. Well worth growing for the striking coloured flowers, probably the best of this shade in the genus. A little difficult to grow in some gardens and sometimes the buds and young growth are frosted. Often cultivated under L&S 2896. AM 1960.

Has a rather limited distribution from Bhutan and neighbouring areas of south Tibet. Often found as a woodland species in rhododendron, conifer or bamboo forest, on dry or moist hill slopes or occasionally in a scree at 8,000–13,000 ft. (2,439–3,961m).
May

Sub-series Lepidotum

R. lepidotum (*salignum*, *obovatum*, *elaeagnoides*, *sinolepidotum*) H3–4 A0 L1–2 F1–3

Ht 2 in.–5 ft. (5cm–1·50m). Habit low and compact to upright and sometimes rather scraggy; often stoloniferous.

L $\frac{1}{6}$–1 rarely to $1\frac{1}{2}$ in. (0·4–2·6 rarely to 3·8cm) long, $\frac{1}{10}$–$\frac{3}{4}$ in. (0·2–1·8cm) wide, obovate to lanceolate, densely scaly below, green or brown, semi-evergreen or evergreen.

F pink, purple, crimson, rose, yellow, greenish-yellow, cream or white, often spotted, scaly outside, rotate, flattish, $\frac{1}{2}$–1 in. (1·2–2·4cm) across, single or in trusses of 3 or rarely 4. Flower stalk slender, $\frac{1}{2}$–$1\frac{1}{2}$ in. (1·3–2·8cm) long, longer than corolla.

Possibly the most widespread and variable of all species, dwarf or tall. Varies in hardiness as it comes from a great range of altitudes. Heat killed in Washington DC. Unfortunately many of the most attractive-sounding forms are not in cultivation and careful selection in the wild should pay dividends. Dwarfer forms are ideal for rock or peat gardens. The deciduous yellow forms are close to *R. lowndesii*. Some forms are stoloniferous. 'Reuthe's Purple', AM 1967.

Found wild over enormous areas from the north-west Himalayas all the way to Szechwan at 8,000–16,000 ft. (2,439–4,875m). Grows in all sorts of habitats from near the snow-line on open moors, rocks and cliffs which are sometimes limestone, to grassy hillsides, scrub jungle with other dwarf rhododendrons and in various types of forest. Can tolerate dry conditions in the wild.

May–June

R. lowndesii H3–4 A none L1 F1–2 or maybe 3

Ht 2 in.–1 ft. (5–30cm) (in cultivation well under 1 ft. (30cm) so far). Habit usually dense and prostrate and much wider than tall with crowded little branchlets. Stoloniferous.

L up to 1 in. (2·4cm) long, usually less in the open, oblanceolate to obovate, bristly all over, completely deciduous.

F pale yellow, lightly spotted carmine, $\frac{1}{2}$–1 in. (1·2–2·4cm) across, rotate-campanulate, solitary or in pairs.

Unfortunately this pretty little plant with the flat yellow flower is rather hard to please and seems to need perfect drainage. While it is apt to suffer die-back from unseasonable frosts and dampness it is well worth covering it with a cloche during all the time of likely frosts. The flowers, often plentifully produced, are small and short-lived in very sunny weather. Grows in peat walls or rock gardens, north facing if available but with plenty of light and no overhang. Only recently introduced. Closely related to *R. lepidotum*.

Comes from central and western Nepal in drier areas at 10,000–15,000 ft. (3,048–4,571m) on shady rocky ledges, sometimes hanging

III 'Pipit' (*lowndesii* x *lepidotum*). Natural Lepidote hybrid

over the edge, rock crevices, peaty banks, grass slopes and under the shelter of boulders.

May–June

MADDENII SERIES (L)

Sub-series Ciliicalyx

A large sub-series of the rather tender Maddenii series. The majority of species have large white or white tinged pink, more or less scented flowers but are unfortunately too tall to include here. The four described are rather different. Three are yellow and show a relationship with the yellow-flowered members of the Boothii series. The fourth, *R. ciliatum*, is a fairly hardy outlier from the west end of the distribution of the sub-series. Stamens usually 10.

R. fletcherianum

R. burmanicum H2–3 A+15 L1–2 F2–3

Ht 4–6 ft. (1·20–1·83m). Habit usually compact but tends to straggle in shade. A few hairs on young shoots.

L up to 3 in. (7·5cm) long, oblanceolate to obovate, densely scaly above and below, dark green, with some hairs on margins.
F yellow, greenish-yellow or greenish-white, up to 1½ in. (3·8cm) long, campanulate, 5–10 per truss. Some forms are scented.

A fine species for mild sheltered gardens. Rather bud tender, even in warmer areas. Good for San Francisco Bay district.

Rare in the wild, only found on Mount Victoria, south-west Burma, at 9,000–10,000 ft. (2,743–3,048m), on the windward side and along fringe of forest on leeward slopes. Many are being scorched by grass fires.

April–May

R. ciliatum H3–4 A+10 L1–2 F2–3

Ht usually 3–5 ft. (90cm–1·50m), occasionally to 6 ft. (1·83m) in shade. Habit compact in the open to straggly in shade. Bark peeling. L 1½–3½ in. (3·8–8·8cm) long, up to 1½ in. (3·8cm) wide, elliptic to oblong-elliptic, hairy above and fringed with longer stiff hairs.
F white or pink tinged, 1½–2 in. (3·8–5cm) long and up to 2½ in. (6·3cm) wide, narrowly campanulate to campanulate, 2–4 per truss. Calyx ⅓ in. (0·8cm) long, densely fringed with hairs.

A well-known species, long in cultivation, which naturalizes itself in some gardens. Variable in time of flowering and size of flower. Flower buds are very susceptible to frost once they start to swell. Sometimes proves a hardier and better plant in an exposed position. Will survive in most parts of Britain. AM 1953, white flowers with pink tinge.

Found wild in east Nepal, Sikkim, Bhutan and adjoining areas of south-east Tibet at 8,000–12,000 ft. (2,439–3,657m) in and around upper forest areas, steep rocky hillsides, hanging over cliff faces, beside streams and waterfalls and in boggy ground.

March–May

R. fletcheranum (affiliated to *valentinianum*) H4 A+10 (I suggest +5) L1–2 F2–3   *March 29, 74*

Ht up to 4 ft. (1·22m). Habit compact when young, leggy with age.
L up to 2 in. (5cm) long and 1 in. (2·5cm) wide, oblong-lanceolate to oblong-elliptic, bristly at margins.
F pale yellow, nearly 2 in. (5cm) long, up to 2 in. (5cm) across, widely

funnel-shaped, in compact trusses of 2–5. Calyx up to $\frac{1}{2}$ in. (1·3cm) long, hairy.

A recently named species previously known as Rock's form of *valentinianum* but quite different from that species. Quite hardy with us but said to be tender at Windsor Park. Foliage apt to be spotted, perhaps due to the necessity of perfect drainage. The largest-flowered yellow lepidote species for outdoors in east Scotland and very pretty when it escapes the frost. Closely related to *R. ciliatum*. 'Yellow Bunting', AM, is a fine form.

Appears to be rare in the wild, found only by R in Tsarung Province, south-east Tibet, in alpine regions at 13,500–14,000 ft. (4,113–4,265m).

March–May

R. valentinianum H3 A+10 L1–2 F2–3

Ht to 3 ft. (90cm). Habit fairly compact.
L up to 1$\frac{1}{2}$ in. (3·8cm) long, $\frac{3}{4}$ in. (2cm) wide, elliptic to oblong-elliptic, dark green above, densely scaly below, with golden hairs at margins and above.
F bright butter-yellow, about 1$\frac{1}{2}$ in. (3·8cm) long, tubular-campanu-late, 2–6 per truss.

A pretty dwarf which does well in west Scotland and thrives on old tree stumps. Just survives in east Scotland in a sheltered nook but rarely flowers. Good for San Francisco area. AM 1936.

Only found wild in a small part of west Yunnan, in open scrub, rocky slopes and on cliffs, sometimes limestone, at 9,000–12,000 ft. (2,743–3,657m).

March–April

MOUPINENSE SERIES (L)

A small distinctive series of three species, only one of which is in cultivation unfortunately. Nearest allies are the Maddenii and Triflorum and perhaps the Boothii series.

Low-growing, usually epiphytic, with bristly branchlets. Leaves very thick and stiff, fringed with hairs. Flowers 1–2, white to pink to rose-red. It is worth describing the two species not in cultivation as they seem to be deserving of introduction. *R. dendrocharis* has very small leaves and bright rosy-red flowers almost as large as *R. moupin-ense*. *R. petrocharis* has even smaller narrower leaves and red or white flowers. Both are found in Szechwan.

R. moupinense H4 A0 L1–2 F3–4

Ht to 5 ft. (1·50m). Habit usually sprawly, but fairly compact in the open. Branchlets bristly. Bark peeling.

L 1–1½ in. (2·5–3·8cm) long, ½–1 in. (1·3–2·5cm) wide, elliptic to ovate-elliptic, usually very dark green and shiny above and densely scaly below. Extremely thick and stiff for their size.

F white, white tinged pink, pink or deep rose, with or without spots, about 1½ in. (3·8cm) long and up to 2 in. (5cm) across, funnel-shaped, solitary or up to 3 per truss. Stamens 10.

This beautiful species is surprisingly hardy but unfortunately flowers very early. The buds and opened flowers are relatively tough and may survive a few degrees of frost but nothing prolonged. In east Scotland we see at least a few unspoilt flowers most seasons. Needs perfect drainage and is remarkably drought resistant. Try growing it on old logs, tree stumps, etc. It is the parent of many early flowering hybrids. Seems sensitive to heat and shoots are easily broken. Excellent in the San Francisco area and makes a fine pot plant. Slightly tender when young. AM 1914, white flowers; AM 1937, suffused rose-pink and spotted crimson.

Found wild in several parts of Szechwan and in Kweichow, China, at 6,500–10,000 ft. (1,980–3,048m), usually epiphytic on evergreen oaks and other broad-leaved trees but also on rocks and cliffs.

February–March and occasionally April

NERIIFLORUM SERIES (E)

This large series, divided into four sub-series, is one of the most important in the genus, containing many of our finest red-flowered species. The chief characteristics are a loose, often few-flowered truss, the usually unspotted corolla, and the hairy or glandular ovary. Many have a thin to very dense indumentum. The tubular flowers are mostly red, scarlet or crimson and have a fleshy texture. Habit is prostrate to just beyond our maximum for the book of 5 ft. (1·50m). They belong to the wetter regions.

All the series are sensitive to nitrogen (ammonia), will produce leaf-burn if over-fertilized and can be killed or severely damaged by dogs' urine. They appreciate an abundance of organic matter, and good drainage and none can tolerate hot summers.

Sub-series Forrestii

A small sub-series with only two very variable species in cultivation. Four others, not yet introduced, are rare to very rare in the wild, with either unusual foliage or rose or yellow flowers.

These are dwarf or creeping plants from the high mountains of east NEFA, south-east Tibet, north-east Burma and Yunnan. They need excellent drainage, yet abundant moisture in summer and some shade in all but the wettest places such as parts of west Scotland.

Really hot sunny districts are unsuitable for their culture, and if tried, plenty of shade is needed. Almost all flower and grow early in the season so are not for low-lying frosty gardens. The susceptibility of the young growth to frost is perhaps one of the reasons why *R. forrestii* and varieties have the reputation of being shy-flowering in cultivation. If the first flush of growth is frosted, practically no flower buds will be set that year. Also, flower buds readily abort and may appear to be hollow. But if well-grown and covered in flowers, these are possibly the gems of all dwarf rhododendrons. It can be worth while covering them for protection against spring frosts. Another point, be careful of an accumulation of soggy leaves which may fall on and rot out the centres of the plants.

Botanically, this sub-series is closest to the Sanguineum sub-series and some forms of *R. chamae-thomsonii* grow larger than *R. aperantum* of the Sanguineum sub-series, but usually their characteristic foliage and low or prostrate habit makes them easily identifiable. Those in cultivation have leaves with a rounded apex with little or no indumentum.

R. chamae-thomsonii H4 A probably −5 or 0 L1–2 F2–3

Ht certain forms to 3 ft. (90cm), others less. Habit dense and compact but sometimes rather open in shade. Fairly erect but often with creeping outer branches.
L $1\frac{1}{4}$–$3\frac{1}{2}$ in. (3–9cm) long, $\frac{3}{4}$–$1\frac{1}{2}$ in. (2–4cm) wide, obovate to oblong-obovate, usually glabrous underneath, thick and leathery.
F crimson, rosy-crimson, bright scarlet, rose-pink, sometimes orange-crimson and occasionally white; very fleshy, $1\frac{1}{4}$–2 in. (2·8–4·8cm) long, tubular-campanulate, solitary or to 4 per truss.

Very variable. A small-leaved form is called var. *chamaethauma* (AM 1932) but it is hard to distinguish between this and *R. forrestii*

R. chamae-thomsonii

var. *tumescens*. Does best on a cool north-facing bank in a little shade, or plenty of shade in hot sunny areas.

Found wild in east NEFA, south-east Tibet, Yunnan and north-east Burma at 11,000–15,000 ft. (3,353–4,571m), in dense thickets clothing steep flanks of hillsides, cliff ledges, among snow on moist alpine meadows, on boulders and lying or sprawling over rocks, often near *R. forrestii* var. *repens*.

March–May

R. forrestii H4 A+5 L1–2 F1–4

Ht 2–3 in. (5–7·5cm) to 6 in. (15cm) or a little more. Habit creeping, with prostrate branches often rooting as they grow. Foliage dense on well-grown specimens.

L ½–2 in. (1·3–5cm) long, ¼–1¼ in. (0·6–3·1cm) wide, broadly obovate to orbicular, dark green above, purple below, leathery. The largest-leaved forms are not in cultivation.

F bright scarlet, about 1½in. (3·8cm) long, tubular-campanulate, single or in pairs, very fleshy.

Very few *R. forrestii* flower freely if at all in cultivation, and the freer-flowering forms of var. *repens* and var. *tumescens* are recommended instead. Some have very small leaves and are exceedingly slow-growing, and these are usually the ones that will not flower.

Found wild in south-east Tibet, Yunnan and north-east Burma at 11,000–15,000 ft. (3,353–4,571m). Habitat as *R. chamae-thomsonii*, usually on granite and other non-calcareous rocks.

April–May if at all

R. forrestii var. *repens*. Also of creeping habit. Underside of leaves green, not purple. Some forms tend to grow and flower more freely than *R. forrestii* itself. Otherwise similar botanically to *R. forrestii*.

This variety does well in not more than 6 in. (15cm) of soil on top of solid rock at Glenarn, west Scotland and on low shady walls at Kilbryde, Northumberland. Try planting it in peaty pockets on a shaded rock-face, on rotten stumps or trunks or where it can grow vertically down a mossy wall. Do not place it where it has to compete with a rank growth of weeds and could be smothered. A few pine needles or some well-rotted leafmould pushed in under the branches is beneficial.

Grows wild under similar conditions to *R. forrestii*, often spreading flat for several feet along moss-covered rocks, flowing with the contours with the plant pointing downhill. FCC 1935.

R. forrestii var. *tumescens*. Similar to var. *repens* except that it has larger leaves and flowers, develops a dome in the middle of the plant with creeping outer branches and tends to be stronger growing. Very easily confused with *R. chamae-thomsonii* var. *chamaethauma*. Various plant collectors have gone into ecstasies over seeing whole hillsides covered by these plants in full flower. Kingdon Ward gave them names like 'Scarlet Runner' and 'Scarlet Pimpernel'. Plant var. *tumescens* on north-facing peat walls. AM 1957.

Both varieties April–May

Sub-series Haematodes

A distinctive sub-series with nearly all members having a thick indumentum. Leaf shape is oblong to obovate or elliptic. Nearly all have a fleshy corolla, red to deep crimson. One aberrant species, *R. mallotum*, is too tall for this book and some others occasionally grow to 6 ft. (2m) or more. The red flowers are all showy and, in most species, freely produced, although it may take a number of years to reach flowering size. With the exception of *R. beanianum*, all species described merge botanically into one another. Most require some shade, even in Scotland, and full shade in very hot sunny districts away from Britain. All need abundant moisture in the growing season and excellent drainage. Some species, notably *R. chaetomallum*, are inclined to die suddenly for no apparent reason but may be especially susceptible to *Phytophthora* root rot and honey fungus (*Armillaria mellea*). They are liable to suffer from bark-split although generally hardy otherwise. Most flower rather early in the season.

Distribution largely confined to upper Burma, south-east Tibet and Yunnan, with one discovery in east NEFA.

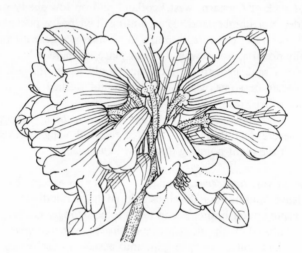

R. haematodes

R. beanianum H3–4 A+10 L2–3 F1–3

Ht usually 5–6 ft. (1·52–1·83m) occasionally to 8 ft. (2·44m) or more. Habit usually rather straggly in old age. Branches *bristly*.
L up to 4 in. (10cm) long, 1½ in. (3·8cm) wide, oblong-elliptic to oblong, dark green and rugose above and with rich red-brown indumentum below.
F scarlet, crimson or sometimes an inferior pink or ivory, up to 1½ in. (3·8cm) long, tubular-campanulate, waxy, 6–10 per truss, which in the poorer forms hangs down between the leaves.

The leaves have one of the most striking indumentums in the genus and when young and compact, makes a first-class foliage plant. Sometimes the flowers open very early and these turn black at the slightest hint of frost. A very distinct species. AM 1953.

IV *R. moupinense*. Moupinense series

Rare in the wild, only being found so far in two areas, one in east NEFA in the Delei Valley and the other in north-east upper Burma in the Seinghku Valley. Pink forms are from the latter. Grows from 9,000–11,000 ft. (2,743–3,353m), scattered under bamboo on steep flanks of ridges or in granite gullies, or as prostrate tuffets on alpine slopes and edges of forest.

March–April, occasionally May

R. beanianum var. *compactum*. Very different from the above and possibly deserving specific status. Leaves not so rugose above but more shiny, with thicker indumentum and fewer short bristles on the branches. Indumentum a paler colour. Hardly lives up to the name of *compactum* as the rather angular growth produces an open bush. Also scarce in the wild in south-east Tibet.

Flowering time as above

R. catacosmum H4 A none L2–3 F2–3

Ht 6–9 ft. (2–3m). Habit fairly compact. Branches *thicker* than *R. haematodes* or *R. chaetomallum*. Young growths clad with brownish or white wool.
L 2⅓–4⅓ in. (6–11cm) long, 1¼–2 in. (3–5cm) wide, obovate, leathery, underside with woolly indumentum, pale to dark cinnamon.
F deep crimson, crimson-rose or scarlet, 1½–1¾ in. (4–4·5cm) long, broadly campanulate, 5–9 per truss. Calyx large and petaloid with uneven lobes. Flower stalk 1 in. (2·5cm) long.

A fine species, rare in cultivation, rather tall for mention here. Closely related to *R. haematodes* and *R. chaetomallum*.

Of limited distribution in south-east Tibet and adjoining Yunnan, at 13,000–14,000 ft. (3,961–4,265m), amongst scrub and margins of forest and cliff ledges in alpine side-valleys.

March–April

R. chaetomallum H4 A+10 L2–3 F2–3

Ht 4–5 ft. (1·30–1·60m) sometimes more. Habit fairly compact to open and leggy.
L up to 4½ in. (11·3cm) long, 2⅓ in. (6cm) wide, obovate or oblong-obovate. Often has vestiges of juvenile indumentum above, with more or less dense woolly indumentum below, pale to dark fawn. Leaves and stems not sticky to touch.

F blood-red crimson or rarely deep rose, fleshy, about 1⅗ in. (4cm) long, tubular-campanulate, 4–7 per truss, often hanging between the leaves.

A well-known species in cultivation, quite free-flowering from a reasonably young age. Odd branches are liable to die off and the whole plant is often short-lived. It is attractive with fine flowers and handsome foliage. Seems to appreciate shade. AM 1959, turkey-red flowers.

Exceedingly widespread in the wild, being the commonest of the series over large areas of west Yunnan, north-east Burma and south-east Tibet at 10,000–15,000 ft. (3,048–4,571m). Grows on open bouldery slopes, alpine meadows, cliffs, thickets and scrub, and in *Abies* forest or cane brakes. Several varieties occur, not surprising in such a widespread species. All appear to be rare in cultivation.

R. chaetomallum var. *chaemaephytum*. More or less prostrate, 1–2 ft. (30–60cm) high, leaves glabrous beneath. South-east Tibet, 13,000 ft. (3,961m).

R. chaetomallum var. *glaucescens*. Leaf upper surface with a wax-like glaucous bloom. F deep rich crimson. North-east upper Burma, 13,000 ft. (3,961m).

R. chaetomallum var. *hemigymnum*. Leaf underside with a thin veiling of indumentum. F crimson. AM 1957, to form of F 25605. South-east Tibet and upper Burma. 12,000–14,000 ft. (3,657–4,265m).

R. chaetomallum var. *xanthanthum*. F creamy-yellow, flushed rose-pink, or striped or margined pale rose. South-east Tibet, 12,000–14,000 ft. (3,657–4,265m).

March–May for all varieties.

R. chionanthum H4 A none L1–2 F1–2

Ht about 3 ft. (90cm). Habit fairly compact.
L about 2½ in. (6cm) long, 1 in. (2·5cm) wide, clustered at ends of shoots, obovate to oblanceolate, with thick continuous or patchy tawny indumentum below. Leaf stalk very short.
F *white* (very unusual colour for the series), 1½ in. (3·8cm) long, campanulate, 4–6 per truss. Calyx ¼–½ in. (0·6–1·3cm) long, with uneven lobes.

Possibly not in cultivation.

A rare species in the wild, found in upper Burma at 13,000–14,000 ft. (3,961–4,265m) on alpine meadows, rocky slopes and scrub-clad cliffs.

April

R. coelicum H4 A none L2–3 F2–3

Ht a low bush but occasionally reaches 15 ft. (4·60m). Habit often compact but sometimes thin and erect. Branchlets neither hairy nor sticky to touch.

L about 2¾ in. (7cm) long, 1½ in. (4cm) wide, obovate; stiff, thick and leathery, with thick cinnamon-coloured indumentum below.

F bright scarlet to deep crimson, fleshy, 1½in. (4cm) long, tubular-campanulate, 6–15 per truss, often forming a compact rounded truss.

Very similar to *R. pocophorum* but smaller in most parts and usually dwarfer and more compact. A nice foliage plant. AM 1955.

Has a limited distribution in Yunnan and upper Burma and possibly south-east Tibet at 12,000–14,000 ft. (3,657–4,265m). Grows in alpine scrub in corries, cliff ledges and in cane brakes. Farrer saw it flowering in the snow, visible for miles.

April

R. haematodes H4 A0 L2–3 F3–4

Ht usually 3–5 ft. (90cm–1·50m), occasionally more. Habit dense and compact in the open, looser in the shade.

L up to 3½ in. (9cm) long, 1⅔ in. (4·5cm) wide, oblong to obovate, leathery, dark green above and covered with thick woolly rufous indumentum below.

F scarlet to crimson, occasionally deep pink, about 2 in. (5cm) long, tubular-campanulate, 6–12 per truss, sometimes hanging down between the leaves. Stamens 10–12.

An excellent species in foliage and flower which needs shade in America but will grow happily in nearly full sun in Scotland and northern England. Takes a few years to flower freely. FCC 1926.

Quite plentiful in Yunnan at 11,000–14,000 ft. (3,353–4,265m). Very variable in the wild in height, leaf shape and indumentum, but many of these forms are probably not in cultivation. Rocky moist Alpine meadows.

May–June

R. hemidartum H3–4 A none L2–3 F2–3

Ht 4–6 ft. (1·30–1·83m). Habit usually fairly compact.
L about 4 in. (10cm) long, 1½ in. (3·5cm) wide, oblong to obovate, leathery, dark green above, with brown *patchy* indumentum below.
F deep rich crimson, about 2 in. (4·5cm) long, tubular-campanulate, 4–10 per truss. Calyx uneven.

Rather subject to bark-split. Probably close to Neriiflorum sub-series.

Wild in south-east Tibet at 13,000–14,000 ft. (3,961–4,265m) in mixed rhododendron scrub on rocky slopes and alpine meadows.
April

R. pocophorum H3–4 A none L2–3 F2–3

Ht 4–10 ft. (1·22–3·05m). Habit rather erect and apt to become leggy. Branchlets sticky to touch.
L 4–6½ in. (10–16·5cm) long, 1½–2⅔ in. (4–7cm) wide, oblong to oblong-obovate, thick and leathery, dark green above, often with a waxy bloom, and covered below with a thick brown woolly indumentum.
F deep crimson or crimson-scarlet, about 2 in. (5cm) long, tubular-campanulate, fleshy, 10–20 per truss, occasionally compact.

A fine species in foliage and flower but all too easily frosted, with often only a portion of the truss opening. Can grow rather large for the purpose of this book. Closely related to *R. coelicum*. The giant of the series after *R. mallotum*.

Quite common in Tsarong Province, south-east Tibet at 12,000–15,000 ft. (3,657–4,571m), where it grows on margins of cane brakes, fir forest, thickets on rocky alpine meadows and gullies, and on limestone crags.
March–April

Sub-series Neriiflorum

This, the central part of the series, contains a group of fairly closely allied species. These can be divided into two groups, those with no indumentum or only a trace on the mid-rib and those with a definite indumentum, although it is sometimes very sparse. The corolla is always fleshy and, while usually scarlet to deep crimson, can appear in various colours or mixtures of colours in *R. floccigerum* and *R. phaedropum*. Those with indumentum usually have narrow pointed

21 *R. chaetomallum.* Neriiflorum series, sub-series Haematodes

22 *R. Forrestii* var *tumescens*. Neriiflorum series, sub-series Forrestii

23 *R. neriiflorum*. Neriiflorum series, sub-series Neriiflorum

leaves while those without have a more or less glaucous underside. The ovary is densely covered with a mat of hairs. The truss is never full and the flowers are usually unspotted.

Some forms will outgrow what can be considered dwarfs and all species are verging on the tender side for eastern Britain and are subject to bark-split. All are worth trying as certain introductions are hardier than others. The best forms include some of the finest reds or scarlets in cultivation.

Distribution from Bhutan eastwards to Yunnan, south-east Tibet and Burma.

R. floccigerum

R. albertsenianum H4 A none L1–2 F1–2

Ht 4–7 ft. (1·22–2·13m). Habit stiff straight branches.
L 2½–4 in. (6–9·5cm) long, ⅔–1 in. (1·5–2·5cm) wide, narrow-oblong to sub-lanceolate. Upper surface with vestiges of juvenile indumentum, and clad with a loose brown woolly indumentum below.
F bright rose-crimson, about 1–1¾ in. (3cm) long, campanulate, 5–6 per truss.

A rare species similar to *R. neriiflorum* but with an indumentum. Seems to be closely related to *R. sperabile*.

Rare in the wild in west Yunnan on the Mekong–Salween Divide at 10,000 ft. (3,048m) – where it grows in open forests.

April

K

R. floccigerum H4 occasionally 3 A—10 L1–2 F1–3

Ht 3–6 ft. (90cm–1·83m). Habit a nice rounded bush in the open, fairly compact; more leggy in shade.

L 2–5 in. (5–12cm) long, $\frac{1}{3}$–$\frac{3}{4}$ in. (1–2cm) wide, narrowly oblong to semi-lanceolate. Glabrous above and with a *speckled* floccose indumentum below varying in density, glaucous underneath, the indumentum often shedding on old leaves.

F very variable in colour, more commonly rose to deep crimson, or can be mixtures of orange, yellow and pink, about 1$\frac{1}{2}$ in. (3·5cm) long, tubular-campanulate, 4–7 per truss, usually hanging down between the leaves. Calyx small, saucer-shaped.

Quite a well-known species in cultivation, easily recognised by the unusual sparse indumentum and narrow leaves. The crimson forms are the most desirable and some of the mixed or rose colours can be definitely muddy. Flowers open rather early in the season. Closely related to *R. neriiflorum* ssp. *phaedropum*.

Common in Yunnan and south-east Tibet at 9,000–13,000 ft. (2,743–3,961m), growing in the open amongst scrub and boulders, on cliffs, in thickets or in scattered conifer forest or cane brakes.

March–April

R. floccigerum var. *appropinquans*. Lacks the indumentum and is probably identical to *R. phaedropum*. AM 1957.

R. neriiflorum H3–4 A+5 L1–2 F3–4

Ht 3–9 ft. (90cm–2·74m). Habit dwarf and compact to loose and upright.

L 2–4 in. (5–10cm) long, 1–1$\frac{1}{2}$ in. (2–3·5cm) wide, oblong to oval, upper surface dark green and smooth; lower, pale green to glaucous waxy white.

F bright scarlet, crimson or deep rose, 1$\frac{1}{4}$–2 in. (3–4·5cm) long, fleshy, tubular-campanulate, 5–12 per truss. These are either in 1–2 tiers or hang down between the leaves in the poorer forms. Calyx fleshy, coloured like the corolla.

A very well-known species of excellent garden value although certain introductions are rather tender. There are several so-called sub-species which are really extreme or geographical forms.

R. neriiflorum typical is found wild in Yunnan, south-east Tibet and the Burma–Tibet frontier at 7,000–12,000 ft. (2,132–3,657m), on open mountain meadows and thin rocky pine forests, often amongst scrub.

April–May

R. neriiflorum ssp. *euchaites*

Ht some forms as tall as 15 ft. (4·57m), straggly with age.
L very glaucous underneath.
F many forms are a fine glowing scarlet.

Really just a large-growing *R. neriiflorum* also with tender forms prone to bark-split. AM 1929.

Often found in more western areas than type, in NEFA and Burma as well as Yunnan, at 9,000–11,000 ft. (2,743–3,353m), commonly growing in forests.

R. neriiflorum ssp. *phaedropum* H3–4 L1–2 F1–2
Ht to 15 ft. (4·57m).
L long and narrow, up to 5 in. (13cm) long.
F colour variable, from straw-yellow, tawny orange to scarlet and can be muddy as in related *R. floccigerum*. Some introductions are too tender for northern and eastern Britain.

Found wild in Bhutan, NEFA, Burma and Burma–Tibet frontier. Habitat as type.

R. neriiflorum ssp. *phoenicodum* H3–4 L1–2 F1–2

Ht 6–8 ft. (1·83–2·44m).
Similar but inferior to *R. euchaites* with smaller leaves and flowers which are more of a deep rose.

Upper Burma at 10,000 ft. (3,048m) growing in a warm gully.
March–May

R. sperabile H3–4 A+15 L1–3 F2–3

Ht 3–6 ft. (1–1·83m). Habit compact and often dense but can get thin and weedy-looking with age. Young growth covered with white woolly indumentum.
L 2–4 in. (5–10cm) long, ⅔–1¼ in. (1·5–3cm) wide, margins often recurved, elliptic to lanceolate, with sparse white indumentum above when young, semi-bullate; indumentum thick and woolly below, at first whitish which later turns to pale cinnamon to tawny.

F scarlet to deep crimson, about 1½ in. (3·5cm) long, tubular-campanulate, fleshy, in loose trusses of 3–5 or more, often hanging down between the leaves. Calyx short and cup-like.

A pretty, neat little shrub when well grown, with interesting foliage. Unfortunately most forms are not really suitable for cold gardens, being subject to bark-split. Best grown in a little shade in all districts except west Scotland. AM 1925 to a form of Farrer 888 with scarlet flowers.

Fairly limited natural distribution in small parts of north-east upper Burma and north-west Yunnan at 10,000–12,000 ft. (3,048–3,657m). Grows as an under-shrub on granite screes, rocky slopes, cliff ledges, humus-covered boulders and in scrub or thin bamboo.

April–May

R. sperabile var. *weihsiense*. Ht to 7 ft. (2·13m). Habit liable to be rather open. L longer than type, up to 4½ in. (11cm) long to about 1¾ in. (4·4cm) wide. Indumentum paler and not so dense. Also liable to bark-split. Free-flowering. Comes from Yunnan and south-east Tibet at 9,000–13,000 ft. (2,743–3,961m) on cliffs and rocky slopes.

April–May

R. sperabiloides H3–4 A+15 L1–2 F2–3

Ht 2–4 ft. (60cm–1·22m). Habit compact and spreading, usually wider than tall. 1st year shoots with white scurfy indumentum.
L 1½–3 in. (3–7cm) long, about 1 in. (2–3cm) wide, oblong-elliptic to oblanceolate, semi-bullate above, with interrupted scurfy indumentum below, less thick than *R. sperabile*.
F deep to light crimson, just over 1 in. (2·5–3cm) long, tubular-campanulate, fleshy, 6–8 per truss. Calyx with unequal petaloid lobes.

Rather similar to *R. sperabile* but tending to be dwarfer and with smaller leaves and less indumentum and glands in all parts.

Of very limited distribution in south-east Tibet at 12,000–13,000 ft. (3,657–3,961m), in alpine scrub in side-valleys.

March–April

Sub-series Sanguineum

Of all the groups of rhododendron species, this is perhaps the most confusing. No one really knows where one species begins and another ends and what or which are natural hybrids. Some people may say that there is only one variable species in the whole sub-series, and it is true that nearly all have intermediate forms. In the herbarium of the Royal Botanic Garden, Edinburgh, it has so far been impossible to determine nearly a third of the wild collected specimens in this sub-series, which goes to show how botanically muddling they are. From the horticulturalist's point of view, it is better to ignore the in-between forms and only cultivate and propagate those typical of a named species or variety. This would avoid much confusion in the future. All this sub-series can be termed low-growing with stiff ever-green leaves and waxy flowers in small loose trusses. Many have beautiful flowers but these can be on the small size for the size of the leaves and may take many years to appear. The majority are hardy throughout Britain. In some gardens they flower better than in others. For the real enthusiast, they are a fascinating group, well worth persevering with. Several so-called subspecies will in future be reduced in botanical rank.

Really good forms of the yellow species or sub-species are very elusive in cultivation. Some have in fact proved difficult to grow and may have been lost. This is very sad, especially as they would have given new blood for the never-ending effort to produce the ideal yellow hybrid. Distribution from east NEFA to south-east Tibet, Yunnan and Burma.

R. aperantum H4 A—5 L1–2 F2–3

Ht up to 2 ft. 9 in. (84cm). Habit dense and compact when well grown, much wider than high with a flat top. Bud scales persistent for several years. Very slow-growing.
L 1–2 in. (2–5cm) long, $\frac{1}{3}$–$\frac{3}{4}$ in. (1–2cm) wide, oval to obovate to oblanceolate, almost in *whorls* at the ends of the shoots. Somewhat rugose above, glaucous waxy whitish below.
F white, yellow, orange-red, pink, rose or most commonly dark crimson, up to 2 in. (4·5cm) long, tubular-campanulate, up to 6 per truss.

Rather a difficult species, liable to die-back in parts, especially when reaching flowering size and inclined to be a poor flowerer at the best of times. It might be an idea to place many plants together in an open situation (in the north only) so as to form a table top. Trials have been made pushing peat or leafmould up to the tips of the

R. sanguineum

branches to make it flower, with promising results. AM 1931, crimson flowers.

Found in north-east upper Burma and neighbouring Yunnan at 12,000–14,500 ft. (3,657–4,417m) where it covers miles of open alpine slopes or rough scree, mixed with other species, in every colour imaginable. Also grows on cliff ledges and under bamboo where it becomes leggy. E. H. M. Cox estimates that he saw 20–30 per cent with yellow flowers when in Burma in 1919.

April–May

R. citriniflorum H4 A none L1–3 F1–3

Ht 2–4 ft. (60–1·22m). Habit compact if well grown, or leggy.
L up to 3½ in. (9cm) long, usually much less; and ½–1 in. (1·3–2·5cm) wide, leathery, obovate to oblong-obovate or occasionally oblanceolate, covered below with moderate to thick fawn, brown or grey indumentum.
F bright lemon-yellow, greenish-yellow, yellow flushed or margined rose, yellowish-crimson or yellowish-red, up to 1½ in. (4cm) long, campanulate, 4–6 per truss.

Although quite widespread in nature, the best yellow forms seem very rare in cultivation and most are flushed rose. Typically, the leaves should be small, about 2 in. (5cm) long with a thick indumentum, and the best forms are really worth growing if they can be found. Needs some shade and perfect drainage. Merges with *R. sanguineum* and others.

Quite common in north-west Yunnan and south-east Tibet at 13,000–16,000 ft. (3,961–4,875m), on alpine moorland, cliffs, boulders, screes, sometimes just above the forest or in open cane brakes.

April–May

R. citriniflorum ssp. *horaeum*. Similar to *R. citriniflorum* but the flowers are deep crimson, orange-crimson, or deep carmine. Can be regarded merely as a colour form. Some extreme variations approach *R. chaetomallum* of the Haematodes sub-series.

R. dichroanthum H3–4 A0 L1–2 F1–3

Ht 2–6 ft. (60cm–1·83m). Habit a spreading bush.
L 1½–4 in. (4–10cm) long, 1–1½ in. (2–4cm) wide, oblong, obovate, elliptic-obovate to oblanceolate, with a thin but even white to greyish-white indumentum below.
F deep orange in the best forms, creamy-rose, yellowish-white, washed rose, dull orange flushed rose, rose or red; waxy, up to 1½ in. (4cm) long, tubular-campanulate, in loose trusses of 4–8.

Seems to be rare in gardens compared with the following sub-species and is a fine plant at its best. Typically, it is taller with larger leaves. The sub-species are all closely related and often hard to tell apart. All are liable to bark-split in cold areas. The parent of many hybrids. Some forms of this and the sub-species have poor muddy-coloured flowers. AM 1923, orange-red flowers.

Found wild in Yunnan, mostly confined to the Tali Range at 9,000–12,000 ft. (2,743–3,657m). Grows on rocky open slopes, margins of cane brakes, cliff ledges and shady situations.

May–June

R. dichroanthum ssp. *apodectum* H4 L1–2 F1–2

Ht 4 ft. (1·22m) or under.
L shape more oval than type, shiny above with a long leaf stalk about ½ in. (1·3cm) long. Indumentum below fawn to dull grey or dull brown, thicker and paler than other sub-species.

F deep rose flushed orange, deep crimson, pale orange flushed rose or purplish-rose, deep dull orange or cherry-scarlet.

Distribution west of *R. dichroanthum* near the Burmese border of Yunnan at 10,000–12,000 ft. (3,048–3,657m).

R. dichroanthum ssp. *herpesticum*

Habit usually smaller than type.
L up to 4 in. (10cm) long, more lanceolate and a thinner indumentum than others in the group, silvery to fawn. Not shiny above. Leaf stalk ¼–⅓ in. (63–80mm) long.
F pure deep orange, yellowish-crimson at base, pale yellow margined rose, and crimson.

Found in north-east upper Burma into neighbouring Yunnan at 12,000–14,500 ft. (3,657–4,417m).

R. dichroanthum ssp. *scyphocalyx*

Ht 4–5 ft. (1·22–1·50m).
L usually obovate, indumentum thinnish, fawn to grey. Not shiny above. Very similar to *R. herpesticum*.
F shades of bronze, apricot and yellow, crimson with orange base or yellow flushed rose-crimson.

Common in the wild. Distribution as *R. herpesticum*.

R. dichroanthum ssp. *septentrionale*

L mostly elliptical, indumentum patchy, silvery or brown.
F yellow flushed rose or dull lemon-yellow.

Comes from north Burma and Yunnan at 12,000–14,000 ft. (3,657–4,265m), rarer than the others.

R. eudoxum H4 A none L1–2 F1–2

Ht may reach 6 ft. (1·83m). Habit fairly dense.
L 1¼–3 in. (3–7cm) long, ⅔–1 in. (1·5–2·5cm) wide, obovate to oblong-oval, not as thick as most others in the sub-series. Indumentum hardly noticeable, leaf stalk ¼–⅓ in. (5–7mm) long.
F usually bright rose, but sometimes creamy-white flushed rose with no spots, up to 1½ in. (3·8cm) long, campanulate or tubular-campanulate, in a loose truss of 5–6, sometimes hanging down between the leaves. Calyx long and fleshy.

Quite a free-flowering species once it starts and a good grower. Nearest relations are some forms of *R. temenium* which also have little indumentum. AM 1960.

Found in east NEFA, Yunnan and south-east Tibet at 11,000–14,000 ft. (3,353–4,265m), on open rocky slopes, rhododendron thickets, shady gullies and on cliffs.

April–May

R. eudoxum var. *brunneifolium*. More indumentum, calyx smaller, flowers rose-crimson. Found in south-east Tibet and adjoining Yunnan in cane brakes and margins of thickets; not common.

R. fulvastrum H4 A none L1–2 F1–2

Ht up to 5 ft. (1·50m). Habit as *R. sanguineum*. Young shoots with thin indumentum.

L 1–2½ in. (3–6·5cm) long, ½–¾ in. (1–1·7cm) wide, oblong-oval, with a *thin cobweb-like* indumentum below, Leaf stalk ¼ in. (5mm) long. F pale lemon-yellow or creamy-yellow, 1¼–1½ in. (3–3·5cm) long, open campanulate, about 4 per truss.

Separated from the others by its thin scurfy indumentum. Seems to be rare in cultivation.

Quite scarce in the wild in south-east Tibet at 12,000–14,000 ft. (3,657–4,265m) on rocky slopes and cliff ledges.

May

R. fulvastrum ssp. *mesopolium*. Very similar to type in foliage but flowers rose or pink, lined or margined a deeper shade, or almost white at base. Distribution similar at 12,000–13,000 ft. (3,657–3,961m).

R. fulvastrum ssp. *trichomiscum*. Young shoots clad with bristly glands. Flowers pale rose or orange-red. Indumentum hardly noticeable. Leaves 2 in. (5cm) or less long, ⅓ in. (1cm) wide. Very rare in cultivation. From 13,500–14,000 ft. (4,113–4,265m) in cane brakes and rhododendron thickets above fir forest.

R. parmulatum H4 A none L1–2 F1–2+

Ht 4 ft. (1·20m) or a little more. Habit erect and rigid but quite compact. Reddish papery peeling bark.

L up to 3½ in. (8·5cm) long, 1½ in. (3·8cm) wide, ovate, *rugose* above, glaucous below with next to no indumentum. Leaf stalk $\frac{1}{8}$–$\frac{1}{5}$ in. (3–5mm) long.

F pale creamy-white or white (KW) or creamy-yellow or white tinged pink or rose-red at tip of corolla (L&S); both heavily spotted crimson, about 2 in. (5cm) long, tubular-campanulate, 3–5 per truss.

A fairly distinct species for the series, with slightly wrinkled leaves and heavily spotted flowers which are quite striking and unusual. Unfortunately, like most of the series, it is rather slow to reach flowering size.

A small distibution known at present in a very wet region south of Doshong La Pass and Tsangpo Gorge, south-east Tibet, at 10,000–14,000 ft. (3,048–4,265m). Fairly abundant on steep slopes among other rhododendrons in a tanglewood, or on cliffs or rocks.

March–May

R. sanguineum H4 A+5 L1–2 F1–3

Ht occasionally to 6 ft. (1·83m) in shade. Habit compact in the open, leggy in shade, shoots thin.

L up to 2$\frac{1}{2}$ in. (6·3cm) long, occasionally more, 1 in. (2·5cm) wide, obovate, oval or narrowly oblong, generally dark green above and with a thin skin of indumentum below, grey to pale fawn.

F commonly bright crimson, waxy, about 1$\frac{1}{2}$ in. (3·8cm) long, tubular-campanulate, in loose trusses of 3–6. Calyx lobes bright red, woolly at base.

A very variable species merging with several others in the subseries and with many so-called sub-species to which it is very similar. The attractive shiny waxy flowers are often freely produced on mature plants. This and its relations need shade in America to survive as they come from naturally wet areas. Will grow in the open in Scotland.

Widespread and common in south-east Tibet and Yunnan at 11,000–14,500 ft. (3,353–4,417m) in open rhododendron scrub and rocky pastures, peaty meadows, cliffs, by alpine streams, margins of forest and cane brakes.

March–May

R. sanguinem ssp. *cliophorum*. Very variable, some forms merging into other species such as *R. citriniflorum* and maybe *R. fulvastrum*. Is most likely a hybrid swarm. F various combinations of rose and yellow. Quite common on rocky slopes and cliff ledges in south-east Tibet.

R. sanguinem ssp. *consanguineum*. Similar to *R. haemaleum*.

R. sanguinem ssp. *didymum*. Differs from *R. haemaleum* in the smaller leaves and very glandular ovary but from a horticultural point of view, in the very late flowering season in *June* and *July*. F black-crimson, best seen with the sun shining through them. Some introductions flower very freely from a young age. Habit often open. Frequently attacked by rabbits.

R. sanguinem ssp. *haemaleum*. Very similar to *R. sanguineum* with darker flowers which are black-crimson or almost black. Some of R's 1948 introductions are very good. Said to be hardy in Washington DC. Otherwise as *R. sanguineum*.

R. sanguinem ssp. *himertum*. Near *R. citriniflorum* with leaves like this species or *R. sanguineum*. F bright to dull pale yellow. Comes from north-west Yunnan and south-east Tibet border at 12,000–15,000 ft. (3,657–4,571m). Not uncommon in nature but rare in gardens.

R. sanguinem ssp. *leucopetalum*. The white equivalent of *R. sanguineum*. Rare in the wild and gardens. 12,000–13,000 ft. (3,657–3,961m).

R. sanguinem ssp. *mesaeum*. Seems identical with *R. himertum* in the yellow forms. Crimson forms as *R. haemaleum*.

R. sanguinem ssp. *roseotinctum*. All ranges of colour combinations of white, pink and rose; beautifully margined rose-crimson, magenta–rose or rose. Some are very pretty and worth propagating. A few are closely related to *R. citriniflorum* and *R. himertum*. From Yunnan south-east Tibet and upper Burma.

R. sanguineum ssp. *sanguineoides*. Similar to *R. sanguineum*.

R. temenium H4 A none L1–2 F2–3

Ht up to 3 ft. (90cm), rarely to 5 ft. (1·509m). Habit usually compact and dome-shaped.
L up to 3 in. (7·5cm) long, 1 in. (2·5cm) wide, oblong or oblong-oval, clustered at ends of shoots. Upper surface often a paler green than other species in the sub-series, usually glaucous below with little or no indumentum. Growth bud rather long and pointed and *leaf stalk very short*.

F deep or purplish-crimson, tubular-campanulate, fleshy, 6 or more per truss. Some forms from R's last expedition have openly campanulate flowers of red or scarlet.

Makes a neat little bush but is slow to flower. More distinctive and less variable than most of the sub-series. Some introductions hide the flowers under the leaves.

Comes from south-east Tibet and north-west Yunnan where it is not very common or widespread. Grows on open moorland, rocky meadows and cliffs at 13,000–15,000 ft. (3,961–4,571m).

April–May

R. temenium ssp. *albipetalum*. Ht 3–4 ft. (90cm–1·22m). F white. Found in south-east Tibet in alpine regions. Rare.

R. temenium ssp. *chrysanthemum*. F sulphur-yellow or yellow tinged pink. Rare in cultivation especially the excellent yellow 'Cruachan', FCC 1964, AM 1958. Collected by R under several numbers in a limited area of south-east Tibet, in alpine regions and moss forest.

R. temenium ssp. *gilvum*. Very similar to *R. chrysanthemum* with yellow flowers. Also comes from south-east Tibet on open rocky slopes, cliff ledges and moss forest.

R. temenium ssp. *glaphyrum*. F white, cream or pale yellow, margined or flushed rose or pink; or deep to pale rose. Common in a limited area of south-east Tibet on rocky slopes, screes, moorland or on cliffs.

R. temenium ssp. *pothinum*. One form of this seems quite distinct with an almost orbicular leaf, somewhat rugose above, a ¼ in. (6mm) leaf stalk and pink flowers. Others are very similar to *R. temenium* itself. In some, the young leaves are a deep magenta-purple. F carmine, crimson or light to dark purplish-crimson. Found in north-west Yunnan and south-east Tibet on bouldery slopes, moist peaty meadows, cane brakes, margins of thickets and cliffs.

PONTICUM SERIES (E)

Sub-series Caucasicum

This sub-series contains a rather unsatisfactory selection of species with a widely scattered distribution.

The Ponticum sub-series are too tall for inclusion here as are *R. ungernii, R. smirnowii, R. brachycarpum* and *R. fauriei* of the Caucasicum sub-series. Others are borderline in size but all have certain introductions within our limits. Some members are obviously related to the Lacteum or Taliense series. The only definite characters are a candelabroid inflorescence, stiffly erect capsules and flower stalks and deeply cut corolla lobes.

An extraordinary distribution, mostly from Japan and region with outliers in north-east Turkey and Caucasus, China, Taiwan, and east Asia.

R. degronianum

R. adenopodum H4 A—5 L2–3 F2–3

Ht occasionally up to 8 ft. (2·44m), usually less. Habit spreading, often wider than high.
L 4–7 in. (10–18cm) long, 1–2 in. (2–5cm) wide, oblong-lanceolate, or oblong-oblanceolate, leathery, dark green above, with a grey or fawn felty indumentum below.

F pale rose, more or less spotted crimson, about 1½ in. (4cm) long, funnel-campanulate, in loose elongated trusses of 6–10.

Distinctive for its long narrow leaves, although in some forms they are longer than others. It is becoming popular in the milder parts of the eastern USA. Bears some resemblance to members of the Argyrophyllum sub-series of the Arboreum series. AM 1926.

Comes from east Szechwan and Hupeh at 5,000–7,000 ft. (1,522–2,132m) in thin woods amongst rocks.

April–May

R. caucasicum H4 A—5 L1–2 F1–2

Ht rarely more than 3 ft. (90cm). Habit usually compact and spreading, broader than tall, slow-growing.

L somewhat variable, 2–4 in. (5–10cm) long, ¾–1½ in. (2–4cm) wide, ovate, obovate or oblong, sometimes with margins recurved. Thin more or less plastered indumentum below, fawn to pale rust-coloured.

F pale yellow, or cream, with or without a pink tinge, spotted, of very thin texture, broadly campanulate, on long stalks in a many-flowered fairly compact truss.

The true species is rare in cultivation. Plants I introduced from north-east Turkey in 1962 are now flowering quite freely (1972), but some are susceptible to bud-blast. Also some trusses half open in the autumn. *R.* 'Cunningham's Sulphur' has a narrower leaf than any I found in three different localities and is probably of garden origin. The parent of many old and some newer hybrids. Susceptible to root rot in east USA but otherwise succeeds well there. The seed ripens unusually early.

Found wild over large areas of the Caucasus and north-east Turkey at 6,000–9,000 ft. (1,828–2,743m) from just above the tree line upwards, often surrounded by hard grazed alpine pasture. The soil is not over-rich in organic matter. Often growing in large mats covering several acres with the branches pointing down the hill.

April–May

R. chrysanthum (aureum) H4 A—5 L1–2 F1–2

Ht 1 ft. (30cm) or less. Habit mound-shaped or creeping, dense and exceedingly slow-growing.

L very variable in size and shape, even on one plant, 1–3½ in. (2·5–

8cm) long, $\frac{1}{3}$–$1\frac{1}{2}$ in. (1–3·5cm) wide, broadly oblanceolate to obovate, margins recurved, often a palish green above, semi-rugose, with next to no indumentum below.

F pale yellow to cream, of very thin texture, about $1\frac{1}{4}$ in. (3cm) long, widely campanulate, on erect stalks about $1\frac{1}{4}$ in. (3cm) long, 5–9 per truss.

One of the slowest-growing of all species especially for the first few years. Has flowered here in 10 years from seed when 4 in. (10cm) across and 2 in. (5cm) high. Its closest relative is *R. caucasicum*. There could be a good future for it as a parent of a new race of dwarf hybrids but it has a bad habit of very early growth. Stands wind and mineral soil in Sweden better than many other species. Introductions from Japan are said to be easier grown than those from Siberia but the best yellows may come from the latter.

Very common and widespread in east Asia in the Siberian-Mongolian mountains and Manchuria, west to Altai and south to high mountains of central Japan and Korea where it grows mixed with other alpine plants.

March–April

R. chrysanthum var. *niko-montanum*. Taller, more erect and freer-flowering. Reckoned to be worthy of specific status by Leach as it came uniform from seed. The Japanese consider it to be a natural hybrid of *R. chrysanthum* with *R. brachycarpum* or *R. fauriei*. Japan.

R. degronianum (*metternichii* var. *pentamerum*) H4 A—10 L2–3 F1–3

Ht 2–5 ft. (60cm–1·50m). Habit usually compact and rounded, wider than high.

L 3–6 in. (7–15cm) long, $\frac{3}{4}$–$1\frac{1}{2}$ in. (2–4cm) wide, oblong, oblong-elliptic to obovate, margins recurved, deep green above, and clad with thick felty fawn to rufous indumentum below.

F soft pink or rose, often with deeper lines on the corolla, about $1\frac{3}{4}$ in. (3·5cm) long and 2 in. (5cm) across, widely funnel-shaped, in a fairly loose to occasionally dome-shaped truss of about 10–15.

Variable in stature with some very slow-growing alpine forms. Poor types with untidy trusses of an inferior colour are to be avoided as others are very attractive. Closely related to *R. metternichii* and regarded in Japan as a variety of the latter. The usual distinction of the number of lobes to the corolla does not really hold good. This was discovered by the American collector in Japan, F. Doleshy. He has found 5–8 lobes on so called *R. degronianum* and some bore a close resemblance to *R. yakusimanum*. The majority of *R. degronianum* in cultivation have 5 lobes to most corollas. AE. Good in east USA.

Found wild in Japan in north Honshu, forming thickets in areas with few large trees, at 6,000 ft. (1,828m) and below.

April–May

R. hyperythum H3–4 A—10 L2–3 F1–3

Ht to 5½ ft. (1·70m). Habit usually compact and rounded.

L 3–5 in. (7–12cm) long, 1–1½ in. (2–3·5cm) wide, oblong to elliptic or elliptic-lanceolate, leathery, dark green above and more or less glabrous below, sometimes with small red dots on the older leaves. Edges usually recurved.

F in the best forms pure white but can open a dirty off-white, 1¼–2 in. (3–5cm) long and broad, funnel-campanulate 7–10 per truss.

One of the few pure white rhododendrons. Very fine in the largest-flowered forms. Growth comes early but is otherwise reasonably hardy.

Found wild only on Taiwan (Formosa) in the lower northern mountains, at 3,000–4,000 ft. (914–1,218m) in broad-leaved forest. Very local. Wilson never saw it himself.

April–May

R. makinoi (*metternichii* var. *angustifolium*) H3–4 A—10 L2–3 F1–2

Ht occasionally up to 8 ft. (2·44m). Habit compact and rounded. Bud scales persistent for several years.

L 3–7 in. (7–17cm) long, ⅔–1 in. (1–2·5cm) wide, narrowly lanceolate, margins recurved, and curved downwards at tip. Thick tawny indumentum below. Young growth not produced until August–September and covered with loose white indumentum above.

F soft pink, rose to off-white, with or without crimson dots, nearly 2 in. (4cm) long, about 1½ in. (3·5–4cm) across, funnel-campanulate, 6 to occasionally 30 per truss, often compact.

An interesting plant with remarkably narrow foliage and late young growth. Usually of excellent habit. I have so far found it hard to establish at Glendoick. Is said to be closely related to *R. degronianum* by the Japanese as intermediate forms exist. T. G. Nitzelius of Sweden, considers it as a variety of *R. metternichii*. At first sight the foliage is not unlike *R. roxieanum*.

24 *R. chrysanthum*. Ponticum series, sub-series Caucasicum

25 *R. degronianum*. Ponticum series, sub-series Caucasicum

26 *R. makinoi*. Ponticum series, sub-series Caucasicum. Young foliage

27 *R. yakusimanum*. Ponticum series, sub-series Caucasicum

Comes only from a small area in central Honshu, Japan, at 1,500–1,800 ft. (457–548m), often in shady forest, among ferns or rocks.

June

R. metternichii H4 A—15 L2–3 F2–3

Ht 3–12 ft. (90cm–3·66m). Habit rounded and very compact to taller and more open.

L very variable, 4–6 in. (10–15cm) long, 1–1¾ in. (2·5–4cm) wide, oblong or oblong-lanceolate, usually glossy above. The colour and thickness of the indumentum differs considerably, fawn, orange, yellowish to rust-coloured. Margins sometimes recurved. The young leaves may be red or pink tinged.

F pink, rose to nearly red, sometimes with a bluish tinge, occasionally with darker lines, or rarely white, 1½–2 in. (3·8–5cm) long, campanulate, up to 15 per truss, loose to fairly compact. Corolla lobes are typically 7, but can vary from 5–9.

In Japan, the following varieties are recognized by Ohwi: var. *pentamerum* (*R. degronianum*); var. *metternichii*, typical, with thick indumentum; var. *hondoense*, with thinner, paler appressed indumentum; and by Yamazaki, var. *kyomaruense*, for plants with thin indumentum and an open habit (including Wada's 'Metternianum').

Many desirable introductions are now being brought into cultivation to Britain and USA. Doleshy remarks that each isolated population of the various forms is unusually uniform, so it is obviously a case of separated colonies slowly evolving over the years. Good in east USA.

Found wild only in southern Japan on various isolated mountains; in forest or open slopes, often rocky.

April–May

R. yakusimanum (*yakushimanum*) H4 A—15 L2–3 F3–4

Ht to 4 ft. (1·20m) in cultivation. Habit rounded and very compact, fairly slow-growing.

L up to 3½ in. (9cm) long, and 1½ in. (3·8cm) wide, dark green and glossy above but at first with silvery indumentum, and with thick light buff to fawn woolly indumentum below. Margins usually recurved.

F rose in bud, opening pink, fading to pure white in FCC form.

L

Others open pure white, or open and remain pale pink, campanulate, in a compact truss of about 10. Usually 5 lobes to the corolla.

This is now one of the most sought-after of all rhododendrons, having near-perfect habit, foliage and flowers.

It is very hardy and starts to flower fairly young, even from seed. Many plants are now being propagated from Yakushima or hand-pollinated seed or cuttings which root quite easily. Grows well in full sun. Is a success in Washington DC and other eastern parts of the USA even in full exposure, but is not really reliable in the colder north-eastern states. FCC 1947; AGM 1968.

Only wild on Yakushima Island, south Japan, in a small area on and below the tops of the peaks from 4,000–6,000 ft. (1,200–1,860m), mostly amongst wind-beaten conifers, very dwarf on exposed slopes and taller in shelter and shade with less flowers. Rainfall is about 370 in. (9·1m) a year, with rain and mist nearly every day. The American collector, Serbin, reported bright sunshine at the same time as constant rain and very strong winds. In 1959, he recorded 3 leaf forms: *a)* leaf recurved, 3½ in. (8·8cm) long, linear-lanceolate; *b)* slightly recurved, 1½–2½ in. (3·8–6·3cm) long, obovate; *c)* flat, 3–4 in. (7·5–10cm) long, elliptic.

May

Sp. *nov* A possible new species was found in Taiwan in 1969 on Nan-hu-ta-shan by Dr Chien-Chang Hsu, growing at about 10,000–10,500 ft. (3,000–3,200m) in a grassy area above the tree-line. It has rich brown persistent indumentum, 11 or more flowers per truss and may be closely allied to *R. yakusimanum*. The flowers have not been seen yet. Seed was introduced in 1972.

SALUENENSE SERIES (L)

A very distinctive series of closely related species, showing a relationship with the Lapponicum series in *R. fragariflorum* which could be placed in either series. All other species are so nearly connected that they could be classed as extreme variations of one species. On examination of herbarium specimens, I found intermediary types in every case and others which had obviously been placed under the wrong name. They make quite good horticultural, but hardly satisfactory botanical species.

Leaves and branches are often bristly. The former are evergreen, highly aromatic and very scaly. 1–3 flowered, occasionally to 7, purplish-crimson, rose-crimson or pink with a flattish corolla with a short broad tube. Calyx usually large, coloured and fringed with hairs. Style always red. Flower stalks $\frac{1}{5}$–$1\frac{1}{4}$ in. (0·5–3·2cm) long.

They are mostly very free-flowering, hardy and reliable species. One unusual feature is that I can find no reference to any albino forms in the series.

The smaller species are excellent subjects for peat beds and walls and they appreciate a little shade.

Distribution from Bhutan eastwards to Szechwan over a wide area.

E.M.S.

R. calostrotum

R. calostrotum (*riparium*) H4 A—5 L1–3 F2–4

Ht most forms reach 2–3 ft. (60–90cm), others up to 5 ft. (1·50m). Habit usually dwarf and compact, the taller types more open.

L $\frac{1}{2}$–$1\frac{1}{3}$ in. (1·4–3·5cm) long, $\frac{1}{4}$–$\frac{3}{4}$ in. (0·5–almost 2cm) wide, oblong-elliptic to nearly orbicular, usually very *glaucous* above, densely scaly and glaucous below, with fawn, brown or cinnamon scales.

F bright rose-crimson to rich purple with deeper spots, 1–1$\frac{1}{2}$ in. (2·5–3·8cm) across, widely funnel-shaped or rotate, softly pubescent outside, solitary or 2–3 per truss, rarely to 5. Calyx coloured.

A really beautiful plant in the 'Gigha' FCC 1971 clone (AGM

1968), which has rose-crimson flowers in great abundance, fine glaucous foliage and a compact habit. One of the best of all dwarfs. Other colours are inferior but an R introduction with deep purple flowers, larger leaves and a taller habit is well worth growing.The flowers come out in succession in the autumn as well as spring. AM 1935, deep rosy-mauve to magenta flowers. All forms start flowering 1–3 years from a cutting. A few plants formerly known as *R. riparium* are nearer *R. saluenense* than *R. calostrotum* and many could be placed in either species.

Common and widespread in north-east upper Burma, Yunnan, east NEFA and south-east Tibet at 10,000–15,000 ft. (3,048–4,571m), usually as a tufted or matted cushion in masses on open moist rocky moorland, screes, on boulders and cliffs, by streams, in a swamp and even as an epiphyte on another rhododendron.

May

R. calostrotum var. *calciphilum*. L smaller, elliptic, rounded at both ends, up to ½ in. (1·3cm) long. F *pink* produced 10 days later than *R. calostrotum*. Often flowers in autumn. Pretty but not as showy as *R. calostrotum* itself. Found wild only in a small area in north-east upper Burma at 13,000–14,000 ft. (3,961–4,265m) and possibly in Yunnan, on limestone screes in tight mats where it is locally quite plentiful.

Late May

R. chameunum H4 A none L1–2 F2–3

Ht 5 in.–2 ft. (12–60cm). Habit fairly compact, flat-topped without creeping branches. Branchlets bristly.

L ¼–1 in. (0·5–2cm) long, ⅙–½ in. (0·4–1·1cm) wide, elliptic, oblong-elliptic or ovate-elliptic, shiny above, densely scaly below, with yellowish or brown scales; margins often bristly. Leaves turn an attractive shining copper or purple hue in winter.

F deep purple-rose or purplish-crimson with a frilled edge, ⅔–1¼ in. (1·7–2·9cm) long, 1–1½ in. (2·5–3·8cm) across, widely funnel-shaped, solitary or 2–6 per truss. Calyx coloured.

Closely related to *R. prostratum* and *R. saluenense*. Varies in the number of bristles present. The deeper-coloured forms are the best and it is worth growing for the winter foliage as well as the flowers. A clone known as *R. saluenense* 'Exbury' belongs to this species AM 1945. Often blooms in autumn.

A common and widespread species in Yunnan, north-east upper Burma, south-east Tibet and Szechwan at 11,000–17,000 ft. (3,353–5,179m), on open rocky pastures, on boulders and cliffs, or sometimes on shady margins of pine forests.
Late April–May

R. fragariflorum H4 A none L1–2 F1–2

Ht 6–8 in. (15–20cm). Habit dense and carpet-forming.
L ¼ to barely ½ in. (0·5–1cm) long (⅛–¼ in. (3–6mm) wide, obovate to elliptic, shining above, with prominent shiny scales; dark brown and yellow scales below.
F pinkish-purple or purplish-crimson, well described by KW as 'crushed strawberry', about ½ in. (1·1–1·5cm) long, widely funnel-shaped or almost rotate, 2–6 per truss. Calyx pink or crimson, 3–5mm long.
This is the aberrant member of the series, resembling *R. setosum* of the Lapponicum series. Of lesser garden value than others of the series and with smaller flowers. Quite rare in cultivation. Common in a limited area of Bhutan, west NEFA and nearby south-east Tibet, sometimes co-dominant with *R. paludosum*, carpeting open hillsides, rocks and boulder scree and even in a swamp, at 11,500–15,000 ft. (3,502–4,571m).
May–June

R. keleticum H4 A—10 L1–2 F1–3

Ht 1 in.–1¼ ft. (3–38cm). Habit mound-forming, often with creeping edges. Dense growth.
L ⅓–nearly 1 in. (0·7–2·1cm) long, ⅛–⅖ in. (0·3–1cm) wide, oblong to elliptic to lanceolate (near *R. radicans*), shiny or mat above, with brown or fawn scales below. The few hairs on young leaf-margins often shed later.
F deep or paler purplish-crimson with crimson spots, up to 1¼ in. (1·6–3cm) long, to 1½ in. (3·8cm) across, widely funnel-shaped or rotate, singly or 2–3 per truss.
An easily grown species of great value as a ground-cover, with fine, freely produced flowers. The best introduction is R No. 58 which is variable in height but has much larger, better-coloured flowers than older collections.
Some forms merge with *R. radicans*. Does well in the Schachen

Alpine Gardens in Bavaria, at 5,100 ft. (1,704m) and has survived with plastic shelters in Washington DC. Is moderately successful in other parts of east USA. AM 1928, lilac flowers with red spots.

Fairly widespread in nature in south-east Tibet, Yunnan and upper Burma at 11,000–15,000 ft. (3,353–4,571m), on moist stony moorland, screes and precipitous rocks and cliffs.

May–June

R. nitens H4 A—10 L1–2 F1–2

Ht 1–1½ ft. (30–45cm). Habit erect and inclined to be sparse-foliaged. L ⅓–1 in. (0·7–2·5cm) long, ⅙–½ in. (0·4–1·1cm) wide, oblong-obovate to oblong-elliptic, shining and scaly above, densely covered with fawn or brown scales below. Usually not bristly.
F deep pinkish-purple or deep pink-magenta with crimson spots, ¾–1¾ in. (1·8–2·8cm) long, 1–1½ in. (2·5–3·8cm) across, widely funnel-shaped or rotate, singly or 2–3 per truss. Pubescent on outside.

Useful for its late flowering, the last in the series, and one of the latest of all dwarfs. Much more erect than *R. keleticum*. Inclined to partial die-back.

Only collected under KW 5482 in north-east upper Burma at 12,000 ft. (3,657m) where it sprawls more or less in the open over boulders and ledges surrounded by bamboo.

June–July

R. prostratum H4 A0 L1–2 F1–2

Ht 1 in.–1½ ft. (3–45cm). Habit prostrate with woody semi-erect shoots. Branchlets bristly and bud scales persistent.
L ⅙–⅗ in. (0·4–1·5cm) or more long, ⅛–⅓ in. (3–9mm) wide, elliptic, oblong-elliptic to ovate-elliptic, shining above, with dense brown scales below. Margins bristly.
F crimson or deep purple-rose with crimson spots, ⅔ to nearly 1 in. (1·6–2cm) long, about 1⅓ in. (3·3cm) across, widely funnel-shaped, singly or 2–3 per truss. Pubescent on outside.

Distinct for the bristly branchlets and leaves. The latter are smaller than in *R. chameunum* and the plant is much less dense than *R. keleticum* and is also liable to flower in the autumn. Not as good a plant as *R. radicans* or *R. keleticum* and earlier flowering.

Comes from Yunnan, Szechwan and south-east Tibet, sometimes almost to the limit of vegetation at 12,000–16,000 ft. (3,657–4,875m), on rocks and peaty open stony pastures where it is quite widespread and plentiful.

April–May

R. radicans H4 A—5 L1–2 F2–3

Ht 1–8 in. (3–20cm). Habit completely prostrate in F 19919 to a low mound with creeping edges. Branchlets not bristly.

L $\frac{1}{4}$–$\frac{3}{4}$ in. (0·6–1·7cm) long, $\frac{1}{12}$–$\frac{1}{4}$ in. (2–6mm) wide, lanceolate to narrowly oblong or oblanceolate, shiny above, fawn or brown below, densely scaly and ciliate.

F pale to dark rosy-purple to purple, with or without spots, $\frac{3}{5}$– nearly 1 in. (1·5–2cm) long, widely funnel-shaped, usually solitary. Pubescent on outside.

This species reaches about the ultimate in dwarfness and small size of leaves in the genus. The prostrate mats, dotted with flowers, are very charming. Best planted on sloping peat beds or rock-garden banks in a little shade. Roots along the ground as it creeps. Do not allow bulbs or other plants to interfere with the growth. Closely related to *R. keleticum* but has narrower leaves. AM 1926 for form of F 19919 with rosy-purple flowers.

Found sparingly in south-east Tibet on open stony and peaty moorlands at 14,000–15,000 ft. (4,265–4,571m).

May–June

R. saluenense H4 A—5 L1–2 F2–3

Ht 2–4 ft. (60cm–1·20m). Habit erect, usually compact but sometimes open and sprawly with age. Branchlets bristly.

L 1–1$\frac{1}{2}$ in. (2–3·6cm) long, $\frac{1}{3}$–1 in. (0·8–2·4cm) wide, elliptic to ovate-elliptic, sometimes shiny or hairy above, and scaly; yellowish-brown or brown below, densely scaly. Margins often bristly. Leaf stalk bristly.

F deep pinkish-purple to deep purple-crimson with crimson spots, about 1 in. (2·1–3cm) long and about 2 in. (5cm) across, widely funnel-shaped, solitary or 2–7 per truss. Pubescent on outside.

The largest of the series in height and leaf size, but very variable in these features and in hairiness. Quite attractive in the best, freest-flowering forms. Merges with *R. chameunum* and *R. calostrotum* (*R. riparium*).

Very common and widespread in Yunnan, Szechwan and south-east Tibet, at 11,000–14,500 ft. (3,353–4,417m) on open stony, rocky or boggy moorland, by streams, on boulders and cliffs, in scrub and on margins of conifer forest. Sometimes on limestone.

April–May

SCABRIFOLIUM SERIES (L)

The chief characteristic of this series is the presence of axillary flowers. These are usually in several clusters towards the apex of the branchlets. The only other series to have this trait are the Virgatum series and a few members of the Triflorum series.

Several members of this series are pubescent and have pale green undersides to the leaves while *R. racemosum* and *R. hemitrichotum* are glaucous and glabrous underneath. The species vary in size from 6 in. to 8 ft. (15cm–2·40m) and sometimes up to 15 ft (4·60m). The calyx is small to minute. Altogether, it makes a fairly distinctive group. *R. spinuliferum* is too tall to be included.

E.M.S.

R. racemosum

28 *R. calostrotum*. Saluenense series

29 *R. prostratum*. Saluenense series

30 *R. callimorphum*. Thomsonii series, sub-series campylocarpum

31 *R. williamsianum*. Thomsonii series, sub-series Williamsianum

Distribution is confined to west China (Yunnan, Szechwan and Kweichow), usually in dryish areas.

Most are free-flowering from an early age and while the flowers are on the small side, their abundance makes a fine show in the best forms. They appreciate sun and are apt to become leggy in shade.

R. hemitrichotum H4 A—5 L1–2 F2–3

Ht 10 in.–7½ ft. (25cm–2·40m). Habit fairly compact to rather open, with occasional strong-growing shoots. Branchlets pubescent.
L ½–nearly 2 in. (1·2–4·5cm) long, ⅛–½ in. (0·3–1·3cm) wide, lanceolate to oblong, *pubescent above, glaucous beneath (not pubescent),* margins recurved, slightly aromatic.
F rose to pink or white edged with pink, with or without purple spots, ⅓–⅔ in. (0·9–1·4cm) long, widely funnel-shaped, axillary with the uppermost few leaves, 1–3 per leaf axil.

Closely related to *R. racemosum* which is generally less pubescent. *R. racemosum* has a wider leaf in most forms in cultivation, but some with narrow leaves merge with *R. hemitrichotum.* Quite pretty in the better forms.

Comes from Szechwan where it is common at 8,000–13,000 ft. (2,439–3,961m), in dry open rocky pastures, amongst scrub or in sheltered oak or fir forest, on limestone or slate rocks.

April

R. mollicomum H3–4 A0 L1–2 F2–3

Ht 2–5½ ft. (60cm–1·68m). Habit often erect, branchlets densely pubescent.
L ½–1½ in. (1·2–3·6cm) long, ⅛–½ in. (0·3–1·3cm) wide, lanceolate or rarely oblong, pubescent above and below. *Green, not glaucous below.* Margins recurved. *Few or no bristles present.*
F pale to deep rose, no spots, ⅔–1¼ in. (1·7–2·8cm) long, narrowly tubular funnel-shaped, axillary with uppermost leaves, 1–3 per leaf axil. A pretty plant rather similar to *R. hemitrichotum* but without the glaucous leaf underside. *R. spiciferum* has wider open flowers and more bristly leaves. Unfortunately some forms are rather tender. AM 1931, bright rose flowers.

Fairly widespread in Yunnan at 8,000–10,000 ft. (2,439–3,048m) on dry bouldery hillsides, open thickets and margins of pine forest.

April

M

R. mollicomum var. *rockii.* F reddish or reddish-purple, larger than type, $1\frac{1}{4}$–$1\frac{1}{2}$ in. (2·7–3·4cm) long.

R. racemosum H4 A—5 L1–2 F1–3

Ht 6 in.–15 ft. (15cm–4·60m). Habit low and compact to tall and leggy. Strong-growing shoots often spoil the shape of a plant. Branchlets more or less glabrous and frequently red.

L $\frac{1}{2}$–$2\frac{1}{4}$ in. (1–5·4cm) long, $\frac{1}{6}$–1 in. (0·4–2·6cm) wide, elliptic, obovate, oval to oblong-lanceolate, *more or less glabrous above, glaucous and glabrous beneath.*

F deep rose to pink, white tinged pink or white, $\frac{1}{3}$ to nearly 1 in. (0·8–2·3cm) long, widely funnel-shaped. Axillary with uppermost few leaves, 1–4 per leaf axil.

This well-known species varies tremendously in habit, flower colour and garden value. The best dwarf forms in cultivation come from the F 19404 introduction, which are lovely plants with bright rose-pink flowers produced in great abundance. Other poorer dwarfs occur. Very versatile, and has proved highly adaptable in the warmer parts of eastern USA. The flowers are quite frost resistant. Some clones suffer from a curious kind of flower-bud abortion which has never been explained to date, and these unopened buds remain for years. The prodigious quantity of seed capsules are unsightly. Occasional pruning will improve its attractiveness. FCC 1892; AM 1970, 'Rock Rose'; AGM 1930.

One of the commonest of all species in the wild, found at 6,000–14,000 ft. (1,828–4,265m), in Yunnan and Szechwan. Often grows as does heather in Scotland, masses of colour being visible for miles, flowering February to October or even later. Grows on dry stony foothills, chalky alpine meadows, dry limestone hills and cliffs, mountain pasture, in reddish clayey loam, amongst rocks and boulders, in peat or boggy situations or in pine forests. Some dwarf compact forms not in cultivation have leaves $\frac{1}{5}$ in. (0·5cm) wide and $\frac{3}{5}$ in. (2cm) long.

March–May with odd flowers at other times

R. scabrifolium H3 A none L1–2 F1–3

Ht 1–8 ft. (30cm–2·44m). Habit often ungainly.

L 1–$3\frac{3}{4}$ in. (2·3–9·5cm) long, $\frac{1}{4}$–$1\frac{1}{4}$ in. (0·6–2·8cm) wide, lanceolate, oblong-lanceolate or sometimes elliptic. *Bullate* above, usually *bristly and pubescent*; pubescent below. In typical forms, the leaves

are not so much recurved as *R. spiciferum* or *R. mollicomum*.
F crimson, rose or white, or white flushed pink, $\frac{2}{5}-\frac{3}{4}$ in. (1–1·7cm)
long, widely funnel-shaped. Axillary with uppermost few leaves,
1–3 per leaf axil.

Closely related to *R. spiciferum* but the latter has smaller and often
much narrower leaves. The flowers are usually small in comparison
with the leaf size and many forms are tender.

Comes only from Yunnan at 5,000–11,000 ft. (1,522–3,353m),
where it is very common and widespread, in open scrub or oak woods
on dry sandstone hills, or in dry pine forests.

March–April

R. spiciferum (*pubescens*) H3–4 A—5 L1–2 F1–3

Ht 6 in.–6 ft. (15cm–1·83m) or more in shade. Habit low and compact
to leggy with long shoots. Branchlets usually bristly and pubescent.
L $\frac{1}{2}-1\frac{1}{2}$ in. (1·2–3·5cm) long, $\frac{1}{12}-\frac{1}{2}$ in. (0·2–1·3cm) wide, lanceolate,
linear-lanceolate to oblanceolate; slightly bullate above, usually
bristly and pubescent above and below, often recurved.
F rose to pink or white, $\frac{1}{5}-\frac{3}{5}$ in. (1–1·5cm) long, widely funnel-shaped.
Axillary with uppermost few leaves, 1–4 per leaf axil.

Leaves smaller than *R. scabrifolium*. Beautiful in the best rose-
coloured forms. Some are tender while others are leggy with small
paler flowers and are hardly worth growing. The latter were formerly
known as *R. pubescens*. 'Fine Bristles', AM 1955, flowers white
suffused rose.

Comes from Yunnan, Szechwan and Kweichow, at 5,000–10,500
ft. (1,522–3,200m), growing abundantly in scrubby thickets on dry
rocky slopes, sometimes limestone.

March–May

TALIENSE SERIES (E)

Sub-series Roxieanum

A fairly distinctive group of slow-growing species, with thick
indumentum and leaves. In most species, the leaf-bud scales persist
for several years and the leaves are often narrow and recurved.
Sometimes the indumentum is patchy, especially on young plants or
on second growth after frost.

It is sad that all the typical members of this series are so desperately
slow to flower from seed. The compact golf-ball-like trusses of white

or pale yellow to rose-spotted flowers are most attractive, set on top of the narrow dark green leaves, which are usually slightly rugose above. Many make rather striking foliage plants. Have proved to be heat-resistant in the Sydney district of Australia.

There are four aberrant members of the sub-series. *R. gymnocarpum* and the closely related, possibly conspecific *R. microgynum* are much nearer the Sanguineum sub-series of the Neriiflorum series. Two others, *R. comisteum* and *R. perulatum*, not in cultivation, appear to be most interesting and well worth introducing. They too have a trend towards the Sanguineum sub-series. Many species tend to merge into one another.

Some start into growth early in the spring so need protection from frost. Be careful of the use of nitrogen which can so easily cause leaf-scorch.

I like this long-lived sub-series very much and wish to encourage people to grow them for posterity. Unfortunately young plants are scarce as cuttings are mostly hard to root. Grafted specimens can sometimes be bought.

Distribution confined to south-east Tibet, Yunnan and Szechwan and just into north-east upper Burma.

R. bathyphyllum H4 A—5 L2–3 F1–2

Ht 3–5 ft. (90cm–1·50m). Habit dense and compact. Leaf-bud scales persistent or deciduous. Young shoots moderately woolly.

L up to 5 in. (13cm) long, usually considerably less and up to 1½ in. (3·8cm) wide, oblong, thick, with a dense woolly dark fawn to rust indumentum below which rubs off quite easily. Mat above and margins recurved.

F white with many crimson spots, about 1½ in. (4cm) long, campanulate, 10–15 per truss.

The foliage is not so unusual as others in the sub-series. Seems to be comparatively unknown in cultivation.

Very common and widespread in south-east Tibet, Yunnan and Szechwan at 11,000–14,000 ft. (3,353–4,265m) in thickets on open rocky and bouldery slopes, on and at the base of cliffs and on margins of forest.

April–May

R. globigerum H4 A none L1–3 F1–3

Ht 3–6 ft. (90cm–1·83m). Habit slow-growing with gnarled thick branches. Persistent leaf-bud scales and with indumentum on young branches.

L 1¼–3 in. (3–8cm) long, ⅗–1¼ in. (1·5–3cm) wide, oblong-oval to obovate, dark green above with vestiges of juvenile indumentum, and with thick woolly fulvous indumentum below.

F white with crimson markings, just over 1 in. (about 2·7cm) long, campanulate, in compact trusses of about 15.

The true plant seems rare in cultivation and in the wild. Merges with *R. roxieanum*. Variable in the species collection at Windsor Park but has fine foliage. From Muli Mountains, Szechwan at 11,000–12,000 ft. (3,353–3,657m).

March–April

R. gymnocarpum H4 A —5 L2–3 F2–3

Ht up to 5 ft. (1·50m). Habit a good umbrella shape, often wider than high.

L up to 4½ in. (11·5cm) long, and to 1½ in. (4cm) wide, oblong-elliptic to oblong, leathery, dark green above, with fawn semi-woolly indumentum below, margins recurved.

F pale to deep *claret-crimson* with deeper markings, 1½–2 in. (3·8–5cm) long, funnel-campanulate, in loose trusses of up to 10.

A good species, in my view belonging to the Sanguineum subseries. The flowers are freely produced from a fairly early age and are a fine rich colour. Easily grown and cuttings root with little difficulty. Seems to be indistinguishable from *R. microgynum*. AM 1940, deep, rich crimson flowers.

Rare in the wild, coming from the north-west Yunnan–south-east Tibet border at 12,000–14,000 ft. (3,657–4,265m). Found in cane brakes, open pine forest and amongst rocks.

April–May

R. iodes H4 A none L1–2 F1–2

Ht 6–8 ft. (1·83–2·44m). Habit bushy with short annual growth. Branchlets with rusty indumentum and without persistent leaf-bud scales.

L 2½–4⅖ in. (6–11cm) long, ⅗–1 in. (1·5–2·5cm) wide, lanceolate or rarely oblanceolate, thick and leathery, rust-coloured indumentum below and margins slightly recurved.

F white with crimson spots, nearly 1½ in. (3·5cm) long, funnel-campanulate, 10–12 per truss.

Does not appear to be a very distinctive species and is not well known in cultivation.

Rare in the wild in south-east Tibet at 12,000 ft. (3,657m) in open cane brakes and thickets.

April–May

R. microgynum H4 A none L2–3 F2–3

Ht, habit, leaves and flowers as *R. gymnocarpum* but the last are sometimes soft dull rose, faintly spotted. Appears to be indistinguishable from *R. gymnocarpum* in every respect. Comes from exactly the same locality on Ka-gur-pu, on open rocky slopes at 12,000 ft. (3,657m). Also rare in the wild.

April

R. pronum H4 A none L2–3 F1–2

Ht up to 1 ft. (30cm). Habit *prostrate* and *compact* with short growth and gnarled branches. Leaf-buds scales persisting for *many* years.
L 1¼–2½ in. (3–6·5cm) long, ⅖–1¼ in. (1–3cm) wide, oblong-elliptic to lanceolate or oblanceolate. Indumentum thick, dull grey to fawn below. Margins recurved.
F white, creamy-yellow or pink, heavily marked crimson or purple, about 1½ in. (3·5cm) long, campanulate, 8–12 per truss. Stamens and ovary glabrous.

A slow creeper, very rare in cultivation and has seldom flowered to date. Quite attractive blue-green leaves. Seems quite a stable plant and differs from the other low-growing species by the wider leaves and more prostrate habit. Young growth comes early. There is a fine specimen at Kilbryde, Northumberland.

Found wild in Yunnan, south-east Tibet and Szechwan at 12,000–15,000 ft. (3,657–4,571m), on moist rocky slopes and humus-covered boulders and on cliffs.

Said to flower April–May

R. proteoides H4 A+5 L2–3 F1–2

Ht 1–3¼ ft. (30cm–1m). Habit usually very compact and *slow-growing*. Persistent leaf-bud scales.
L ¾–1½ in. (2–4cm) long, ⅕–⅖ in. (0·5–1cm) wide, *oblong or linear*, mat above with vestiges of juvenile hairs, and thick rufous woolly indumentum below. Margins recurved. Leaf stalk densely woolly.

F creamy-yellow or white, sometimes flushed rose with many crimson spots, about 1¼ in. (3cm) long, funnel-shaped, in compact trusses of 8–10. Leaves shorter and with a blunter tip than *R. roxieanum* var. *oreonastes* or *R. recurvoides*. A most enchanting little foliage plant but also slow to flower. Introduction from R's last expedition is dwarfer and with smaller leaves.

Comes from Yunnan, Szechwan and south-east Tibet at 12,000–14,000 ft. (3,657–4,265m) on open stony slopes, amongst boulders, on rocks and cliffs. Quite common and widespread.

April

R. recurvoides H4 A0 L2–3 F2–3

Ht occasionally up to 5 ft. (1·50m). Habit compact, usually wider than high with dense foliage. Persistent leaf-bud scales and *hairy branchlets*.
L up to 4½ in. (11·4cm) long, and 1¼ in. (3·2cm) wide, lanceolate, or oblanceolate, rugose and shiny above, with thick tawny indumentum below. Margins recurved. Young leaves *hairy* on upper surface and leaf stalks *hairy*.
F white or rose, spotted, 1½ in. (3·8cm) long, about 2½ in. (6·3cm) across, funnel-campanulate, in compact trusses of 4–7.

Fairly closely related to the dwarf forms of *R. roxieanum* but is hairy and usually more compact than those. Has flowered rather younger in several cases than the other members of the sub-series and can be most fascinating when flowering well. Leaves longer than *R. proteoides*. Young growth is liable to be frosted, hence no flowers the following year. Could be useful for hybridizing. AM 1941, pale rose flowers.

A rare species in the wild, so far only recorded from the Di Chu valley in upper Burma, as KW 7184, at 11,000 ft. (3,353m), on steep granite screes and amongst boulders, where it flowered very freely.

April–May

R. roxieanum H4 A0 L2–3 F2–3

Ht very variable, 3–9 ft. (90cm–2·74m). Habit dwarf and compact to tall and leggy. *Densely woolly branchlets*, slow growth and persistent leaf-bud scales.
L 1½–4 in. (4–10cm) long, ⅖–⅘ in. (1–2cm) wide, linear, narrow-lanceolate to oblanceolate, thick and leathery, thick fawn to rust-coloured woolly indumentum below, margins recurved.

F creamy-white or white with rose flush, with or without crimson markings, about 1¼ in. (3cm) long, campanulate, in compact trusses of 10–15.

A variable species, merging with *R. proteoides*, *R. bathyphyllum* and others. Slow to flower but long-lived and hardy. Seems to flower better under light woodland conditions where the annual growth is longer. Foliage liable to scorch in sun. Lacks the hairiness of *R. recurvoides*. Very widespread and plentiful in Yunnan, Szechwan and south-east Tibet at 11,000–14,000 ft. (3,353–4,265m), on boulder-strewn slopes, open rocky pastures or in or around open pine forest or cane brakes.

April–May

R. roxieanum var. *oreonastes*. The *narrow* leaves make the plant look as though it is related to a porcupine or sea-urchin. It is excellent for foliage alone but the globular trusses are lovely, perched like round candles on the pin-cushions of leaves. Otherwise similar to *R. roxieanum* with which it tends to merge. Variable in height and size of truss. Quite plentiful in the wild in similar situations to the type species and also on cliff ledges and in fir forest.

R. russotinctum H4 A none L1–3 F1–3

Ht 6–12 ft. (1·83–3·66m). Habit dome-shaped and can become leggy in shade. Leaf-bud scales persisting for a year or two. Longer annual growths than *R. roxieanum*. Very thin indumentum on branchlets. L 2–7 in. (5–18cm) long, ⅗–1½ in. (1·5–3·8cm) wide, thick and leathery, indumentum fawn to rusty below, not very thick. Margins less recurved than *R. roxieanum* or not recurved.

F white or white flushed rose with a few crimson spots, about 1½ in. (3·8cm) long, campanulate, in a compact or more loose truss of up to 20. This is a less alpine equivalent of *R. roxieanum* with a general tendency to larger leaves and less indumentum, but they do merge together. Once again, many years pass before flowers appear and these too are correspondingly bigger. Rather gross compared with the smaller species and a little tall for our limit in this book.

Very variable and plentiful in south-east Tibet and north-west Yunnan at 9,000–14,000 ft. (2,743–4,265m), on open rocky slopes, cane and rhododendron thickets and open pine forests.

April–May

R. triplonaevium and *R. tritifolium* (can be classed together as they may well be the same species) H4 A none L1–2 F1–2

Ht 5–9 ft. (1·50–2·74m). Young shoots at first covered with rufous indumentum.

L 2¾–6 in. (7–15cm) long, ⅖–1½ in. (2–4cm) wide, lanceolate to oblanceolate, thick and leathery, mat above and loose cinnamon to rust-coloured indumentum below. Margins slightly recurved.

F white or white tinged rose with crimson blotch and spots, 1¼–1½ in. (3–4cm) long, campanulate or funnel-campanulate, 12–15 per compact truss.

These appear to be a larger equivalent of *R. roxieanum*, coming from more wooded areas and with thinner indumentum.

They come from north-west Yunnan only, at 11,000–12,000 ft. (3,353–3,657m).

Sub-series Wasonii (*E*)

A small sub-series, three of which are dwarf enough for inclusion. They tend to flower at a somewhat younger age than the Roxieanum sub-series and have broader leaves. The habit is more open and the flower trusses less compact. Those described here are confined to Szechwan.

R. wasonii

R. inopinum H4 A none L1–2 F1–2

Ht to 6 ft. (1·83m). Habit fairly compact and wide-spreading, with loose indumentum on the young shoots, white when young and very conspicuous, later brown.

L1½–4¾ in. (4–12cm) long, 1–1½ in. (2–4cm) wide, dark green above and thin patchy drab-coloured indumentum below.

F white to cream, with or without blotch, about 1 in. (2·5cm) long, funnel-campanulate, in loose trusses of about 10. Calyx small, anthers black-purple.

A rare species, originally introduced in mixed seed including *R. wasonii* under W 1866A. The flowers often hang down amongst the foliage. Closely related to *R. paradoxum*.

Found only in Szechwan.

April–May

R. paradoxum H4 A none L2–3 F2–3

Ht 3–7 ft. (90cm–2·13m). Habit fairly compact. Young shoots with dense white indumentum.

L 2–5 in. (5–12·5cm) long, 1–2 in. (3–5cm) wide, slightly rugose above with veins conspicuously grooved. Loose patchy indumentum below, very sparse on maturity, grey or brown.

F white or pink with blotch, 1½ in. (4cm) long, campanulate, in loose trusses of 6–8. Calyx larger than *R. inopinum* and anthers also black-purple.

Also rare and again introduced in mixed seed including *R. wiltonii* (which belongs to this sub-series) under W 1353. Likewise hides the flowers under the leaves. Has distinctive foliage buds which are conical, with outer scales densely woolly, and long curved tips.

Szechwan only.

April–May

R. wasonii H4 A none L2–3 F2–3

Ht usually 3–5 ft. (90cm–1·50m), occasionally more. Habit fairly dense in the open, sparser in shade. Foliage buds have pale fawn indumentum.

L 2–4 in. (5–10cm) long, 1–2 in. (2·5–4·5cm) wide, oval or broadly lanceolate, dark glossy green above, indumentum below at first white, to uniform rich brown or rusty red on maturity.

F cream or pale yellow, lightly spotted, 1¼–1½ in. (3–4cm) long, funnel-campanulate, in loose to fairly compact trusses of 6–10. Anthers black and style pale yellow.

A fine foliage plant with attractive yellow flowers freely produced from a moderately young age. Hardy, easily grown and very distinct. Comes only from west Szechwan, south-east of Tatsienlu at 9,000–10,000 ft. (2,743–3,353m) where it is common in a limited area. Grows in forests on cliffs and boulders.

R. wasonii var. *rhododactylum*. Similar to the type except for pinkish instead of yellow flowers.
April–May

THOMSONII SERIES (E)

This large series includes many well-known and very beautiful species, nearly all of which are too tall to include here. Much of the Selense sub-series is borderline, but owing to lack of space and the fact that many are of little garden value, none are mentioned.

Subseries Campylocarpum

Four members of this sub-series are low-growing and are very closely related. The other species are also of very near kinship. It could be said that the four yellows are all extremes of one species. All are evergreen and without indumentum. Those mentioned have orbicular leaves, a small calyx, yellow, pink or white flowers and a slender, often curved capsule.

Distribution of the whole sub-series is from east Nepal eastwards to south-east Tibet, Yunnan and upper Burma.

R. callimorphum H3–4 A0 L2–3 F3–4

Ht to 9 ft. (2·74m). Habit dome-shaped if well grown but can become scrawny.
L 1–3 in. (2–7cm) long, ⅔–2 in. (1·5–4·8cm) wide, orbicular to ovate or elliptic, leathery, glabrous and glossy above, glaucous below.
F pink to deep rose, with or without a crimson blotch, 1½–2 in. (3·8–5cm) long, openly campanulate, 5–8 per truss.

An excellent plant with neat foliage, unfortunately liable to lose branches from bark-split but rarely killed here. Smothers itself in

R. caloxanthum

flowers from quite a young age. Many forms grow rather over 5 ft. (1·50m).

Found wild in Yunnan and north-east Burma at 9,000–11,000 ft. (2,743–3,353m) on open rocky slopes, mountain pastures, margins of thickets, cliff ledges and amongst scrub and cane brakes.

April–June

R. caloxanthum H3—4 A–5 L2–3 F2–3

Ht 3–6 ft. (90cm–1·83m). Habit as *R. callimorphum*.

L 1¼–3 in. (3·2–8cm) long, 1–2¼ in. (2·6–5·6cm) wide, leathery, orbicular to ovate or broadly elliptic, glabrous, and often glaucous above and pale glaucous green below.

F creamy- to sulphur-yellow, often orange-scarlet in bud and later tinged pink or rarely remaining orange, 1–1½ in. (2·5–4cm) long, campanulate, 4–9 per truss.

An attractive species with nice foliage and very free-flowering, but unfortunately can be short-lived. Best planted in open woodland. Is liable to bark-split and needs perfect drainage to avoid the base of the trunk rotting. Very closely related to *R. telopeum,* which has slightly smaller leaves AM 1934, deep yellow flowers suffused red.

Quite plentiful and widespread in north-east Burma, south-east

Tibet and Yunnan at 11,000–13,000 ft. (3,353–3,961m), often in dense masses on rocky slopes and cliffs, in mixed scrub and in or on margins of conifer forest.

April–May

R. myiagrum H4 A none L1–2 F2–3

Ht 2½–5 ft. (76cm–1·50m). Habit as *R. callimorphum*.
Similar to *R. callimorphum* but with less flowers to the truss. Flowers white, with or without spots and crimson blotch. Flower stalks sticky. Very closely related to *R. callimorphum*, the only constant distinction being flower colour.

Found in a small area on the Burma–Yunnan frontier at 10,000–13,000 ft. (3,048–3,961m), in open cane brakes and thickets.

May

R. telopeum H4 A+5 L1–2 F1–2

Very similar to *R. caloxanthum* but the leaves are 1–2 in. (2·5–5cm) long, ⅔–1½ in. (1·7–3·5cm) wide. Often has less flowers to the truss and is usually an inferior garden plant.

From south-east Tibet and Yunnan at 12,000–14,000 ft. (3,657–4,265m).

May

Sub-series Williamsianum

R. williamsianum H3–4 A−5 L2–3 F2–3

Ht 2–5 ft. (60cm–1·50m). Habit exceptionally dense and spreading but can grow into a dome. Branchlets thin.
L ⅗–1¾ in. (1·5–4·2cm) long, ½–1½ in. (1·3–4cm) wide, ovate to orbicular to broadly elliptic, base often cordate, glabrous.
F pale pink to rose, 1¼–1½ in. (3–4cm) long, campanulate, in small trusses of 2–3 rarely to 5. Lobes usually 5, occasionally up to 7.

A really beautiful species when well-flowered and happy. Very attractive bronzy to chocolate young growth. Varies very much in freedom of flowering, and susceptibility to frost damage from clone to clone. Those with hardier or later growth give good results. Best grown in full sun for perfect habit and plentiful flower. Complete failure is often met with in woodland frost pockets, with young growth always getting damaged and therefore no flowers produced. Does well in southern Sweden. Borderline in east USA. Those with pale-coloured flowers are inferior. The parent of many hybrids. Cuttings root easily. AM 1938. Cannot be confused with any other species but could be related to *R. martinianum* of the Selense sub-series which has a similar small truss of pink flowers but a more open habit.

Has only been found on Wa-shan Mountain, west Szechwan, at 8,000–10,000 ft. (2,439–3,048m) in isolated places on cliffs by W.

April–May

TRICHOCLADUM SERIES (L)

Quite a distinctive series with largely deciduous leaves, and all but one with yellow flowers. Several of the deciduous so-called species have few horticultural and not many botanical characters to separate them. The flowers are solitary, in pairs or up to 5 in a truss, and are precocious. The calyx is well developed, with or without hairs, even on the same plant, so in this case it is a poor character for differentiating between species. The style is frequently curved. Most species have an erect habit, grow to 5–7 ft. (1·52–2·13m) and flower in April–May.

While quite pretty in a delicate sort of way, in only a few cases can they be called really showy.

Distribution from Nepal, south-east Tibet, Burma and Yunnan, often in dry areas.

Instead of listing the species as usual in alphabetical order, here only well-defined species are treated this way and all the rest are grouped along with *R. trichocladum* with which they are very closely connected.

R. caesium H4 A none L1–2 F1–2

Ht up to 4 ft. (1·22m). Habit erect and spreading. Bark pale brown and shiny.

L largely evergreen, 1½–2 in. (3·8–5cm) long, elliptic to oblong-elliptic to oblong-lanceolate, very glaucous below, aromatic.

F greenish or pale yellow, spotted green, about ¾ in. (2cm) long, widely funnel-campanulate, rather pendulous, usually 3 per truss.

Grows early in the season and is not very showy.

Comes from a small area in mid-west Yunnan at 8,000–10,000 ft. (2,439–3,048m), on rocky slopes amongst scrub in side-valleys.

May

R. trichocladum

R. cowanianum H3–4 A none L1–2 F1

Ht up to 8 ft. (2·44m). Habit erect; open and straggly in shade.

L deciduous, 1–2½ in. (2·5–6·3cm) long and up to 1¼ in. (3cm) wide, oblong to oblong-obovate, hairy at margins. Sometimes colours well in autumn.

F precocious, pink, purplish-magenta or deep wine, ⅘ in. (2cm) long, shortly campanulate, 2–4 per truss. Calyx large, sometimes hairy, up to ⅖ in. (1cm) long. The first flower to open often drops before the last is out in each truss.

A very distinct species but of little garden value. The small flowers shed quickly and it is not even all that easy to grow. Only a collector's piece.

Found wild in central Nepal at 10,000–13,000 ft. (3,048–3,961m), and not introduced until 1954. Grows in clearings or on the edge of forest, along rocks in river-beds and in deep wet tree-covered gorges. Introduced under SS&W 9097.

May

R. *lepidostylum* H4 A0 L3–4 F1–2

Ht 1–4 ft. (30cm–1·22m). Habit very compact and dome-shaped.
L evergreen, about 1½ in. (3·8cm) long, and ⅗ in. (1·5cm) wide, ovate to obovate, ciliate, extremely glaucous above when young, moderately so on maturity. Leaf stalk hairy. Aromatic.
F yellow, about 1 in. (2·5cm) long, widely funnel-shaped, single or in pairs.

A magnificent foliage plant with silvery-blue young leaves. Grows best in a sunny position. Easily grown and excellent for an open border. This and *R. viridescens* are the only completely evergreen members of the series. It is a well-defined species quite unlike any other. The flowers, when produced, do not blend well with the leaves and are not very attractive. The finest specimen I know is at Brodick, Isle of Arran, West Scotland. AM 1969, for foliage.

Found wild in a limited area of Yunnan at 10,000–12,000 ft. (3,048–3,657m), on humus-covered boulders, cliff ledges and crevices in ravines.

June

R. *melinanthum* H4 A none L1–2 F2–3

Ht 6–8 ft. (1·83–2·44). Habit upright and open. Branchlets with long bristles.
L deciduous, up to 2½ in. (6·3cm) long, 1¼ in. (3cm) wide, narrowly obovate, or oblanceolate, hairy on margins when young.
F precocious, yellow or bright yellow, about ⅘ in. (2cm) long, widely funnel-shaped, 3–4 per truss.

The largest member of the series in all parts, and has the most showy flowers. Takes a little while to flower freely and is best planted in a reasonably open situation to flower well. Fairly closely related to *R. trichocladum*.

Comes from a small area of the Yunnan-Burma frontier at 11,000–14,000 ft. (3,353–4,265m) where it is uncommon, in *Abies* forest, dense thickets and margins of rhododendron forest.

April–May

R. *trichocladum* H4 A none L1–2 F1–2

Ht 3–8 ft. (90cm–2·44m). Habit usually open and erect.
L deciduous, about 1½ in. (3·8cm) long, and ⅘ in. (2cm) wide, oblong,

32 (*left*) *R. mekongense*. Trichocladum series in wild (G. Sherriff)

33 *R. lepidostylum*. Trichocladum series

34 (*above*) *R. hanceanum* 'Nanum' Triflorum series, sub-series Hanceanum

35 (*right*) *R. ludlowii*. Uniflorum series in wild (G. Sherriff)

usually fringed with hairs and pubescent above. Sometimes colours well in autumn.

F greenish-yellow, spotted, about 1 in. (2·5cm) long, widely funnel-shaped, 3–5 per truss. Flower stalks hairy. Style bent.

This is the type species of the series. The following closely allied species may mostly lose their specific status and become synonymous with *R. trichocladum*.

Quite pretty when flowering well in an open situation. We have a very late-flowering pale yellow introduction from the KW 1953 Triangle Expedition to upper Burma.

A very widespread and common species found as far west as east Nepal, throughout south-east Tibet, north-west Yunnan, and north Burma at 7,500–13,000 ft. (2,284–3,961m). Found on open rocky hillsides, grassland, moorland, screes, cliff ledges, on rocks, margins of thickets and forests, cane brakes, along rivers, and in boggy pasture.

April–May, KW Triangle form June–July

The following so-called species are at present divided by a few, often inconstant features, chief of which are mentioned below. Otherwise they are all virtually identical with *R. trichocladum*. The presence or absence of scales on the ovary and elsewhere are also liable to be poor differentiating characters.

R. chloranthum. Small non-hairy calyx.

R. lophogynum. Calyx lobes densely covered with curly hairs. Leaves hairy on both surfaces.

R. mekongense. Calyx with long bristles.

R. oulotrichum. Calyx well developed with long hairs. Leaves and plant smaller than *R. trichocladum*.

R. rubrolineatum. Leaves usually semi-deciduous. Style straight. Calyx very small.

R. semilunatum. Leaves and plant small.

Of the above, only *R. rubrolineatum* appears to have reasonable grounds for specific status.

N

R. viridenscens. H4 A none L2–3 F2

Ht up to 4 ft. (1·22m). Habit erect shoots but spreading outwards. Branchlets hairy.

L evergreen, up to 2 in. (5cm) long, 1 in. (2·5cm) wide, oblong-elliptic, very glaucous above becoming glaucous green with age, moderately glaucous below. Margins with or without bristles.

F pale yellow with green spots, about ¾ in. (2cm) long, widely funnel-shaped, 4–5 per truss.

An under-rated species with fine glaucous foliage, good habit and pleasant flowers produced very late in the season, often flowering on the young wood even later. Very distinct and handsome but loses some glaucousness as a mature specimen. Should be planted more often. 'Doshong La' AM 1972.

Rare in the wild, only having been found so far on the Doshong La Pass, south-east Tibet, at 10,000–11,000 ft. (3,048–3,353m).

June–August

TRIFLORUM SERIES (L)

This large series consists mostly of rather tall species with small flowers and leaves for the size of the plant. Only three species can truly be classified as dwarf. Two belong to the small and distinctive Hanceanum sub-series and one to the Triflorum sub-series.

Sub-series Hanceanum

There are two species, widely sparated geographically, with white, cream, greenish-white or yellow flowers. Inflorescence racemose, 5–15 flowered.

R. afghanicum H4 A none L1–2? F1–2?

Ht about 1 ft. (30cm). Habit rather straggly in the wild with prostrate ascending branches.

L 1¼–3 in. (3–8cm) long, ⅖–1 in. (1–2·5cm) wide, lanceolate or oblong-lanceolate, with scales of unequal size below, yellowish or pale brown.

F pure or greenish-white, ⅓–½ in. (0·8–1·3cm) long, campanulate, in a racemose truss of 8–15. Calyx 1–4mm long. Style sharply bent.

A very interesting species, only found in east Afghanistan and the

Afghanistan–Pakistan frontier. Lost to cultivation and only re-introduced by Hedge and Wendelbo in 1969. They report that it is a species of no real beauty, but in their second and new location the flowers were pure white and larger than the original introduction. The foliage bears some resemblance to *R. keiskei*. Very poisonous to livestock.

Always found in fairly dense forest, usually *Abies*, in soil overlying gneiss or limestone, at 7,000–9,000 ft. (2,132–2,743m), on rock walls and cliff ledges.

July–August in the wild, probably June in cultivation

R. hanceanum H4 A+5 L1–2 F2–3

Ht 6 in.–5 ft. (15cm–1·50m). Habit dome-shaped and compact or very dense in 'Nanum'. Others with large leaves more open or straggly.
L 1–5 in. (2·5–12·8cm) long, $\frac{3}{4}$–2$\frac{1}{4}$ in. (1·6–5·5cm) wide, ovate, ovate-lanceolate to obovate, thick and rigid. Young leaves bronzy-brown.
F white to yellow, $\frac{1}{2}$–$\frac{7}{8}$ in. (1·3–2·1cm) long, funnel-campanulate, in racemose trusses of 5–11. Style slender and straight.

Another aberrant species with no known close relation. The usual form in cultivation has relatively small leaves, fine bronzy-brown young growth and creamy flowers which are pretty but not out-standing. This form received an AM in 1957 under the name 'Canton Consul' and was wrongly called 'Nanum'. Tall forms with large leaves and yellow or cream coloured flowers are rare in cultivation. Needs protection to survive in Washington DC. 'Nanum' is possibly a clone but more probably applies to several low compact variants. It is very dwarf with small leaves and bright yellow flowers and is a free-flowering charming little plant, being one of the best yellow dwarfs. Slow-growing and still quite scarce. Later flowering than type.
From Mount Omei, west Szechwan at 5,000–13,000 ft (1,522–3,961m) in thickets.
May–June

Sub-series Triflorum

R. keiskei (*laticostum, trichocalyx*) H4 A—15 (tall form) —5 (dwarf form) L1–2 F1–3

Ht 1–6 ft. (30cm–1·83m). Habit dwarf and compact to open and leggy.

L 1–3 in. (2·3–7·3cm) long, ⅓–1 in. (0·8–2·6cm) wide, lanceolate to oblong-lanceolate, olive to medium green above; with large brown scales below, mid-rib puberulous.

F pale to lemon-yellow, not spotted, ½–1 in. (1·4–2·7cm) long, widely funnel-shaped, 3–6 per truss. Calyx variable, usually small. Style slender.

Very variable in leaf size and shape and in habit. Captain Collingwood Ingram has named two extreme forms (see under synonyms above). It is true that three obvious variations stand out in cultivation. (1) The original introduction with large long leaves and an open habit. (2) Medium-sized leaves and fairly compact. (3) Small leaves and prostrate. (2) is commonly grown as 'dwarf form' which does well in America and is the only dwarf yellow species for many eastern areas. Needs shade and shelter in Washington DC, and is a slow starter. This form grows very poorly in many parts of Britain. Especially hardy variations have been raised by G. G. Nearing by growing several generations of seedlings. These include two doubles named 'Ramsay Gold' and 'Ramsay Tinsel'. The species does not succeed in hot dry lowland Japan. (3) Is a new introduction from Yakushima Island which is so far proving to be a much better plant than either (1) or (2) and may well become a valuable parent for hybridizing. AM 1970 as 'Yaku Fairy'. An old clone received the AM in 1929.

Only found wild in Japan from central and southern regions of the main islands to Yakushima, growing in hilly country on sandstone and shale rocks and even as an epiphyte.

March–May

UNIFLORUM SERIES (L)

A closely related group from or near to the eastern Himalayas, on the edge of an area unexplored botanically. They are dwarf species, 6 in.–2 ft. (15–60cm) high, often spreading, with evergreen, oblanceolate to obovate leaves. Flowers 1–2 (rarely 3), campanulate or funnel-shaped, densely hairy outside.

There are two sets of so-called species which are extremely closely related. The first group includes *R. pemakoense* and *R. uniflorum*, the second *R. imperator* and *R. patulum*. All have been collected only one to three times each, so more material is badly needed. Unfortunately, owing to political instability, there is little hope at present of getting this. It could be that one or more of these species are quite plentiful which could even bring about the amalgamation of all four species once ample specimens are collected.

The whole series is exceptionally free-flowering from a very early age but the flowers are subject to frost damage. *R. imperator* and *R. pumilum* are slightly tender as plants.

E.M.S.

R. pemakoense

R. imperator H3–4 A+5 L1–2 F2–3

Ht 6 in.–1 ft. (15–30cm). Habit dwarf or prostrate with spreading branchlets.
L ½–1½ in. (1·3–3·8cm) long, ⅛–⅓ in. (4–10mm) wide, margins slightly recurved, lanceolate to oblanceolate. Brown or clear scales below, 2–6 times their own diameter apart.
F bright or pinkish purple, not spotted, about 1 in. (2·3–3cm) long, and about 1½ in. (3·8cm) across, narrowly funnel-shaped, densely hairy outside, 1–2 flowered.

A pretty little plant where it grows well. Unfortunately it is rather tender, often being cut back almost to ground-level in many winters.

We now cover it with a cloche when there is a danger of frost. Apparently does well in parts of southern Sweden and Copenhagen where it may get a better snow-cover than here. The old leaves sometimes colour well in autumn. AM 1934, rosy-purple flowers.

KW found this at the low elevation of 10,000–11,000 ft. (3,048–3,353m) where the snow lingers late, in the Seinghku Valley in upper Burma, growing on bare ledges of granite cliffs in flat mats where it gets little sun. He only found one plant with flowers on it.

April–May

R. ludlowii H4 A none L1 F2–3

Ht up to 1 ft. (30cm). Habit very slow-growing and somewhat twiggy, with a weak root system.
L about ½ in. (1·2–1·4cm) long, about ⅓ in. (8–10mm) wide, obovate, margins with very small teeth. Brown scales below, 2–3 times their own diameter apart.
F yellow with reddish-brown spots, ⅗–1 in. (1·5–2·5cm) long, about 1 in. (2·5cm) across, deeply saucer-shaped, hairy and scaly outside, 1–2 flowered. Flower stalks about ⅔ in. (1·5–1·9cm) long. Calyx large, 5–7mm long, margins ciliate.

A beautiful little gem when in full flower with astonishingly large flowers for the size of the plant. Unfortunately it rarely thrives, usually growing into a rather sparsely foliaged plant. Try planting it in partial shade with plenty of organic matter and with 3–4 stones surrounding the neck of the plant to keep the roots cool in summer. Well worth every effort and usually flowers after the danger of frost is over. It is my favourite parent for hybridizing dwarf yellow lepidotes, having produced *R.* 'Chikor' FCC and *R.* 'Curlew' FCC.

Found only in a small area of south-east Tibet in Packakshiri and Tsari Sama at 13,000–13,400 ft. (3,691–4,113m), on open rocky hillsides creeping over rock-faces in moss, amongst *Cassiope* and other dwarf rhododendrons. Common locally.

May

R. patulum H4 A none L1–2 F2–3

Ht up to 2 ft. (60cm). Habit dwarf or prostrate with spreading branchlets.
L as *R. imperator* but scales on underside 1–1½ times their own diameter apart.

F as *R. imperator* although KW said that they were such a delicate shade of purple, that they were almost pink. Another reference described them as old rose, spotted or unspotted.

Rare in cultivation and almost identical with *R. imperator*. Some plants growing under this name are *R. pemakoense*.

Found only in the Mishmi Hills, east NEFA at 11,000–12,000 ft. (3,353–3,657m), growing as a thin spreading mat in extensive drifts on steep mud slides and rocks in full exposure.

May

R. pemakoense H4 A0 L1–2 F2–3

Ht up to 2 ft. (60cm). Habit usually dense, forming a low mound. Often stoloniferous.

L $\frac{1}{2}$–1$\frac{3}{4}$ in. (1·3–3cm) long, $\frac{1}{4}$–$\frac{3}{5}$ in. (0·6–1·5cm) wide, obovate to oblong-obovate, with brown scales below, unequal in size, $\frac{1}{2}$ to 1$\frac{1}{2}$ times their own diameter apart.

F pale pinkish-purple or light purple or near pink, 1–1$\frac{1}{4}$ in. (2·5–3·5 cm) long, up to 2 in. (5cm) across, broadly funnel-shaped and densely hairy outside. 1–2 flowered. Calyx small.

Very closely related to *R. uniflorum* judging from the herbarium specimens. One of the most free-flowering of all dwarfs with foliage often hidden by the comparatively large flowers. Easily grown and usually hardy as a plant. Unfortunately, once the flower buds start to swell, they are very susceptible to frost damage. Old leaves sometimes colour well in autumn. Surprisingly variable in flowers and foliage. Does well in southern Sweden but is unsatisfactory in east USA. AGM 1968.

Found only in the Tsangpo Gorge, south-east Tibet at 10,000 ft. (3,048m) by KW. Fairly common up the side-valleys forming carpets on steep, damp moss-clad slabs or rock. Two L&S specimens collected nearby are probably referable to this species.

March–April

R. pumilum H34 A none L1–2 F1–3

Ht up to 6 in. (15cm) or a little more. Habit dwarf or prostrate.

L $\frac{1}{3}$–$\frac{3}{4}$ in. (0·8–1·9cm) long, 4–11mm wide, elliptic or obovate-elliptic, or almost orbicular, slightly glaucous below with brown scales.

F pink or rose, $\frac{2}{5}$–$\frac{4}{5}$ in. (1–2cm) long, campanulate, hairy and scaly outside. 1–3 flowered.

184 Species

A distinct, slow-growing little plant which KW called his 'pink baby', an apt description. The smaller, narrower flowers and smaller leaves separate it from the other species in the series. Although it comes from high elevations, the growth often proves tender and it is rarely seen looking really happy. But the little pink bells are so charming, it is worth trying to please it. Odd leaves sometimes colour well in autumn. AM 1935, pinkish-mauve flowers and a dark red calyx.

Comes from east Nepal, Sikkim, north-east Bhutan and is quite widespread and common in south-east Tibet at 11,000–14,000 ft. (3,353–4,265m). Grows on bare hillsides, beside snow, on wet mossy rocks, screes, amongst grass with *Cyananthus*, *Primula* and *Cassiope* species and by waterfalls. L&S found an interesting group of 12 white-flowered plants, which regrettably were not introduced.

April–May

R. uniflorum H4 A0 L1–2 F2–3

Ht up to $3\frac{1}{2}$ ft. (1m). Habit low-growing or nearly prostrate to leggy in woodland.

L $\frac{1}{2}$–1 in. (1·3–2·4cm) long, $\frac{1}{4}$–$\frac{1}{2}$ in. (0·6–1·2cm) wide, obovate or oblong-obovate. In the type specimen the scales are brown and 3–6 times their own diameter apart but on a clone cultivated at Windsor Park, under this name and the type number of KW, the scales are very small, light brown-coloured and about their own diameter apart with occasional large brown scales. Is this plant a natural hybrid or what? It seems to be distinct in leaf and habit from *R. pemakoense*. A plant with larger leaves but the correct scales, grows at Gigha, West Scotland.

F mauve-pink or purple, about 1 in. (2·3–2·8cm) long, broadly funnel-shaped, densely hairy outside. 1–2 flowered (Windsor form 1–3 flowered). From the above leaf descriptions, the identity of the true species is in doubt and it is difficult to know whether *R. pemakoense* should be included in it or not. In southern Sweden it is said to be deciduous.

Comes only from the Doshong La Pass, south-east Tibet, at 11,000–12,000 ft. (3,353–3,657m). KW described it as having small regular lilac-purple flowers, spreading itself over some of the moraines and gravel. One of the rarest species he found, flowering more freely in October than in June in the wild.

April–May

VACCINIOIDES SERIES (L)

A series of small-flowered evergreens, usually epiphytic, very different from plants we usually recognise as rhododendrons, but closely related to the Malesian species. The branchlets are usually *rough*, leaves have a curious fleshy texture and the seeds have long thin tails at each end. Most members are not in cultivation, are probably of little garden value with very small flowers and are all most likely tender. Their chief value could be for use in hybridization with the finer Malesian species. This might produce hybrids adaptable to temperate regions with proper winter and summer seasons, where light frosts can occur in winter.

R. *vaccinioides* is the aberrant species of the series as the leaves are scattered up the stem, while in the other species they are in *whorls* at the ends of the branches.

R. kawakamii ratings not yet known

Ht 3–5 ft. (1–1·5m). Habit bushy, usually epiphytic in nature. Branchlets not rough.
L about 2 in. (5cm) long, $\frac{3}{5}$–$1\frac{1}{5}$ in. (2–3cm) wide, obovate, thick and leathery.
F yellow or white, $\frac{2}{5}$ in. (1cm) long, widely funnel-shaped, 3–4 per truss. Flower stalks 1 in. (2·5cm) long.

This species could possibly prove hardy in Britain. Only very recently introduced into Britain and USA by John Patrick of California. May prove useful for hybridizing although the first efforts have resulted in cases of apomixy or a failure to set seed.

Endemic to Taiwan at 6,000–8,600 ft. (1,828–2,632m) where it is moderately plentiful as an epiphyte on trunks in rich rain-forest, high up in trees, especially *Chamaecyparis*.

R. santapauii H probably 2–3 L1–2 F2

Ht to 2 ft. (60cm) in the wild. Habit epiphytic in the wild, hanging from large tree-trunks. In cultivation, slow-growing and sparsely branched. Branchlets slightly rough.
L up to $1\frac{1}{2}$ in. (4cm) long, $\frac{4}{5}$ in. (2cm) wide, thick and leathery, dark green above. Scales twice their own diameter apart.
F pure waxy white, about 1 in. (2·5cm) across, with a short tube, $\frac{1}{5}$ in. (5mm) long and spreading lobes. Red scales on outside of corolla.

Stamens white, anthers at first yellow, later brown-red. Stigma red. Capsule dehisces right back when opened. Seeds with long tails. A new species collected by the author on the Cox and Hutchison expedition to Assam and NEFA in 1965. Found near the Apa Tani valley NEFA, at 5,400 ft. (1,644m) as C&H 459, on large broad-leaved forest trees with little moss present.

This has proved quite easy to grow in a pot or bed in a cool greenhouse. The thick waxy pure white flowers, while small, are most attractive, set off by the browny-red anthers and red stigma. Still very rare in cultivation. Very late-flowering.

July–August

R. vaccinioides H3 L1–2 F1

Ht 1 ft. (30cm) or more. Habit compact or more open growing, epiphytic in nature in masses of moss. Branchlets very rough to touch.

L ¼–1 in. (0·6–2·5cm) long, spathulate–oblanceolate, without visible lateral nerves. Shiny above. *Leaves scattered up stem.*

F lilac-pink or white tinged pink, ⅖ in. (1cm) long, campanulate, 1–2 flowered.

Of little horticultural value, with flowers amongst the smallest and most insignificant in the genus. Very long flowering season. The little box-like leaves are pleasant and unusual for a rhododendron.

Has a very wide distribution from Nepal, through Bhutan, NEFA, and south-east Tibet to Burma and north-west Yunnan at 6,000–14,000 ft. (1,828–4,265m). Has a small range of altitude in the Himalayas and a much larger one in south-east Tibet and adjoining Yunnan. A very common epiphyte on various species of trees, fallen rocks, cliff ledges and crevices, usually in moist shady places.

July–September

VIRGATUM SERIES (L)

Only one very widespread species is now left in this series. Differs from the Scabrifolium series, which also has an axillary inflorescence, in the sprawly habit, the presence of pubescence on the corolla and the generally larger corolla and larger calyx.

R. virgatum

R. virgatum (*oleifolium*) H2–3 A+10 L1–2 F2–3

Ht 1–8 ft. (30cm–2·44m). Habit often ungainly and straggly, some-times having long arching branches.

L $\frac{2}{3}$–3 in. (1·8–8cm) long, $\frac{1}{5}$–$\frac{4}{5}$ in. (0·5–2cm) wide, oblong or oblong-obovate, rarely obovate. Margins recurved. Pale green or pale glaucous green below with flaky brown unequal scales.

F pink, rose, lilac, purple or white, $\frac{1}{2}$–1$\frac{1}{2}$ in. (1·4–3·8cm) long, funnel or tubular funnel-shaped, pubescent and scaly outside, axillary, 1–2 flowered per leaf axil, with flowers occurring for several inches up robust young shoots. Fragrant.

It is a pity that this very floriferous species is so tender, only the hardiest forms being at all reliable in eastern Britain. The most tender introductions can even be killed in the west but are easily reproduced by cuttings. Best grown on a bank where it can sprawl and a fine specimen can be literally a fountain of flowers. The white forms are very beautiful.

Has a very wide distribution from east Nepal, through Bhutan,

NEFA, south-east Tibet into Yunnan at 6,000–11,000 ft. (1,828–3,353m) where it is largely confined to dry areas. Found on dry open pastures, by and on rocks, by streams and waterfalls, hanging from cliffs, on margins of and in forests and cane brakes and often in sunny situations.

March–May

Malesian Species

This group includes a large assemblage of about 300 species which are mostly found in Malaya, Borneo, Sumatra, Java, Celebes and New Guinea; with a few species in other East Indian Islands, Siam, Philippines and one in Australia. According to Dr H. Sleumer, the Vaccinioides series is included in this section which he calls Vireya. A few Malesian species belong outside the section Vireya but they will not be mentioned here.

The chief distinction of this section is that the seed has a long tail at each end. Many have tubular flowers and the leaves are often in whorls. In contrast to Asiatic species, many of the flowers have a colour which deepens with age and are notable for their long-lasting qualities.

As these species nearly all grow near the equator, they are not subject to any winter resting period. Although many are found at considerable elevations, especially in Borneo and New Guinea, they are proving virtually impossible to grow outside in our temperate climate.

In the middle of the last century, between 1840 and 1860, a few Malesian species were introduced, mostly from Java and Malaya, and were extensively hybridized. These hybrids were extremely popular in hot-houses for a while and then the craze died out and the majority were lost by 1914. Most were raised by Veitch of Chelsea, London.

Recently, with much of Asia being closed to collectors, attention has been diverted to New Guinea and Borneo, resulting in the introduction of a large number of species, many new. Especially noteworthy gatherings have been made by Dr Sleumer, Michael Black and P. J. B. Woods. Much remains to be collected particularly in Sumatra, west New Guinea and Celebes.

Experiments in Britain at cultivating these plants have proved that most will survive and often flourish in greenhouses with very little heat. In parts of Australia and the San Francisco area of the USA, many will do well outdoors and have proved remarkably drought- and heat-resistant. The Strybing Arboretum under the Recreation and Parks Department, Golden Gate Park, San Francisco, has one of the finest collections of Malesian species and hybrids growing out of doors. Peter Sullivan has grown these very successfully almost single-handed. While a little frost is experienced, if given a site with excellent air drainage, the climate of San Francisco suits them admirably. Most varieties will stand to a minimum of 30°F (−1°C) while a few such as *R. macgregoriae* and *R. retusum* survive to 25°F (−4°C).

Many varieties are grown terrestrially in well-aerated and drained soil. It has been proved that these plants appreciate more light and less water than ordinary rhododendrons. They tend to form more of a tap root especially if not watered too much.

All plants are grown to a gallon-can size before planting out, and are hardened off in raised beds in a lath house in three-quarters pine needle mould and one-quarter wood shavings.

Some successful hybridizing is being carried out using hitherto unused species such as *R. leucogigas*.

Most Malesians in the Melbourne area of Australia are grown in shade-houses or under trees to protect them against mild frosts, also from the sun which is much more severe than in San Francisco. They are grown on fern logs and in raised beds and are also planted out only when well established. Many grow much better outdoors in Sydney.

The old Veitch hybrids grow very well and flower freely and are easier than many of the species. The bigger species grow better than the alpines which resent the heat and strong sunlight.

Sheltered parts of the North Island of New Zealand, especially the northern half, is another area suitable for Malesians.

Unfortunately most species have a tendency to straggliness and many have rather uninteresting narrow tubular flowers, but there is a great diversity of foliage. It is even harder in this section to decide where a dwarf begins and ends. Many are epiphytic or terrestrial and vary considerably in height. Little is known yet of the behaviour of many in cultivation.

These plants appreciate perfect drainage. Some are proving very prone to chlorosis in cultivation, especially a few of the Borneo species. Michael Black grows many very successfully in the Lake District, north-west England, in greenhouses in beds of bracken soil, on a slope covered in growing moss. I have found that, in pots, most species grow best if sphagnum moss is actually growing in the pot. They can either be grown in pure sphagnum or in various mixtures of sphagnum, leafmould, pine needles, peat, loam and fibre. An occasional liquid feed is usually beneficial but it has been found that certain Borneo species resent any at all. In the Royal Botanic Garden, Edinburgh, some do well in hanging baskets and as epiphytes on tree trunks. As some of the Borneo species grow in an exceptionally low pH, it may be worth trying acidifiers such as sulphur and only using rainwater even in districts where the local supply is usually satisfactory for other rhododendrons. It has not been found necessary to give extra light in winter or to adjust the day lengths at all. The flowering season is more or less scattered throughout the year, according to species, even in cultivation.

For erect growing species, a suggested cultural hint is to lay the branches flat to induce the production of more shoots. Some respond to pruning. One way of pruning is to make a cutting of the top few inches of young growth. This encourages branching better than pinching out the growing point and also should provide an additional plant. Many, especially those with narrow foliage like *R. hooglandii*, could make good bonsai plants.

The following is an alphabetical list of species in the section Vireya, paying no attention to Sleumer's sub-divisions. The first-mentioned countries are where each species is found wild and the last are where they are cultivated. Unless otherwise stated, all species tend to be erect or straggly rather than compact or prostrate. These descriptions are of necessity short and only the commonest leaf shapes, heights and flower colours are included.

R. acuminatum Mount Kinabalu, north Borneo

Small tree or shrub. L 2⅓–4 in. (6–10cm) long, 1–2 in. (2·5–5cm) wide, ovate. F red, scarlet-purple to deep pinkish-orange, tubular, ⅗ in. (1·5cm) long, 10–15 per truss. Good hard foliage. GB, USA, Australia.

R. adinophyllum Sumatra

Ht 3 ft. 4 in.–5 ft. (1–1·5m). L about ½ in. (1·1–1·6cm) long, 2–3mm wide, narrow lanceolate. F bright crimson to scarlet, hanging tubular, ½ in. (1·3cm) long, 6–12 per truss. Worthy of introduction.

R. arfakianum North-west New Guinea

Ht 1 ft. 8 in.–6 ft. 7 in. (0·5–2m). L 1–1½ in. (2·5–4cm) long, oblong-obovate to oblong-elliptic. F deep pink, tubular, 5–7 per truss. Flowers are small and do not promise much for the future. GB, USA, Australia.

R. aurigeranum New Guinea

Ht 3 ft. 4 in.–8 ft. (1–2·5m), shrub or small tree. L 3–4 in. (8–10cm) long, 1–1½ in. (3–4cm) wide, oblong. F orange or yellow-orange, 2¼–3 in. (6–7cm) long, 8–10 per truss. Has fine showy flowers but is undistinguished in foliage and habit. Disappointing in San Francisco. GB, USA, Australia.

R. brookeanum Borneo

Ht to 6 ft. 7 in. (2m). L 5–10 in. (12–25cm) long, 1½–3 in. (3·5–8cm) wide, oblong-lanceolate. F beautiful orange-pink to orange-red or orange-yellow with white to yellow throat, often scented, 5–14 per truss. Used by Veitch for hybridizing. FCC 1970 'Mandarin', very pale vermilion. GB, Australia.
R. brookeanum var. *gracile*, FCC 1972, 'Rajah', a lovely rich butter-yellow.

R. christi East New Guinea

Ht 1–4 ft. (0·3–1·2m). L 2–4 in. (5–9cm) long, 1–2¼ in. (2·5–6·5cm) wide, ovate. F red or orange-red, tubular-funnel-shaped, about 1½ in. (3·5–4cm) long, 3–4 per truss. Flowers when only about 6–9 in. (15·2–22·8cm) high. Has beautiful flowers of a marvellous glowing colour and has unusual foliage. GB, Australia.

R. christianae South-east New Guinea

Ht to 10 ft. (3m). L 1½–3 in. (4–7cm) long, 1–1¾ in. (3–4·5cm) wide, broadly elliptic. F deep yellow to glowing orange or salmon, widely tubular-campanulate, 3–4 per truss. Very conspicuous in its native habitat and highly thought of in Australia where it is being used extensively for hybridizing. GB, USA, Australia.

R. citrinum West Java and Bali

Ht 2 ft. 4 in.–7 ft. (0·7–2m). L 1–2 in. (2·5–5cm) long, $\frac{3}{5}$–1 in. (1·5–2·5cm) wide, elliptic. F lemon-yellow to near-white, about $\frac{3}{5}$ in. (1·5–1·7cm) long, broadly funnel-campanulate, slightly scented, 2–4 per truss. A pleasant species. GB.

R. commonae New Guinea

Ht 1 ft. 8 in.–5 ft. (0·5–1·5m). L 1–1$\frac{1}{2}$ in. (2–3·5cm) long, $\frac{1}{2}$–1 in. (1·2–2cm) wide, elliptic. F deep blood-red to purple, rather small, tubular, 4–6 per truss. One of the toughest and most alpine of species but not of great merit. Has done well in San Francisco. GB, USA, Australia.

R. culminicolum New Guinea

Ht to 16 ft. 5 in. (5m). L about 1$\frac{1}{2}$–2$\frac{1}{2}$ in. (3·5–6cm) long, about 1 in. (2–3cm) wide, usually elliptic. F red to purple, 1$\frac{1}{2}$ in. (4cm) long, tubular, 4–6 per truss. Very good flower colour. GB, Australia.

R. ericoides Mount Kinabalu, North Borneo

Ht 6 in.–10 ft. (15cm–3m). L very dense, $\frac{1}{6}$–$\frac{1}{4}$ in. (4–7mm) long, $\frac{1}{12}$ in. (1mm) wide. F bright scarlet to purplish-red, $\frac{3}{5}$ in. (1·5cm) long, tubular, pendent, solitary or to 3 per truss. Not in cultivation. Has most interesting heather-like foliage.

R. gracilentum East New Guinea

Ht 8 in.–1 ft. 4 in. (20–40cm). Habit erect to prostrate. L $\frac{1}{3}$–$\frac{1}{2}$ in. (0·8–1·2cm) long, $\frac{1}{12}$–$\frac{1}{5}$ in. (1·1–1·3cm) wide, elliptic-lanceolate. F red to pink, $\frac{3}{4}$–1 in. (1·8–2·4cm) long, tubular, solitary or in pairs. One of the best alpine species now being successfully grown and flowering well in GB. The red forms are the best. Reasonably easy in Australia.

R. herzogii New Guinea

Ht 3 ft. 4 in.–7 ft. (1–2m). L 1$\frac{1}{2}$–2$\frac{1}{4}$ in. (4–6cm) long, 1–2 in. (2–4cm) wide, elliptic. F pure white or tube slightly pinkish, with long narrow tubes, 5–10 per truss, spicy fragrance. Often quite dwarf. Flowers when young. GB, USA, Australia.

36 *R. santapauii*. Vaccinioides series

37 *R. arfakianum*. Malesian species

38 *R. laetum*. Malesian species

R. *hooglandii* New Guinea

Ht 2 ft. 3 in.–6 ft. (0·7–1·8m). L $1\frac{1}{2}$–$2\frac{1}{5}$ in. (3·5–5·5cm) long, $\frac{1}{20}$ in (2–3mm) wide, linear. F pale pink to pinkish-red, 1–$1\frac{1}{5}$ in. (2·8–3cm. long, tubular, 2 per truss. Unusual for the very narrow leaves. Rare in the wild. GB.

R. *inconspicuum* New Guinea

Ht 3 ft. 4 in.–10 ft. (1–3m). L $\frac{1}{2}$–1 in. (1·2–2·4cm) long, $\frac{1}{3}$–$\frac{3}{5}$ in. (0·8–1·5cm) wide, elliptic. F pink, red or bright crimson, about $\frac{1}{2}$ in. (1·1–1·5cm) long, widely tubular, 3–5 per truss. Insignificant flowers. Doing well in San Francisco. GB, USA, Australia.

R. *intranervatum* Borneo

Epiphytic. L 5–6 in. (13–16cm) long, 3–4 in. (8–10cm) wide, with prominent raised mid-rib and veins, elliptic-obovate. F light yellow, 2–$2\frac{2}{5}$ in. (5–6cm) long, funnel-shaped, 2–4 per truss. A fine species with startling foliage. Successfully cultivated in the Royal Botanic Garden, Edinburgh on a trunk in a warm house. GB, Australia.

R. *invasorum* New Guinea, very common

Ht 1–3 ft. 4 in. (30cm–1m). Habit fairly compact. L 1–$1\frac{1}{2}$ in. (2–3·5cm) long, $\frac{2}{5}$–$\frac{4}{5}$ in. (1·5–2cm) wide, elliptic. F deep scarlet to magenta, $\frac{3}{5}$–$\frac{3}{4}$ in. (1·5–1·8cm) long, tubular, 3–4 per truss. Doing well in San Francisco and has a future in Australia. Also GB.

R. *jasminiflorum* Malay Peninsula

Small, mostly epiphytic shrub to 8 ft. (2·5m). L 1–2 in. (2·5–5cm) long, $\frac{3}{5}$–$1\frac{1}{4}$ in. (1·5–3·2cm) wide, ovate. F pure white or flushed pink below throat, about $1\frac{1}{2}$ in. (3·5–4cm) long, tubular-salver-shaped, scented like a narcissus. Has been long in cultivation and used for hybridizing. I consider the flowers dull. GB, USA, Australia.

R. *javanicum* Sumatra, Java

Ht 3 ft. 4 in.–10 ft. (1–3m) with a fair spread. L $1\frac{1}{2}$–6 in. (4–15cm) long, 1–$2\frac{2}{5}$ in. (2·5–6cm) wide, broadly oblong. F usually orange or

o

more rarely yellow or red, fleshy, $1\frac{1}{2}$–2 in. (4–5cm) long, funnel-shaped, 4–20 per truss. A fine plant, previously much used for hybridizing. Good shiny foliage. Grows well in San Francisco. GB, USA, Australia.

R. javanicum var. *teysmanii* Sumatra, Malay Peninsula, Java, Bali

R. konori New Guinea

Ht 3 ft. 4 in.–13 ft. (1–4m). Edie Creek form fairly compact. L 4–7 in. (10–18cm) long, 2–3 in. (5–8cm) wide, elliptic. F pure white or pinkish, 5–6 in. (12–16cm) long, tubular below, funnel-shaped with lobes, 5–8 per truss with a splendid scent. One of the finest species. Flowers at 2–3 ft. (61–91cm). AM 1969, 'Eleanor Black', white flushed red. Often grows better if grafted. GB, USA, Australia.

R. laetum North-west New Guinea

Ht 1 ft. 8 in.–5 ft. (50cm–1·5m). L 2–4 in. (5–9·5cm) long, 1–2 in. (3–5·3cm) wide, broadly elliptic. F deep pure yellow at first, later suffused with red, orange or salmon, $2\frac{1}{2}$–$2\frac{3}{4}$ in. (6·5–7cm) wide, broadly funnel-shaped, fleshy, 6–8 per truss. The lovely yellow flowers have been produced on young plants at Glendoick. Excellent in San Francisco. GB, USA, Australia.

R. leptanthum East New Guinea

Ht 1 ft. 8 in.–7 ft. (50cm–2m). L 1–$2\frac{1}{2}$ in. (3–6·5cm) long, $\frac{3}{5}$–$1\frac{1}{5}$ in. (1·5–3cm) wide, ovate. F deep pink to salmon or carmine, about 1 in. (2·5–3cm) long, tubular, 2–3 per truss. Easily cultivated and the flowers are quite nice. GB, USA, Australia.

R. leucogigas West New Guinea

Ht 3 ft. 4 in.–7 ft. (1–2m). L 8 in.–1 ft. 2 in. (20–36cm) long, $2\frac{2}{5}$–4 in. (6–10cm) wide, oblong. F white suffused with pale carmine, 5 in. (14cm) long, tubular-funnel-shaped, 6–14 per truss, fragrant. The largest flowered and leaved of the Malesians. Just introduced into GB from the Netherlands. Very free-flowering and of good habit. Also USA, and Australia.

R. longiflorum Sumatra, Malay Peninsula, Karimata Arch, Borneo

Ht to 10 ft. (3m). L $1\frac{1}{2}$–$3\frac{1}{2}$ in. (4–9cm) long, 1–$1\frac{1}{2}$ in. (2·5–3·5cm) wide, narrowly obovate. F magenta or coral-red to crimson, $1\frac{1}{2}$–2 in. (4–5cm) long, tubular, 5–10 per truss. Used by Veitch for hybridising. GB, USA, Australia.

R. lochae North-east Queensland, Australia

Ht to about 3 ft. (91·4cm). L up to nearly 4 in. (10cm) long, 1–2 in. (2·5–5cm) wide, broadly obovate. F scarlet-red, $1\frac{3}{4}$ in. (4·5cm) long, funnel-shaped, 2–5 per truss. The only rhododendron from Australia. Quite easily cultivated and flowers freely from a reasonably young age. Attractive. GB, USA, Australia.

R. macgregoriae New Guinea

Ht 1 ft. 8 in.–17 ft. (0·5–5m). L 2–3 in. (5–8cm) long, $1\frac{1}{2}$ in. (3·5cm) wide, ovate-lanceolate. F light yellow to dark orange, about 1 in. (2–2·5cm) long, tubular below expanding to flattened lobes. Very variable, 8–15 per truss. The commonest species in New Guinea. Some forms are good and a few are scented. GB, USA, Australia.

R. maius West New Guinea

Ht to 7 ft. (2m). L $1\frac{1}{2}$–$2\frac{1}{2}$ in. (6–8·7cm) long, 1–$1\frac{1}{3}$ in. (2·5–3·4cm) wide, oblong. F white at lobes, pinkish at tube or red at base, 3–$3\frac{1}{2}$ in. (8–8·8cm) long, salver-shaped, 12–15 per truss. Beautifully polished foliage and a well-proportioned truss. GB, USA. Rare in wild.

R. malayanum South Siam, Malay Peninsula, Sumatra, Java, Borneo and Celebes

Ht occasionally to 17 ft. (5m). L 2–4 in. (5–10cm) long, $\frac{3}{5}$–$1\frac{1}{5}$ in. (1·5–3cm) wide, elliptic. F scarlet or rose-pink, about $\frac{4}{5}$ in. (2cm) long, tubular with spreading lobes, 4–8 per truss. Poor flowers but good foliage. GB, Australia.

R. multicolor Sumatra

Ht 3 ft. 4 in.–5 ft. (1–1·5m). L $1\frac{1}{2}$–3 in. (4–7cm) long, $\frac{2}{5}$–$\frac{3}{5}$ in. (1–1·5 cm) wide, lanceolate. F whitish-cream to yellow, rose or fiery red, sometimes sweetly scented, $\frac{3}{5}-\frac{4}{5}$ in. (1·5–2cm) long, broadly funnel-shaped, 4–6 per truss. GB, USA, Australia.

R. nervulosum North Borneo

Ht small and few-stemmed. L 2–3 in. (5–7·5cm) long, $\frac{2}{5}-\frac{1}{2}$ in. (1–1·4 cm) wide, narrow-lanceolate. F bright scarlet, fleshy and shiny, $1\frac{1}{4}-1\frac{1}{2}$ in. (3–3·5cm) long, campanulate, 2–3 per truss. GB.

R. orbiculatum Borneo

Ht 1–10 ft. (0·3–3m). L $1\frac{1}{2}$–4 in. (4–10cm) long, $1\frac{1}{2}-2\frac{1}{2}$ in. (4–6cm) wide, orbicular. F white or pale pink, $2\frac{1}{2}-2\frac{3}{4}$ in. (6–6·5cm) long, salver-shaped, up to 5 per truss. GB, Australia.

R. pachycarpon East New Guinea

Ht 4–5 ft. (1·2–1·5m). L 2–$2\frac{1}{2}$ in. (5–6·5cm) long, 1–$1\frac{3}{4}$ in. (3–4·5cm) wide, obovate. F sulphur or lemon or lime-yellow, $2\frac{1}{2}$–3 in. (6–7cm) long, tubular-funnel-shaped, 4–8 per truss. Good flowers of excellent colour but difficult to grow. Good firm foliage. USA, Australia.

R. pauciflorum Malay Peninsula

Ht small epiphyte. L about 1 in. (2–3cm) long, about $\frac{1}{2}$ in. (1–1·5cm) wide, obovate. F bright or rose-red, $\frac{3}{5}-\frac{3}{4}$ in. (1·5–1·8cm) long, narrow tubular-campanulate, solitary or in pairs. Quite good with nice foliage. GB, Australia.

R. perakense Malay Peninsula

Ht to 6 ft. (1·8m). L $\frac{1}{2}-\frac{3}{4}$ in. (1·3–1·8cm) long, $\frac{1}{4}-\frac{2}{5}$ in. (0·6–1cm) wide, obovate-spathulate. F white or bright yellow, at least $\frac{2}{5}$ in. (1cm) long, tubular-campanulate, 3–5 per truss. Good foliage and flowers. GB.

R. phaeopeplum

Close to *R. konori*. GB, USA, Australia.

R. rarum New Guinea

Ht to 3 ft. 4 in. (1m). Slender straggly habit. L $1\frac{1}{4}$–$2\frac{3}{4}$ in. (3–7cm) long, $\frac{1}{4}$–$\frac{2}{5}$ in. (0·6–1cm) wide, lanceolate. F pink, crimson, scarlet or blood-red, 1–$1\frac{1}{2}$ in. (2·5–3·5cm) long, tubular, usually solitary or in pairs. Not in fact at all rare. The best forms are quite pretty. Good in San Francisco. GB, USA, Australia.

R. retusum Sumatra and Java

Ht to 13 ft. (4m). L up to $1\frac{1}{2}$ in. (4cm) long, $\frac{3}{5}$ in. (1·5cm) wide, oblong, F light red to bright scarlet, up to 1 in. (2·5cm) long, tubular-funnel-shaped, up to 9 per truss. Not very attractive. GB, USA, Australia.

R. robertsonii Malay Peninsula

Ht to 8 ft. (2·5m). $2\frac{1}{2}$–5 in. (6–12cm) long, 1–$1\frac{1}{2}$ in. (2·5–4cm) wide, elliptic. F golden to deep creamy-yellow, flushed, $\frac{1}{2}$ in. (3·5cm) long and wide, funnel-shaped, 5–8 per truss. Quite pretty. GB.

R. saxifragoides New Guinea

Ht 2–6 in. (5–15cm) forming mats. L 1–$1\frac{1}{2}$ in. (2·3–4cm) long, about $\frac{1}{6}$ in. (3–5mm) wide, linear lanceolate. F blood-red to pinkish-red, 1–$1\frac{1}{5}$ in. (2·5–3cm) long, tubular, solitary or in pairs. The Malesian *R. repens* but more like *R. campylogynum* in impression. A very good species with proportionally large flowers. Comes from very high altitudes. Very slow-growing. USA, Australia only.

R. scabridibracteum New Guinea

Ht to 12 ft. (3·5m). L 3–5 in. (8–13cm) long, $1\frac{1}{2}$–$2\frac{1}{2}$ in. (3·5–6cm) wide, elliptic-oblong. F pale to deep red or crimson, $2\frac{1}{4}$–$2\frac{1}{2}$ in. (5·5–6cm) long, tubular, 6–12 per truss. Very good flowers and nice foliage. GB, USA, Australia.

R. solitarium. East New Guinea

Ht to 5 ft. (1·5m) stiff habit. L 2–3 in. (5–8cm) long, 1–2 in. (3–5cm) wide, oblong elliptic, dark green and glossy. F white and pale pink, scented, about 2 in. (5–5·5cm) long, widely funnel-shaped, 4–6 per truss. Beautiful flowers and good foliage. GB.

R. stenophyllum Borneo

Ht 2 ft.–3 ft. 4 in. (0·6–1m). L 2–3 in. (5–8cm) long, 2–3mm wide, narrow linear. F flame-coloured, about 1 in. (2–2·5cm) long, campanulate to funnel-shaped, mostly in pairs. Most unusually narrow leaves and lanky shoots. Pretty flowers. GB, Australia.

R. suaveolens Borneo

Rather similar to *R. jasminiflorum*. AM 1970 'Painted Snipe'.

R. superbum

Rather similar to *R. konori* with equally fine flowers and excellent scent. GB, Australia.

R. vitisidaea East New Guinea

Ht 2–7 ft. (0·6–2m). L $\frac{3}{5}$–1 in. (1·5–2·5cm) long, $\frac{2}{5}$–$\frac{3}{5}$ in. (1–1·5cm) wide, obovate-elliptic. F bright red or scarlet, $\frac{3}{5}$–$\frac{4}{5}$ in. (1·5–2cm) long, tubular, solitary. Very good flowers. GB.

R. womersleyi East New Guinea

Ht to 7 ft. (2m). Stiff and erect. L dense, about $\frac{1}{3}$ in. (5–8mm) long, $\frac{1}{4}$ in. (4–6mm) wide, ovate. F bright or deep red-scarlet, $\frac{3}{5}$–$\frac{4}{5}$ in. (1·5–2cm) long, tubular, solitary, rarely to 3 per truss. Quite attractive in an unusual stiff manner. GB, USA, Australia.

R. wrightianum var. cyclopense North New Guinea

Ht 8 in.–3 ft. 4 in. (20cm–1m). L about 1 in. (2–3cm) long, $\frac{1}{4}$–$\frac{3}{5}$ in) (0·7–1·7cm) wide, F glossy red to deep crimson, about 1 in. (2·5–3cm. long, tubular, 2–3 flowered. Quite a compact habit flowering freely over a long period. GB, USA, Australia.

R. zoelleri Moluccas and New Guinea

Rather similar to *R. aurigeranum* with yellow to orange flowers, often tinged pink. Promising. GB, USA, Australia.

6 *Hybrids*

Elepidote Hybrids (Red)

RHS Merit Rating	American Merit Rating	RHS Hardiness Rating	American Hardiness Rating	Name	Parents	Colour	Flowering Time	Description	Awards
				April Shower	'Wilgens Ruby' × *williamsianum*	Rich rosy red			D
				Bengal	*forrestii* var. *repens* hybrid	Red			B
				Blood Ruby	*forrestii* var. *repens* × Mandalay	Blood-red	Early May		PA A
x			0	Brickdust	'Dido' × *williamsianum*	Rose-red	Early May	Spreading habit.	A
		H4		Burning Bush	*haematodes* × *dichroanthum*	Tangerine-red			B
xxx	3/3	H4	−5	Carmen	*sanguineum* ssp. *didymum* × *forrestii* var. *repens*	Dark red	Late April–May	Very free-flowering, low compact habit.	B
				Clove	*sperabile* × *sanguineum* ssp. *haemalum*	Dark crimson	Mid-season		B
xxx	2/3	H4	−5	Doncaster	*arboreum* hybrid	Scarlet-crimson	Late May	Medium but spreading, hardy.	B
xx		H4		Elisabeth Hobbie	'Essex Scarlet' × *forrestii* var. *repens*	Scarlet	April–May	Mound-shaped and compact, free-flowering and very hardy. Similar clones are 'Axel Olsen', 'Bad Eilsen', 'Baden Baden' (PC 1972), 'Scarlet Wonder' and 'Spring Dream'. None are heat-resistant in eastern USA. These are some of the best	G

39 *R. leptanthum*. Malesian species

40 *R. zoelleri*. Malesian species

41 (*right*) 'Cilpinense'
(*ciliatum* × *moupinense*).
Lepidote hybrid

42 (*below*) *carolinianum*,
var. *album* × *leucaspis*.
Lepidote hybrid

			Name	Parentage	Colour	Flowering	Description		Group
P		H4	Ems	forrestii var. repens × 'Purple Splendour'	Purplish rose to crimson	April–May	Hardy and free-flowering, a striking colour.		G
	3/3	H3	Ethel	'F. C. Puddle' × forrestii var. repens	Crimson scarlet	Early May	A shy flowering form occurs, not as good as 'Elizabeth'	+5	B
			Fascinator	forrestii var. repens × 'Hiraethlyn'	Carmine shot with turkey-red	April–May	Slow to flower, flowers large with big red calyx.		B
			Gartendirektor Glocker	'Doncaster × williamsianum	Rose-red				G
x		H4	Gertrude Schäle	forrestii var. repens × 'Prometheus'	Scarlet	April–May	Some clones have small flowers, hardy.		G
xxx	3/3	H4	Golden Horn	dichroanthum × elliottii	Orange-red	Late May	Medium compact habit, large calyx	+10 AM 1945	B
			Hyperion	'Cardinal' × forrestii var. repens	Blood-red	April			B
		H4	Ightham Bijou		Orange-scarlet	Mid-season	Petaloid calyx, semi-dwarf.		B
		H4	Ightham Delight	'Hummingbird' × griersonianum	Red	Mid-season	Semi-dwarf.		B
xxx	3/4	H3	Indiana	dichroanthum ssp. scyphocalyx × kyawi	Orange-red, spotted	June–July	Spreading habit, grey-white indumentum, flowers in loose trusses.	+10	B

Elepidote Hybrids (Red) – continued

RHS Merit Rating	American Merit Rating	RHS Hardiness Rating	American Hardiness Rating	Name	Parents	Colour	Flowering Time	Description	Awards
				Isaac Newton	(catawbiense × thomsonii) × forrestii var. repens	Carmine-red			G
	4/2		+5	Jaipur	forrestii var. repens × meddianum	Deep crimson	March	Low open habit, flowers in loose trusses.	B
xxx		H4		Jenny	forrestii var. repens × griersonianum	Light blood-red	April–May	The same grex as 'Elizabeth'. Prostrate habit with creeping branches.	B
	4/3		0	Leaburg	dichroanthum × 'Penjerrick'	Brilliant waxy scarlet	Mid–April	Habit very compact, waxy flowers in flat-topped truss.	PA 1956 A
				Linswegeanum	'Brittania' × forrestii var. repens	Deep scarlet-red			G
xxx	3/3	H4	+10	Little Ben	forrestii var. repens × neriiflorum	Waxy scarlet	April	Dense or loose, low-growing.	FCC 1937 B
	3/3		+10	Little Bert	forrestii var. repens × neriiflorum ssp. euchaites	Crimson scarlet	Late April	More sprawling, free-flowering.	AM 1939 B
	+5			Little Gem	'Carmen' ×	Deep	Early		A

			Name	Parentage	Colour	Flowering	Notes	Award	
		H3–4	Maestro	'Barclayi' × williamsianum	Dark red	April	Attractive foliage.		B
x		H4	Major	haematodes × thomsonii	Brilliant red	April			B
x		H3	Marshall	haematodes × elliottii	Blood-red	May	Blood-red indumentum.		B
xxxx	4/3	H3	May Day	griersonianum × haematodes	Scarlet	May	Many forms, habit usually broader than high, excellent and free-flowering, calyx variable in size.		B
		H3	May Morn	beanianum × 'May Day'	Red	April–May	Good indumentum, a little tender.		B
			Moerheim's Scarlet	'Earl of Athlone' × haematodes	Bright scarlet	April–May			G
	−15		Nodding Bells	red catawbiense × (forrestii var. repens × griersonianum)	Cherry-red	Late April			A
	3/3 +5		Nymph	forrestii var. repens × 'Largo'	Deep red	Early April	Dwarf spreading habit.		B
			Oporto	thomsonii × sanguineum ssp. haemaleum	Fine waxy crimson bells	April–May		AM 1967	B
x		H4	Osfriesland	'Madame de Bruin' × forrestii var. repens	Bright scarlet-red	April–May	Spreading habit.		G

Elepidote Hybrids (Red) – continued

RHS Merit Rating	American Merit Rating	RHS Hardiness Rating	American Hardiness Rating	Name	Parents	Colour	Flowering Time	Description	Awards
			0	Peekaboo	('Carmen × Moonstone') × *elliottii*	Deep blood-red	Early May		A
xx				Persimmon (Golden Horn group)	*dichroanthum* × *elliottii*	Bright scarlet	June–July	Thick rusty indumentum.	B
				Popacatapeti	'Compactum multiflorum' × *forrestii* var. *repens*	Bright scarlet	April–May	Compact.	B
			0	Pygmy	'Moonstone' × 'Carmen'	Dark red	Early May		A
				Red Bells	'Essex Scarlet' × *williamsianum*	Bright red	May–June	Compact habit.	
xxx		H3		Red Cap	*sanguineum* ssp. *didymum* × *eriogynum*	Deep red	July	Very fine late red but a little tender in E. Scotland.	B
			0	Ruby Hart	('Carmen' × 'Elizabeth') × *elliottii*	Blood-red	Early May		A
				Salute	*forrestii* var.	Red			G

RHS Merit Rating	American Merit Rating	RHS Hardiness Rating	American Hardiness Rating	Name	Parents	Colour	Flowering Time	Description	Awards
				The Lizzard	'Mosers Maroon' × 'Carmen'	Dark red	May	Dark leaves, creeping habit.	
		H4		Ursula Siems	'Earl of Athlone' × *forrestii* var. *repens*	Carmine-scarlet	April–May		G
				Vega	'Fabia' × *haematodes*	Scarlet	May		B
				Venapens	*venator* × *forrestii* var. *repens*	Scarlet	May	Free flowering.	B
				Yeoman	'Choremia' × *forrestii* var. *repens*	Turkey-red	April		AM 1947 B

Elepidote Hybrids (Pink)

RHS Merit Rating	American Merit Rating	RHS Hardiness Rating	American Hardiness Rating	Name	Parents	Colour	Flowering Time	Description	Awards
	3/2		0	Adrastia	*neriiflorum* × *williamsianum*	Deep pink	Late April	Rounded habit, small trusses.	B
	3/3	H4	−10	Arthur J. Ivens	*williamsianum* × *houlstonii*	Pale pink	Early May	Habit dome-shaped, good in full sun.	AM 1944 B

Elepidote Hybrids (Pink) – continued

RHS Merit Rating	American Merit Rating	RHS Hardiness Rating	American Hardiness Rating	Name	Parents	Colour	Flowering Time	Description	Awards	
xxx	3/4	H4	0	Bowbells	'Corona' × williamsianum	Pink	Early May	Very popular in W. America, fine flowers and foliage.	AM 1935	B
	3/4		0	Dormouse	'Dawn's Delight' × williamsianum	Pale, flushed deep pink	Late April	Compact habit, small loose trusses.		B
		H3-4	0	Elizabeth Lockhart	sport of 'Hummingbird'	Deep pink	Late April	Red foliage dulling to chocolate-brown. Unusual.	HC 1972	B
		H4		Grayswood Pink	williamsianum × venator	Deep pink	May			B
				Hebe	'Neriihaem' × williamsianum	Deepest rose-pink	April-May			B
	3/3	H3-4	0	Hummingbird	haematodes × williamsianum	Pink to medium red	Late April	Very compact in the open, slow to flower.		B
		H4		Hydon Ball	yakusimanum × 'Springbok'	Pink opening white	April-May			B
		H4		Hydon Dawn	yakusimanum × 'Springbok'	Clear pink	April-May			B
		H4		Hydon Glow	yakusimanum × 'Springbok'	Salmon-pink	April-May			B
x		H4		Jacksonii	caucasicum × 'Nobleanum'	Rosy pink with	April	Habit wider than tall.		B

				williamsianum	*williamsianum* with orange in throat				
H3			John Marchand	*moupinense* (lepidote) × *sperabile*	Pink	March–April	Drought-resistant.	AM 1966	B
			Kimberly	*williamsianum* × *fortunei*		April–May		PA 1963	A
	+5	2/3	Little Bill	*williamsianum* × 'Lady Stuart of Wortley'	Deep rose-pink	Late April	Medium habit, dome-shaped, small loose trusses.		B
	−5	3/4	Mission Bells	*orbiculare* × *williamsianum*	Pale pink	Early May	Compact habit, good in full sun, loose truss.		
H4			x	Moerheim's Pink	*williamsianum* hybrid	Deep pink		Hardy.	AM 1972	G
H3–4				Mystic	'Barclayi' × *williamsianum*	Clear pink	April	Attractive foliage.		B
				Oudijk's Sensation	'Essex Scarlet' × *williamsianum*	Deep pink	Late May	Medium height.		G
				Pink Bountiful	'Essex Scarlet' × *williamsianum*	Bright pink	May–June	Compact habit, bronze young foliage.		G
				Pink Pebble	*callimorphum* × *williamsianum*	Pink	April–May	Good foliage.		B
	−15	4/3		Pink Twins	*catawbiense* × *haematodes*	Light shrimp pink	Late May	Slow-growing compact, flowers hose-in-hose, fleshy.		A

207

Elepidote Hybrids (Pink) – continued

RHS Merit Rating	American Merit Rating	RHS Hardiness Rating	American Hardiness Rating	Name	Parents	Colour	Flowering Time	Description	Awards
				Psyche	*fortunei* 'Sir Charles Butler' × *williamsianum*	Pink	April–May		G
				Riplet	*forrestii* var. *repens* × 'Letty Edwards'	Crimson fading to salmon pink	April–May		PA 1961 A
				Royal Pink	'Homer' × *williamsianum*	Light rose	May	Compact habit.	
				Starlet	'Diva' × *williamsianum*	Deep pink	April–May		PA 1961 A
				Suomi	'Linswegeanum' × 'Metternianum', red	Rose to bright red	April–May	Many forms, flowers usually long lasting.	G
xxx	3/4	H3	–5	Temple Belle	*orbiculare* × *williamsianum*	Pale rose	Early April	Medium-compact habit, flowers in in loose trusses.	B
		H4		Tottenham	unknown parentage	Deep pink	May		
				Veryan Bay	*pseudochrysanthum* × *williamsianum*	Clear pink	April–May	Dense rounded bush.	B
	3/3		+5	Wilbar	'Barclayi' × *williamsianum*	Deep rose-pink	April	Compact habit, dark shiny leaves.	B
				Willbrit	'Brittania' × *williamsianum*	Deep pink	Late May	Leaves light green, medium height, rounded bush.	G

V *R. roxieanum*, var. *oreonastes*.   Taliense series, sub-series
Roxieanum

Elepidote Hybrids (Yellow)

RHS Merit Rating	American Merit Rating	RHS Hardiness Rating	American Hardiness Rating	Name	Parents	Colour	Flowering Time	Description	Awards
				Canary	campylocarpum × caucasicum	yellow	May	Fairly compact, and free-flowering, surprisingly little known.	B
xx	3/2	H4	0	Cowslip	wardii × williamsianum	Cream to flushed pink	Early April	A rounded bush, best in partial shade, loose truss.	AM 1937 B
x	2/2	H4	−5	Cunningham's Sulphur	caucasicum hybrid	Pale yellow in a rounded truss	April–May	Slow-growing, has flowered in Iceland.	B
xx	3/4	H4	0	Devonshire Cream	campylocarpum hybrid	Clear yellow, red throat	Early May	Slow-growing, compact habit and truss.	AM 1940 B
				Doubloons	'Carolyn Grace' × 'Moonstone'	Deep yellow	Early May		A
	3/4		0	Elspeth	campylocarpum × hardy hybrid	Scarlet bud fading to cream	Mid May		AM 1937 B
	4/4		−5	Full Moon	'Crest' × 'Harvest Moon'	Canary yellow	Mid May	Low, sturdy and compact, shiny foliage, best in some shade.	PA 1955 A
				Honeydew	'Moonstone' × 'Carolyn Grace'	Yellow	April–May		A

209

Elepidote Hybrids (Yellow) – continued

RHS Merit Rating	American Merit Rating	RHS Hardiness Rating	American Hardiness Rating	Name	Parents	Colour	Flowering Time	Description	Awards
				Honey Moon	(*wardii*) × 'Devonshire Cream' × *wardii*	Yellow	April–May		A
				March Sun	*caucasicum citrinum* × 'Moonstone'		February–March		PA 1963 A
xx	4/4	H3	−5	Moonstone	*campylocarpum* × *williamsianum*	Pale creamy yellow, cream edged pink, etc.	Mid April–May	Forms a compact mound, highly rated in W. America.	B
				Sweetie Pie	'Cowslip' × *forrestii* var. *repens*	Pale cream flushed pink	April–May		A
	3/4		+5	Tidbit	*dichroanthum* × *wardii*	Apricot and flame turning to straw yellow	May	Good dense foliage and habit, flowers fleshy in loose truss.	PA 1957 A
xxx	3/5	H4	+5	Unique	*campylocarpum* hybrid	Pale yellow, tinged peach	Mid April–May	Very compact, symmetrical habit. FCC 1935 B

Elepidote Hybrids (Orange)

RHS Merit Rating	American Merit Rating	RHS Hardiness Rating	American Hardiness Rating	Name	Parents	Colour	Flowering Time	Description	Awards
x		H4		Berryrose	'Doncaster' × *dichroanthum*	Orange-pink	May		B
xx		H4		Break of Day	'Dawn's Delight' × *dichroanthum*	Yellow-edged orange-pink	May		AM 1936 B
x		H4		Dido	*dichroanthum* × *decorum*	Pink, shaded orange	May–June	Compact sturdy habit, large calyx and loose truss.	B
	4/3		+10	Ella	*dichroanthum* × *wardii*	Orange to yellow	Late May	Shiny leaves, best in partial shade, numerous small trusses.	A
xxx	3/4	H4	+10	Fabia Tangerine	*dichroanthum* × *griersonianum*	Orange-red	Mid May–June	Compact habit.	AM 1940 B
	3/3		+5	Gold Bug	'Fabia' × *wardii*	Orange-yellow spotted changing to gold	Early May	Unusual colour, not liked by all.	A
x		H4		Icarus	A. Gilbert × *dichroanthum* ssp. *herpesticum*	Pale yellow, shaded rose	April–May	Flowers pendulous.	AM 1945 B

Elepidote Hybrids (Orange) – continued

RHS Merit Rating	American Merit Rating	RHS Hardiness Rating	American Hardiness Rating	Name	Parents	Colour	Flowering Time	Description	Awards
xxx				Icarus Organdie	'A. Gilbert' × dichroanthum ssp. herpesticum	Cream, striped pink	April-May		AM 1947 B
x	2/3	H4	−5	Jasper	dichroanthum × 'Lady Bessborough'	Pale orange or cream	Late May-June	Sturdy compact habit, flat-topped truss.	B
	3/3		+5	Medusa	griersonianum × dichroanthum ssp. scyphocalyx	Vermilion	Mid May	Upright but dense habit, grey indumentum, flowers in loose trusses.	B
xx	3/4	H3	0	Nereid	neriiflorum × dichroanthum	Orange-pink	Late May	Very compact habit, flat-topped truss.	B
				Varna	'Carmen' × williamsianum	Yellow, flushed rose	April	Very low and compact, growth and flower buds easily frosted.	B

Elepidote Hybrids (White)

RHS Merit Rating	American Merit Rating	RHS Hardiness Rating	American Hardiness Rating	Name	Parents	Colour	Flowering Time	Description	Awards
				Anna Hall	catawbiense var. album 'Glass' ×				PA 1960 A

	American Merit Rating		American Hardiness Rating	Name	Parents	Colour	Flowering Time	Description	Awards
							May	NE. USA, excellent habit and foliage.	A
	4/4			Great Lakes	catawbiense var. album 'Glass' × yakusimanum	Light pink fading to white	June–July		
			0	Nestucca	fortunei × yakusimanum	White	Early May	Compact and rigid habit, truss dome-shaped.	PA 1960 B
	4/4		0	Olympic Lady (Miss Olympia)	'Loderi King George' × williamsianum	Light pink fading to white	Early May	Good foliage and very free-flowering.	PA 1960 A

Lepidote Hybrids (Blue)

RHS Merit Rating	American Merit Rating	RHS Hardiness Rating	American Hardiness Rating	Name	Parents	Colour	Flowering Time	Description	Awards
xxx	4/4	H4	0	Augfast	augustinii × fastigiatum	Blue or violet-blue	Mid April–May	Good in full sun.	B
				Azamia	augustinii × russatum)	Blue-mauve	April–May		B
xxx	5/3	H4	0	Blue-Bird	augustinii × intricatum	Blue or violet-mauve	Mid April	Not as good as 'Blue Diamond'.	AM 1943 B AGM 1968
xxxx	5/4	H4	0	Blue Diamond	augustinii × 'Intrifast'	Blue or violet-blue	Mid April–May	Compact upright habit, one of the best blues, good in full sun.	FCC 1939 B AGM 1968

Lepidote Hybrids (Blue) – Continued

RHS Merit Rating	American Merit Rating	RHS Hardiness Rating	American Hardiness Rating	Name	Parents	Colour	Flowering Time	Description	Awards
		H4		Blue Gown		Deep lavender-blue	April–May	New semi-dwarf.	
		H4		Blue Star	*impeditum* × 'St Tudy'	Brilliant blue	April	Low.	B
				Blue Stone	*augustinii* × 'Bluebird'	Deep blue	April–May		B
xx	4/4	H4	0	Blue Tit	*impeditum* × *augustinii*	Light grey-blue	Mid April	Good in full sun.	B
	3/4		–10	Bluette	*impeditum* × *augustinii*	Hyacinth blue	Mid April	Twiggy habit, good in full sun and heat.	A
xx		H4		Ilam Violet	'Electra' × *russatum*	Deep violet	May	Taller than 'Blue Diamond' and has larger and darker flowers.	NZ
x		H4		Impeanum	*hanceanum* × *impeditum*	Lilac	April–May	Hardly up to present day standards, free-flowering.	FCC 1934 B
				Inshriach Blue		Mid blue	April–May	Free-flowering.	B
x		H4		Intrifast	*intricatum* × *fastigiatum*	Violet-blue	April–May	Neat glaucous foliage.	B
		H4		Moerheim	*impeditum* hybrid	Lilac-blue	April–May	Floriferous.	
			–5	Oceanlake	'Sapphire' × 'Blue	Deep blue	Early April		A

RHS Merit Rating	American Merit Rating	RHS Hardiness Rating	American Hardiness Rating	Name	Parents	Colour	Flowering Time	Description	Awards
				Favourite	hybrid	blue	May		B
				Pematit Cambridge		Powder blue	April–May	Very free-flowering.	B
				Pematit Oxford		Blue	April	Very free-flowering.	B
xxx		H4		St Breward	*augustinii* × *impeditum*	Violet-blue	April–May	One of the finest of the taller blue hybrids.	FCC 1962 B
xxx		H4		St Tudy	*augustinii* × *impeditum*	Violet-blue	April–May	Similar to St Breward.	AM 1960 B
xxx	4/4	H4	0	Sapphire	'Blue Tit' × *impeditum*	Light blue or blue	Mid April	Low spreading habit in sun, excellent low blue.	B
xxx		H4		Songbird	*russatum* × 'Blue Tit'	Deep violet-blue	April–May or autumn	Fine compact habit, a good plant.	AM 1957 B
		H3–4		Songster	*russatum* × 'Blue Tit'	Mauve-blue	April–May	Not as good as 'Songbird'.	B

Lepidote Hybrids (Yellow)

RHS Merit Rating	American Merit Rating	RHS Hardiness Rating	American Hardiness Rating	Name	Parents	Colour	Flowering Time	Description	Awards
				Baby Lou	((*leucaspis* × *ciliatum*) × *leucaspis*) × *valentinianum* F2		February–March		A

Lepidote Hybrids (Yellow) – continued

RHS Merit Rating	American Merit Rating	RHS Hardiness Rating	American Hardiness Rating	Name	Parents	Colour	Flowering Time	Description	Awards
				Bobbet	campylogynum × campylogynum var. cremastum	Yellow	May–June		A
xxx	3/3	H3	+5	Bo-peep	lutescens × moupinense	Pale yellow	March	Open erect habit, nice with 'Praecox', 'Tessa', etc.	AM 1937 B
				Busaco (Golden Oriole group)	moupinense × sulfureum	Golden-yellow flushed pink	March	Early flowering.	AM 1963 B
xxxx		H4		Chikor	chryseum × ludlowii	Yellow	May	My first real success in hybridizing, becoming one of the most popular dwarf yellows, compact, hardy and free-flowering.	FCC 1968 B Cory Cup
xxx		H4		Chink	keiskei × trichocladum	Pale greenish-yellow	March–April	Semi-deciduous foliage, free-flowering.	AM 1961 B
				Chrysomanicum	chrysodoron × burmanicum	Prim-rose-yellow	April–May	Bud tender.	AM 1947 B
			0	Cream Crest	chryseum × 'Cilpinense'	Creamy-white	March–April	Open upright habit, easily frosted.	A
				Curlew	ludlowii × fletcheranum	Yellow	May	My best cross so far, very large flowers for so small a plant, fairly	FCC 1969 B

VI 'Chikor' (*chryseum* x *ludlowii*). Lepidote hybrid

	Name	Parentage	Colour	Flowering	Description	Award	Rating
	Fine Feathers Primrose	*'Cilpinense' × lutescens*	Pale yellow	March	Rather similar to 'Bo-peep' with heavier foliage.		B
	Golden Gift	*chryseum × leucaspis*	Yellow	February–March			A
	Goldfinger	*burmanicum × valentinianum*	Primrose yellow	April		AM 1965	B
	un-named Reuthe hybrid	*hanceanum × keiskei*	Yellow	May	Very compact, excellent foliage, and free-flowering, first rate.		B
	Lemon Mist	*xanthosteph-anum × leucaspis*	Yellow	February–March		AE 1971	
3/2 -10	Lenape	*speciferum × keiskei*	Light yellow	Early April	Leaves dark bronze-green, free-flowering.		A
	Little Lou	*((leucaspis × ciliatum) × leucaspis) × valentinianum*	Green-ish-yellow	February–March		PA 1963	A
-15	Mary Fleming	*(racemosum × keiskei) × keiskei*	Pale yellow	April–May	Shapely and free-flowering.		A
	Moth	*megeratum × mishmiense*	Lemon-yellow	April–May		AM 1955	B
	Owen Pearce	*burmanicum × 'Saffron Queen'*		April–May			A
H3	Parisienne	*burmanicum × valentinianum*	Cream to yellow	April–May	Bud tender.		B

Lepidote Hybrids (Yellow) – continued

RHS Merit Rating	American Merit Rating	RHS Hardiness Rating	American Hardiness Rating	Name	Parents	Colour	Flowering Time	Description	Awards
x		H3		Quaver	*leucaspis × sulfureum*	Cream	March–April	Brownish young foliage.	B
				Remo	*lutescens × valentinianum*	Deep yellow	April	Inclined to have poor foliage and flowers of thin texture.	B
				R. W. Rye	*chrysodoron × johnstoneanum*	Primrose-yellow	February–March	Bud tender.	AM 1951 B
	4/3		+20	Saffron Queen	*xanthostephanum × burmanicum*	Pale sulphur-yellow	Late April	Best in partial shade, rather bud tender.	AM 1948 B
				Talavera (Golden Oriole group)	*moupinense × sulfureum*	Golden-yellow	March	Early flowering.	FCC 1963 B
				Tow Head	*carolinianum × ludlowii*	Brilliant greenish-yellow	Mid season		A
				Valaspis	*valentinianum × leucaspis*	Pale yellow	April	Pretty but not as good as either parent.	AM 1935 B
xxx	4/3	H4	+10	Yellow Hammer	*sulfureum × flavidum*	Yellow	April and autumn	Straggly erect habit, flowers small but freely produced, stands full sun.	B

Lepidote Hybrids (Lavender to Purple)

RHS Merit Rating	American Merit Rating	RHS Hardiness Rating	American Hardiness Rating	Name	Parents	Colour	Flowering Time	Description	Awards	
		H4		Arbutifolium ('Punctatum')	ferrugineum × minus	Lilac-rose	June–July			B
	4/3	H4	−15	Conemaugh	racemosum × mucronulatum	Lavender-pink	Early April	Semi-deciduous, flowers in a rounded truss.		A
	3/2	H4	−25	Conewago	carolinianum × mucronulatum	Lavender-rose	Early April	Open habit.		A
			−10	Daphnoides	virgatum hybrid	Bright rosy-lilac	Late May	Interesting foliage.		B
		H4		Debijo	carolinianum × saluenense	Lavender-purple	April–May			A
xx		H4		Emasculum	ciliatum × dauricum	Rosy-lilac	April	Very free flowering. Later than Praecox.		B
		H3		Gene	spiciferum × ciliatum	Cyclamen-purple	March–April			A
		H4		Myrtifolium	hirsutum × minus	Lilac-pink				B
		H4		Olive	moupinense × dauricum	Mallow-purple, spotted	March	Free-flowering.	AM 1942	B
	A			Patricia	saluenense × campylogynum	Magnolia-purple	April–May	A striking colour.		A

219

Lepidote Hybrids (Lavender to Purple) – continued

RHS Merit Rating	American Merit Rating	RHS Hardiness Rating	American Hardiness Rating	Name	Parents	Colour	Flowering Time	Description	Awards
				Phalarope	*pemakoense* × *davidsonianum*	Lilac-pink	April-May	Very free-flowering with long lasting flowers.	PC 1968 B
xxx		H4		Pink Drift	*calostrotum* × *scintillans*	Magenta-pink	May	Very compact habit and free-flowering.	B
	3/4		−20	P. J. Mezzit	*carolinianum* × *dauricum*	Light lavender-purple	Early April	Leaves mahogany in winter, compact habit, good in sun, shade or drought. Several clones.	A
xxx	3/3	H4	−5	Praecox	*ciliatum* × *dauricum*	Rosy-purple	March	Upright habit reaching over 6 ft. (2m). Very well known.	AGM 1926B
				Prostigiatum	*fastigiatum* × *prostratum*	Deep or violet-purple	April-May	Very low-growing, neat and compact. Flowers of a good colour.	AM 1924 B
	3/4		−15	Purple Gem	*fastigiatum* × *carolinianum*	Light purple	Mid April	Rounded dwarf habit, good in full sun.	A
	3/4		−25	Ramapo	*fastigiatum* × *carolinianum*	Bright violet-pink	Early April	Attractive glaucous foliage, very compact, very good in sun or shade.	A
xxx	3/4	H4	−5	Tessa	'Praecox' × *moupinense*	Deep lilac-pink	March	Will grow in full sun, vigorous habit.	AM 1939 B AGM 1968

Lepidote Hybrids (Pink and Rose)

RHS Merit Rating	American Merit Rating	RHS Hardiness Rating	American Hardiness Rating	Name	Parents	Colour	Flowering Time	Description	Awards
			−10	Anna Baldsiefen	'Pioneer' selfed	Light rose	April–May		A
		H4		Arden Belle	'Rosy Bell' × glaucophyllum	Rose-pink	April–May	Smooth mahogany bark.	B
	4/2		−10	Brandywine	spiciferum × keiskei	Cream, edged rose	Late April	Leaves dark bronze-green, many flowers per shoot.	A
				Candi	campylogynum var. cremastum × racemosum	Bright rose	April–May	Poor foliage.	A
				Carousel	carolinianum × saluenense	Lavender-pink	April–May		A
		H3		Chaffinch	'Countess of Haddington' × ciliatum	Blush	March–April	Semi-dwarf.	B
xxxx	4/4	H4	+5	Cilpinense	ciliatum × moupinense	Pale pink marked rose	March	Beautiful in the best form, frost protection desirable.	FCC 1968 B AGM 1968
		H3		Cream Cascade	lutescens × leucaspis	Cream flushed pink	March	Free-flowering	
	3/3		−15	Cutie	calostrotum hybrid	Pink, shaded lilac	Early May	Upright habit.	AE 1962 A

221

Lepidote Hybrids (Pink and Rose) – continued

RHS Merit Rating	American Merit Rating	RHS Hardiness Rating	American Hardiness Rating	Name	Parents	Colour	Flowering Time	Description	Awards
		H3		Felise	*ciliatum × burmanicum*	Cream, flushed pink	March–April		B
				Fittra	'Fittianum' × *racemosum*	Rich pink	April–May	Ungainly habit but one of the the pinkest dwarf hybrids	AM 1949 B
				Grievii	*virgatum × ciliatum*	Pale pink	April		B
				Intermedium	*ferrugineum × hirsutum*	Bright rose-pink	June	Natural hybrid.	
				Kim	*campylogynum × campylogynum var. cremastum*	Pink fading to yellow			A
				Laetevirens	synonym of 'Wilsoni'				
		H3		Multiflorum	*ciliatum × virgatum*	Pink	March–April	Free-flowering.	B
	3/3		−5	Pera	*pemakoense × racemosum*	Lilac-pink	April	Very free-flowering and quite vigorous.	A
				Pink Snowflakes	parentage unknown	White flushed pink	April–May	Good deep foliage.	A
				Pipit	*lowndesii ×*	Delicate May–		Natural hybrid, very compact	A

			Name	Parentage	Colour	Flowering	Notes	Award	
	3/4	0	Rose Elf	racemosum × pemakoense	White, flushed bluish-pink	Late April	Flower buds easily frosted, very free-flowering.	PA 1954	A
xx	3/3 H4	−5	Rosy Bell	ciliatum × glaucophyllum	Old rose	March–April	Very free-flowering.	AM 1894	B
xxxx	H3–4		Seta	spinuliferum × moupinense	White or pink flushed deep pink	March–April	Charming flowers very freely produced.	FCC 1960 AGM 1968	B
			Tessa Roza	'Praecox' × moupinense	Deep rosy-pink	March	The pinkest of the early hybrids and a striking colour.	AM 1953	B
	3/2	0	Twinkles	racemosum × spiciferum	Light pink	Mid April	Vigorous with long shoots, good in full sun.		A
			Veesprite	impeditum × racemosum	Rose	Mid May			C
			Waterer's Hybridum	ferrugineum hybrid	Rose-pink	June	Neat habit		B
	H4		Wilsonii	carolinianum × ferrugineum	Rose	June	Still worth growing, very hardy and useful for its lateness.		B
	4/3	−25	Windbeam	carolinianum × racemosum seedling	Opens white and turns to a light pink	April	A bit sprawly with long willowy shoots.		A

Lepidote Hybrids (White)

RHS Merit Rating	American Merit Rating	RHS Hardiness Rating	American Hardiness Rating	Name	Parents	Colour	Flowering Time	Description	Awards	
xx	4/4	H3	+5	Bric-a-Brac	*leucaspis × moupinense*	White or blush pink, dark anthers	February	Flowers need protection from frost.	AM 1945	B
	4/4		−15	Dora Amateis	*carolinianum × ciliatum*	White lightly spotted green	Late April	Very promising, vigorous and free-flowering.	AE	A
				Leucacil	*leucaspis × ciliatum*	Pure white, black stamens	February–March			B
				Lucy Lou	*(leucaspis × ciliatum) × leucaspis*	White	February–March			A
	4/4		0	Maricee	near *sargentianum*	Creamy white	Early May	More vigorous than *sargentianum* and very free-flowering.	AE 1960	A
	3/3		−15	Montchanin	*spiciferum × keiskei*	White	Late April	Graceful habit and free-flowering.		A
xxx				Ptarmigan	*Microleucum × leucaspis*	White	March–April	Plant away from morning sun, compact and spreading.	FCC 1965	B
		H4		Sarled	*sargentianum × trichostomum*	Pale pink	May–June	Neat habit and long-lasting flowers,		B

43 'Tessa Roza' (*praecox* × *moupinense*). Lepidote hybrid

44 'Elizabeth' (*forrestii*, var. *repens* × *griersonianum*). Elepidote hybrid

45 (*above*) *R. kaempferi.*
Azalea series, sub-series
Obtusum

46 (*right*) *R. macrosepalum*
'Linearifolium'. Azalea
series, sub-series Obtusum

				macronulatum	flushed rose			
		Springtime						
5/2	0	Snow Lady	*leucaspis* × *ciliatum*?	White, dark anthers	March–April	Needs protection in E. Scotland, free-flowering.	PA 1955	A
3/4	−25	Wyanokie	*carolinianum* × *racemosum* seedling	White	Early May	Good habit, flowers small in rounded trusses, floriferous.		

Azaleodendrons

RACEMOSUM × OBTUSUM SUB-SERIES

		Hardijzer Beauty	*racemosum* × Obtusum azalea	Light red				D
		Lilian Harvey	*racemosum* × 'Hatsugiri'	White with pink flush		All are new, free-flowering and quite promising.		D
		Martine	*racemosum* × Obtusum azalea	Pink				D
		Ria Hardijzer	*racemosum* × 'Hinodegiri'	Rosy-red				D

ELEPIDOTE RHODODENDRON × LUTEUM AZALEA

xx	2/2 H4	0	Broughtonii Aureum	(*maximum* × *ponticum*) × *molle*	Soft yellow	Late May	Ungainly habit, semi-deciduous, small rounded truss.	FCC 1935	B

225

7 *Obtusum Azaleas (Evergreen)*

OBTUSUM SUBSERIES

This large, very distinct sub-series, is really a group out on its own with only a few relations in other small sections of the Azalea series. They are thus hard to cross with other rhododendrons although a few breakthroughs have been made.

They are much-branched, rather low shrubs, sometimes up to 10 ft (3m) but usually less. The evergreen or semi-deciduous leaves and the shoots are usually covered with appressed (flattened) hairs. Leaves, where evergreen, are retained at the tips of the shoots. Many remain evergreen in mild climates while being completely deciduous in colder areas.

A number of so-called species are not in cultivation, and several that are prove barely hardy. Most need a much hotter summer than than of Britain (especially in Scotland) to ripen the wood. Hence, species satisfactory in the eastern USA, with hotter summers and colder winters, will not flower here and are liable to winter damage. In fact only a handful of species are really suitable for Scotland and all should be grown in full sun, preferably with a wall behind them. One word of warning: some brightly coloured varieties bleach badly in strong sunlight. In hotter climates, dappled shade is ideal.

I have taken the liberty of relegating any so-called species not found in the wild to cultivars of the wild equivalent. Many cultivated varieties were first known to collectors and botanists before the wild types were discovered, hence the muddle in nomenclature. Several of these azaleas have a tendency to sport even in their native habitat. This has resulted in numbers of double and semi-double forms and also striped and parti-coloured varieties.

In identification, points to watch are: 1. the shape of flowers; 2. the colour of flowers; 3. the size and shape of leaves; 4. habit; 5. the number of stamens and 6. the number of flowers per truss. The persistence of the leaves is not really reliable.

There is a great deal of confusion over the Japanese species, with the descriptions in the RHS *Rhododendron Species Handbook* badly needing a complete revision. *R. kiusianum* is an example.*

Distribution is in north-east upper Burma, much of south and south-west China, Taiwan, the Philippine Islands, Korea and all parts of Japan.

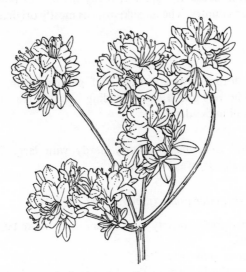

R. kiusianum

R. indicum (*macrantha*) H2–3 A0 L1–2 F2–3

Ht occasionally to 6 ft (1·83m), usually very much less. Habit dense, with slender rigid branches. Sometimes prostrate.

L up to 1½ in. (3·8cm) long, narrow lanceolate to oblanceolate, with scattered hairs on both surfaces. Often dark green above.

---

* There is a most confusing and unfortunate botanical rule in the 1969 Code of Nomenclature which I sincerely hope will be amended some time, which states that the originally described specimen must hold preference over later wild collections even if the former is a cultivated clone, I have more or less followed books of reference such as Ohwi's *Flora of Japan*, Hillier's *Manual of Trees and Shrubs* and Lee's *The Azalea Book* where the wild varieties are generally given specific status. I have done this largely to simplify the nomenclature from a horticultural point of view to show which are the true wild plants and which are cultivars. Hence, *R. linearifolium*, a cultivar of *R. macrosepalum* with narrow leaves and corolla lobes, is the botanically legitimate species. I have relegated it to cultivar status thus, *R. macrosepalum* 'Linearifolium' instead of *R. linearifolium* var. *macrosepalum*.

F rose-red through bright red to scarlet, 2–2½ in. (5–6·3cm) across, broadly funnel-shaped, single or in pairs.

A fine species where it can be grown well, but is of little use in Scotland and other cool areas. Satisfactory only in the warmest parts of England after good summers. Good in Washington DC.

Comes from southern Japan in rocky ravines, torrent sides, and often in open country. The Satsuki azaleas mostly originate from this species.

June–July

'Balsaminaeflorum' (*rosaeflora*). F3 of garden origin, has double salmon-red flowers and a low spreading habit. Is reasonably hardy and successful in Scotland.

'Crispiflorum' (*macrantha*). Fairly hardy with large bright pink flowers with slightly wavy edges.

R. indicum var. *eriocarpum* (*tamurae*) H2–3? A+5

Usually considered a variety of *R. simsii*. Even more tender than *R. indicum* itself.

F reddish, rose, pink or white.

A more southerly form of the above from south Kyushu and the various islands south to Taiwan. Sometimes grows prostrate on the beach of Yakushima. The Gumpo azaleas probably come from this variety.

R. kaempferi (*obtusum* var. *kaempferi*) H4 A−5 L1–2 F3–4

Ht up to 10 ft (3m), often less. Habit loosely branched with erect growth.

L up to 3 in. (7·6cm) long, hairy on both sides. Semi-evergreen or deciduous. Leaves often turn scarlet in autumn.

F salmon-red, orange-red, pink to rosy-scarlet and white, 1¾–2½ in. (4·4–6·3cm) long, and wide, funnel-shaped, 1–4 per truss. Some forms are double or hose-in-hose but may be of garden origin.

A very variable species with many forms and hybrids. Several of these make good garden plants in the sunnier low-lying parts of Scotland and northern England, and of course do well in southern England and eastern USA. The flowers of most forms bleach readily in the sun. 'Eastern Fire', FCC 1955; AM 1953; AGM 1968.

Found wild in the main islands of Japan, often very common, from sea-level to the lower hills below 2,600 ft (800m). Usually grows in sunny positions on hillsides, by the sea, on active volcanos and also in thickets, pinewoods and deciduous forest.
May–June

R. *kanehirai*

Recently introduced from Taiwan. Habit spreading.
L up to 2¼ in. (5·6cm) long, narrowly lanceolate.
F carmine-red to scarlet, narrow funnel-shaped, 1¼–1¾ in. (3·1–4·3 cm) long, solitary or in pairs.

R. *kiusianum* H4 A0 L1–2 F1–3

Ht 2½ ft (76cm) or less. Habit often flat-topped and spreading along the ground.
L up to ¾ in. (1·9cm) long, and ½ in. (1·3cm) wide, elliptic to narrowly obovate, semi-deciduous.
F purple-mauve, rose-pink or rarely white (very fine), ¾–1 in. (1·8–2·5cm) funnel-shaped, almost tubeless, 2–4 per truss but usually in pairs. Stamens 5.

Makes an excellent ground-cover and is attractive in the better recently introduced forms from Japan via the USA. Good in Scotland.

The true species has long been in cultivation, introduced by Wilson. Usually found as an alpine species on bare meadows, pumice flats or among dwarf pines, at 4,000–5,600 ft (1,200–1,700m). At 2,600–4,000 ft. (800–1,200m), hybrid swarms occur of a bewildering array of colours.
May

R. *komiyamae* H4? A0 L1–2 F2?

Ht to 10 ft (3m). Habit upright and vigorous.
L semi-evergreen, acute at both ends.
F rosy-mauve to purple, 1 in. (2·5cm) across. Stamens 10.

Not known by the author but is said to be free-flowering and quite pretty and should be more widely grown.

Found on the summits of two mountains in central Honshu, Japan. Natural hybrids with R. *kaempferi* do occur.
May–June (Japan)

R. macrosepalum H3 A0 L1–2 F1–2

Ht 3–6 ft (1–2m). Habit wide-spreading open bush.
L up to $3\frac{1}{2}$ in. (6·3cm) long, ovate-elliptic or ovate to lanceolate, sometimes colouring to rich crimson-purple in autumn.
F lilac-pink to rose-purple, 2 in. (5cm) across, funnel-shaped, 2–10 per truss. Large green calyx. Stamens usually 5, occasionally up to 10.

A somewhat tender species, only suitable for warmer parts of southern England. Variable, good forms being handsome. Leaves and flowers liable to frost damage.

From central and southern Japan, often in sunny situations, and in pine woods and thickets, frequently in gravelly soil. Grows mixed with *R. kaempferi* by the thousand in places.
April–May

'Linearifolium'. A queer garden clone with extremely narrow leaves up to 3 in. (7·5cm) long, and $\frac{1}{4}$ in. (6mm) wide. The lobes of the pink flowers are exactly the same shape as the leaves. Worth growing as a curiosity. Hardy in lowland Scotland in a warm sheltered position.

R. microphyton H3 A none L1–2 F1–2

Ht to 6 ft (1·83m), but often less. Habit upright, much branched. Shoots densely clothed with appressed brown hairs.
L $\frac{1}{4}$–2 in. (0·6–5cm) long, elliptic to lanceolate, persistent.
F rose to almost white, dotted carmine on upper lobes, $\frac{1}{2}$–$\frac{3}{4}$ in. (1·3–1·9cm) across, funnel-shaped, 3–6 per truss, often clustered at the ends of branches. Stamens 5.

Probably too tender for most parts of Britain but some forms could be worth growing. Possibly not in cultivation.

Widespread and common in Yunnan at 6,000–10,000 ft (1,828–3,048m) on open dry situations, thickets, cliffs and shady rocky places.
April–May

R. mueronatum see *ripense*

R. nakaharai H4 A none L1–2 F2–3

Ht low shrub. Habit creeping and usually prostrate, possibly the dwarfest azalea, forming mats 1 ft (30cm) or more across.

L up to 1 in. (2·5cm) long, oblanceolate, elliptic or elliptic-obovate.
F brick-red to rose-red, 1½ in. (3·8cm) across, funnel-campanulate, in trusses of 2 to 3. Stamens 10.

In the form now well-distributed in cultivation, 'Mariko', AM 1970, this is one of the most valuable introductions of recent years. Its prostrate habit makes it an excellent ground-cover for peat walls, banks and rock gardens. Plant in full sun. Flowers best the year after a hot summer. There is now some doubt if this form is the true species and could be a hybrid raised in Japan. The real wild plant has just been introduced direct from Taiwan but it remains to be seen whether this proves such a good garden plant. 'Mariko' has a great future for hybridization of low late azaleas.

Endemic to Taiwan.

June–August, either all out at once or over a long period

R. obtusum H3–4 A−5 L1–2 F1–3

Ht rarely above 3 ft (1m). Habit spreading and dense.
L up to 1¼ in. (3·1cm) long, oval to elliptic, glossy green above. More evergreen than *R. kiusianum* or *R. kaempferi*.
F reddish-violet, but bright red, scarlet and crimson forms occur, ¾–1 in. (1·9–2·5cm) across, funnel-shaped, 1–3 per truss. Stamens 5. Best known for its garden varieties. Wild in highly acid soil on three mountains on Kyushu, Japan; may be a natural hybrid. AM 1898.

R. obtusum var. 'amoenum' has rich magenta hose-in-hose flowers and sports occur with reddish-violet and light carmine-red ('coccineum') flowers. There is also form 'album', white. AGM. Placed under *kiusianum* by Ohwi. These are just garden forms, not valid wild varieties. Old gardens such as Caerhays in Cornwall have magnificent tiered specimens of 'amoenum' which are very fine, but for the average garden there are better azaleas. Sometimes suffers winter damage in Scotland. Flowers May.

'Macrostemon'. Low, spreading, late, flowers single, salmon-orange.

R. oldhamii H2–3 A+5 L1–2 F2–3

Ht 4–10 ft (1·22–3m). Habit much branched and spreading with young shoots densely clothed with red-brown hairs.
L to 3½ in. (8·8cm) long, and 2½ in. (6·3cm) wide, with spreading hairs, at first white, later golden.

F salmon-red with lilac-pink blotch, to bright brick-red, 1½–2 in. (3·8–5cm) across, funnel-shaped, 1–3 per truss.

A fine species. Forms some time in cultivation are only suited to mild districts, but those recently introduced may be hardier. Does well in Washington DC. Used at Exbury, England, for hybridizing.

Endemic to Taiwan, from sea-level to 8,000 ft (2,439m) on wind-swept grassy slopes, sandstone cliffs and thickets around lakes. The common red azalea of Taiwan.

May

R. poukhanense H4 A—5 to −10 L1–2 F2–3

Ht up to 6 ft. (1·83m), usually much less. Habit low and spreading or even prostrate (in the wild).
L to 3½ in. (8·8cm) long, usually less, and 1 in. (2·5cm) wide, oblan-ceolate to lanceolate or ovate-lanceolate, semi-deciduous to com-pletely deciduous in cold climates.
F rose to lilac-purple, 2 in. (5cm) across, broadly funnel-shaped, 2 or more per truss. Slightly fragrant. Stamens 10. Opening with or before the leaves.

From central and south Korea and islands off the coasts and Tsushima Islands off Kyushu, Japan, on rocks, in scrub, in light shade and around water courses to summits of hills.

April–May
'Yedoense' ('Yodogawa'). AM 1961. Double form of the above with rosy-purple flowers.

R. pulchrum. Not a wild species but probably a hybrid group.

R. ripense H3–4 A0 L1–2 F2–3

Ht to 6 ft. (1·83m) or more, usually much less. Habit spreading.
L ⅖–2¼ in. (1·1–5·7cm) long, ¼–1 in. (0·6–2·5cm) wide, partly per-sistent, clothed with grey or grey-brown hairs.
F pale mauve or white, 1½ in. (3·8cm) occasionally to the exceptional size of 4½ in. (11·4cm) across, widely funnel-shaped, 1–3 flowered, scented? Stamens 8–10.

This is thought to be the wild form of the well-known 'Mucro-natum' (*ledifolia alba*), only known in several cultivars and therefore not valid as a wild species. *R. ripense* is attractive itself and worth growing in mild districts. AM 1933.

Grows wild in southern Honshu, Shikoku and Kyushu, Japan.

R. mucronatum is a fine azalea with large white flowers and is fairly hardy throughout Britain. Other clones are 'Noordtianum' with even larger flowers sometimes partly rose-coloured, but more tender. Rather open habit. 'Bulstrode' has a faint chartreuse blotch. 'Delaware Valley White' is said to be hardier than *mucronatum*.

The purple or lilac ancestry of 'mucronatum' shows up when it is used for hybridizing, proving that the white genes are subordinate.

May

R. rubropilosum H3 A+10 L1–2 F1–2

Ht 3–10 ft. (1–3m). Habit upright and twiggy or spreading. Young shoots densely clad with appressed hairs.

L up to 2 in. (5cm) long, and $\frac{3}{4}$ in. (1·9cm) wide, convex, oblong-lanceolate to elliptic-lanceolate, crowded at the ends of branchlets. Nearly deciduous or persistent.

F mauve or pink, spotted with mauve, $\frac{3}{5}$–1 in. (1·4–2·5cm) across, 2–4 per truss. Stamens 7–10.

Hardly known in cultivation but probably hardy in warm areas. Wilson says it is very floriferous and should be worth cultivating. Very variable. Endemic to Taiwan, on open grassy slopes, common towards Mount Morrison.

May–June?

R. sataense. A species newly named by the Japanese, seen by American collectors and recently introduced into cultivation. I only mention this because it is now thought to be closer to the Kurumes than either *R. kaempferi* or *R. kiusianum*. It grows on mountains in southern Kyushu with a dense mound-like habit with flowers from pink to purple with broadly overlapping petals and shiny flat to convex leaves. Found on open meadows from 1,500 ft (500m).

R. scabrum H2 A+10 L1–2 F2–3

Ht 3–6 ft. (1–2m). Habit loosely branched.

L large for the series, up to 4 in. (10cm) long and 1½ in. (3·8cm) wide, elliptic-lanceolate to lanceolate.

F rose-red to brilliant scarlet with purple dots, about 2½ in. (6·3cm) across, broadly funnel-shaped, 2–6 per truss. Calyx green, large, up to ½ in. (1·3cm) long. Stamens 10.

A very fine large-flowered species, unfortunately barely hardy anywhere in Britain with flower buds liable to frosting and abortion. Some forms in southern USA are shy-flowering.

Comes from Liu Kiu and Okinawa and other Ryukyu Islands south of Japan on scrubby hillsides and south-facing cliffs.

May

R. serpyllifolium H3–4 A−10 L1–2 F1

Ht up to 4 ft. (1·22m). Habit very thin twiggy growth, much branched. L ¼–½ in. (6–12mm) long, obovate or elliptic, possibly the smallest in the genus, bright green, partly persistent or deciduous.

F rosy-pink or occasionally dark pink or white (var. *albiflorum*), about ½ in. (1·3cm) across, solitary or in pairs. Stamens 5.

This is a dainty plant, not of great garden value but worth growing to add variety to a mixed collection, and certain landscape gardeners may like it. Soft growth in autumn and spring liable to frost damage. Does well in Washington DC. Pretty in the white form.

Wild in central and southern Japanese mountains on volcanic soils and moss-covered boulders.

R. simsii H2 A+10 L1–2 F2–3

Ht to 6 ft. (1·83m). Habit much branched.

L up to 2 in. (5cm) long and ¾ in. (1·9cm) wide, elliptic to oblong-elliptic, dull green above, evergreen or semi-evergreen.

F rose-red to bright or dark red, spotted, 1½–2½ in. (3·8–6·3cm) across, broadly funnel-shaped, 2–6 per truss. Stamens usually 10, rarely 8–9.

This is the chief parent of the popular large-flowered greenhouse azaleas which we all flower in our houses in winter. It is barely hardy anywhere in Britain. These so-called 'Indica' azaleas are a success out of doors in south-east USA. The species received an FCC in 1933 with bright rose flowers.

It has the widest distribution of the series, occurring throughout China except the northern provinces, also being found in Taiwan, and north-east upper Burma at 1,000–8,000 ft. (304–2,439m). Grows in conifer and other forests, thickets, on dry slopes, cliffs, boulders and shingle banks by rivers.

May

R. subsessile

L $\frac{3}{5}$–1$\frac{1}{2}$ in. (1·5–3·8cm) long, $\frac{1}{3}$–$\frac{1}{2}$ in. (1–1·3cm) wide, elliptic to lanceolate, densely clothed with prominent hairs. Persistent.
F lilac to violet-purple, $\frac{3}{4}$ in. (1·9cm) long and about 1 in. (2·5cm) across, funnel-campanulate, 2–4 per truss. Stamens 6–10.

Only just introduced from the highlands of north Luzon in the Philippine Islands. Is unlikely to prove very hardy but is interesting for being the southernmost-growing azalea species. Grows in pine, oak and mossy forest.

R. tosaense H3–4? A0 L1–2 F1–2

Ht 5–7 ft. (1·5– rarely 2·1m). Habit much branched and often erect.
L $\frac{1}{2}$–1$\frac{1}{2}$ in. (1·3–3·8cm) long, $\frac{1}{4}$–$\frac{1}{2}$ in. (6–12mm) wide, lanceolate, elliptic-lanceolate or oblanceolate, evergreen or deciduous, crowded at the ends of branches. Leaves sometimes change to purplish-crimson in autumn.
F lilac-purple to rose-pink, about 1$\frac{1}{4}$ in. (3·1cm) across, funnel-shaped, 1–6 per truss. Stamens 5–10.

Can only be grown successfully in south-west England or in very favoured positions.

Abundant in Shikoku, Honshu, and Kyushu at 0–1,000 ft (0–304m) on exposed slopes or amongst trees and shrubs. Very free-flowering and admired by Wilson.

April–May

R. tschonoskii H4 A—10 L1–2 F1

Ht 1–5 ft. (30cm–1·52m) or rarely to 8 ft (2·44m). Habit erect to a low broad mat. Shoots densely clothed with appressed rufous hairs.
L $\frac{1}{4}$–1$\frac{1}{4}$ in. (0·6–1·9cm) long, $\frac{1}{5}$–$\frac{2}{5}$ in. (0·4–1·1cm) wide, narrow-lanceolate to elliptic-lanceolate, almost completely deciduous, colouring well in autumn.
F white, about $\frac{1}{3}$ in. (0·8cm) across, funnel-shaped, 3–6 per truss. Stamens 4–5.

Very hardy but not of much garden value.

From Hokkaido to southern Japan and south Korea, wide-spread. On rocky mountain tops, shady rocks, cliffs and moist woods.

June

R. tsusiophyllum (tanakae) H4 A none L1 F1–2

Ht to 1½ ft (50cm). Habit prostrate or nearly so, much branched, branchlets covered with brown hairs.
L ⅓–⅖ in. (0·7–1cm) long, ⅛–¼ in. (4–6mm) wide, elliptic to narrowly elliptic, sometimes obovate, rather thick and with a very short leaf stalk.
F white, ⅓–⅖ in. (0·7–1cm) long, tubular-campanulate. Stamens 5.

Usually placed in a separate monotypic genus as *Tsusiophyllum tanakae*. One of the dwarfest of the series, not very showy but is a neat little rarity for the front of the border, peat walls or rock garden.
Mountains of Honshu, Japan, rare.
June–July

AZALEA SERIES (E)

Sub-series Canadense

R. canadense (Rhodora) H4 A—30 L1–2 F1–2

Ht up to 3 ft. (1m). Habit upright and much branched, often stoloni-ferous, sending up shoots some way from the main plant.
L ¾–2¼ in. (1·9–5·7cm) long, ⅓–¾ in. (0·8–1·9cm) wide, elliptic to oblong, dull bluish-green above, completely deciduous.
F various shades of rosy-purple, about ¾ in. (1·9cm) long with a deeply divided corolla, distinct from all other azaleas, in trusses of 3–6. There is a lovely pure white form (var. *albiflorum*) which if isolated, comes true from seed.

A pretty little azalea which should be more often grown. The darkest-flowered forms are the most desirable. Extremely hardy and likes moist situations.

Comes from north-east North America, from Labrador to north-east Pennsylvania and New Jersey, west to central New York. The most northerly azalea species.
April–May

Obtusum Azalea Hybrids

The hybrids of this series are so numerous that it is only possible to mention some of the hybrid groups and a few varieties of each. The vast majority have been raised in Japan and the USA.

KURUME GROUP

Mostly fairly low-growing, with dense habit, flowers single or hose-in-hose, $\frac{1}{2}$–1$\frac{1}{2}$ in. (1·3–3·8cm) across. Early to mid-May. Many are not suitable for northern Britain where the summers are too cool to ripen the wood. Grow in light or heavier shade in warm districts, light shade in southern Britain and full sun in the north where a border against a south or west wall is excellent.

xxx	H3	Azuma-kagami (Pink Pearl), deep pink, hose-in-hose. AM 1960; AGM 1968.
xxx	H4	Hatsugiri, purplish-crimson, low and compact. AM 1956. Fairly hardy in Scotland.
xxx	H3	Hinodegiri, bright crimson, low and compact. AM 1956.
xxxx	H4	Hinomayo, soft pink. FCC 1945; AGM 1968. Fairly hardy.
xxx	H4	Iro-hayama, white margined pale lavender. AM 1952.
xxx	H3	Kirin, deep rose shaded silvery rose, hose-in-hose. AM 1952; AGM 1968.
xxx	H4	Kure-no-yuki, white, hose-in-hose. AM 1952; AGM 1968. Fairly hardy.
xxx	H4	Vida Brown, rose-pink, large flowers, small bush. AM 1960.

KAEMPFERI HYBRIDS

Taller and more upright. Flowers single, 1$\frac{1}{2}$–2$\frac{1}{2}$ in. (3·8–6·3cm) across, mid to late May. These are generally better plants for northern districts than the Kurumes and flower well most seasons in a sunny position. Most have good autumn colour.

xxx	H4	Addy Wery, bright scarlet. AM 1950.
xxx	H4	Betty, orange pink. AM 1940.
xx	H4	Favorite, deep rosy-pink.
xxxx	H4	Fedora, dark pink. FCC 1960.
xxx	H4	John Cairns, Indian red, excellent in north. AM 1940; AGM 1952.
xxx	H4	Kathleen, rosy-red. AM 1962; AGM 1968.
xxx	H4	Naomi, salmon-pink, late. HC 1964.
xxx	H4	Orange Beauty, orange-pink. AM 1945; AGM 1968.
xx	H4	Willy, clear pink, very hardy, excellent in north.

GLENN DALE HYBRIDS

Very numerous, raised in east USA, mostly quite hardy with large flowers. The following have been tested in Scotland.

New H3   Everest, white, very fine large flowers, needs a warm corner.
New H4   Gaiety, pink, late May, good in north, low-growing.
New H4   Galathea, brick-red, unusual colour, good foliage.
New H4   Megan, amaranth-pink with rose dots, free-flowering in north.

GABLE HYBRIDS

American. Several excellent, reasonably hardy varieties.

New H4   Elizabeth Gable, light red, large, hardy.
xx   H4   Rosebud, double rose-pink, pretty, fairly late. AM 1972.

VUYK HYBRIDS

Raised in the Netherlands, similar to *R. kaempferi* hybrids.

xxxx H3–4   Palestrina, pure white, faint green eye. Unsatisfactory in east Scotland. AM 1944; FCC 1967; AGM 1968.
xxx   H4   Vuyk's Rosy Red, rose-red. AM 1962.
xxxx H4   Vuyk's Scarlet, deep red, an excellent variety. AM 1959; FCC 1966; AGM 1968.

There are many other hybrid groups, often suited to the locality in which they were raised.

OTHERS

New H4   Chippewa, rose-pink, hardy, very late.
F3   H3–4   Maxwellii, bright rose-red.
xxx   H4   Mothers Day, red semi-double. AM 1959; AGM 1968.

Indian Hybrids, largely derived from *R. simsii* plus other species. Too tender for culture outdoors in Britain where they are very widely grown as pot plants. Some are hardy as far north as Washington DC in the USA.

Gumpo and Satsuki groups, late flowering, frequently large-flowered and often striped. Only suited to warm districts where there is sufficient sun heat to ripen the wood.

Hirado Hybrids originated from the island of Hirado, Japan. There are many clones, evolved from several species, with large single flowers of many colours, often over 4 inches (10 centimetres) across. Some have been introduced into the USA and Britain but are of doubtful hardiness for the latter. Many are very fine.

8 *Hybridization and its Future*

Aims of Hybridizers

There is much controversy as to what the future holds for rhododendron hybridization. Some people say that there are plenty of hybrids now, that all the best combinations have already been made and that there is little point in carrying on further. Others feel that successful crosses already tried should be remade. Still others hope that by using cold-hardy, drought-resistant or lime-tolerant species, it will be possible to plant rhododendrons over a much greater part of the earth's land surface.

I personally would go so far as to say that rhododendron hybridizing is still in its infancy and that if sufficient skilled knowledge is applied to the subject, many breakthroughs can be made. These would increase enormously the variety of hybrids available for all the growing areas.

Those endeavouring to hybridize with a purpose (there is no point in starting if there is no plan of campaign) should concentrate their efforts towards producing better plants for their own areas or for those with a comparable climate. As rhododendrons are grown in more and more districts, borderline for their successful culture, it becomes increasingly obvious that very specialized hybridizing is necessary. Luckily, there are various known species which show definite resistances to drought, cold, heat, calcium and other extreme conditions. To give an example: in Japan, K. Wada has been working with the heat-tolerant *R. tashiroi* and a special early-flowering form of *R. metternichii*. The latter opens its flowers before the summer heat arrives in lowland Japan. While selected clones of this type may be invaluable for Japan, parts of Australia and the southern states of the USA, they would be of little or no value in Scotland, Scandinavia and north-west America.

In Chapter 3, I have tried to make comparisons between the various rhododendron-growing areas of the world. Those people who find that they have a very similar climate to someone in another country or even continent should get together, compare notes, and co-operate in every possible way to their mutual advantage.

While I do not wish to condemn the very useful groundwork done by past hybridizers such as the great rhododendron garden owners of Britain, I wish to take them to task for lack of foresight. They had little consideration for others who might wish to grow their hybrids. Far too much attention was paid to large gaudy trusses, capable of winning their own hybrid classes at shows, and not enough thought to garden value. Many are of course excellent garden plants, but I feel that this came about as a matter of chance rather than design.

The hybridization policy of Antony Waterer at Knaphill was kept in notebooks by the apprentice, W. C. Slocock, the founder of the nursery of that name. One clue that he gave was always to breed like with like; pinks with pinks, blotched for bigger blotches and so on. This shows good sense.

With the general tendency all over the world to smaller gardens, and the unavailability of hired labour, the great want for the future will be low compact bushes, easily grown and capable of covering the ground to the extent of suppressing weeds under their canopy. Also, people are impatient these days and must have a flower quickly. Far too many old hybrids take years to flower from a cutting and even some dwarf varieties are guilty of this. What will be most sought after will be hardy bushes with nice foliage, that will flower freely at the best season (after frost or before heat) from a young age, will need the minimum of attention to do well and will be easily propagated. I am not saying that other types of plant will no longer be wanted. I sincerely hope that there will always be a demand by the connoisseur for species and the more unusual hybrids.

I shall now suggest a few ideas which are in many cases already being tried out. It must be made clear here that several large species are mentioned. Many of these are represented in the ancestry of quite dwarf hybrids.

DWARF ELEPIDOTES

I feel there is a need here for new blood from species little used in crossing in the past. Certain species such as *R. griersonianum*, *R. discolor*, *R. dichroanthum*, *R. wardii*, *R. forrestii* var. *repens*, *R. williamsianum* and *R. catawbiense* (typical) have been used over and over again, often with excellent results, but these hybrids tend to have

R

that 'I have seen something very similar before' feeling about them. The very best of hybrids from these species, crossed with the new blood suggested below, could bring good results.

Owing to lack of space, staff and, I am afraid, enterprise, enthusiasts in Britain are doing little worthwhile hybridizing these days apart from in a few isolated cases. Chief of these are the Crown Commissioners at Windsor Park who are pioneering with excellent, hitherto rarely used species. *R. yakusimanum* is, of course, being used virtually everywhere that hybridization is going on. While the F1 (first generation) seedlings may be rather disappointing, I feel sure that subsequent generations will produce outstanding results.

A brief list of these little-tried species and some of their virtues may be of some use.

R. aberconwayi, beautiful saucer-shaped flowers. *R. anwheiense*, fine pink flowers freely produced. Hardy. Tough foliage. *R. roxieanum* var. *oreonastes*, most interesting narrow foliage and small globular white trusses. *R. recurvoides* is similar. *R. pseudochrysanthum*, excellent thick handsome foliage, and beautiful flowers. *R. thayerianum*, late white with fine narrow foliage. *R. chrysanthemum* 'Cruachan', FCC, lovely yellow flowers. *R. hyperythrum*, fine pure white flowers and interesting recurved leaves. Can tolerate heat. *R. tsariense*, magnificent indumentum on small leaves. *R. wasonii*, yellow flowers and fine foliage with rufous indumentum.

The main drawback of many species is their slowness to flower, but it may be possible to overcome this failing with less difficulty than imagined. *R. forrestii* var. *repens* and *R. aperantum* are notoriously shy-flowering and yet many of their progeny flower with great abandon. Needless to say of course, always use the best available forms of any species.

LIME-RESISTANT HYBRIDS

Several species have proved more or less tolerant of calcium carbonate and with repeated crossing and re-crossing, great strides could be made. The following species are now being used for this purpose: *R. fargesii*, *R. dichroanthum* ssp. *scyphocalyx*, *R. traillianum*, *R. insigne*, *R. fortunei*, *R. williamsianum*, *R. vernicosum*, *R. decorum*, *R. sanguineum* ssp. *didymum*, *R. wardii*, *R. lutescens*, *R. rubiginosum*, *R. ambiguum*, *R. ciliatum*, *R. hirsutum*, and *R. hippophaeoides*. They are reputed to pass on lime-tolerance to their hybrids. People actually living on alkaline soil should carry out this project themselves.

DROUGHT- AND HEAT-RESISTANCE

I have already mentioned the valuable work being done by K. Wada in Japan. *R. arboreum* and relations are sometimes found at low elevations in parts of the Himalayas, Ceylon and south India where both hot and dry conditions can occur. Wada has found that a low elevation blood-red form is a useful parent and also *R. fortunei* and *R. ponticum*. One plant which possibly has a great future is the low-land form of *R. catawbiense* named var. *insularis*, and the Taliense series shows some promise.

Captain Collingwood Ingram finds *R. moupinense* and its hybrids very drought-resistant. It might be worth crossing this species with late-flowering lepidotes to produce mid-season drought-resisters. *R. racemosum* does very well in north-east USA under hot conditions.

Another species of probable use is *R. chapmanii*, which grows wild (very rare) in the Gulf of Mexico on sand-dunes, where it has to stand considerable heat and drought.

The Malesian species show promise for hot areas where they can be grown outside. Lastly, many Obtusum azaleas bred from such species as *R. simsii* and *R. indicum* can stand considerable heat.

BREEDING FOR INDUMENTUM

Indumentum has proved to be recessive. Species with a dense indumentum such as *R. yakusimanum* at once lose practically all traces of it if crossed with a glabrous-leaved rhododendron. Little work has been done until very recently on crossing species with foliage entirely covered with indumentum. As there are many to choose from, both large and small, there is ample scope and I am sure some interesting results could be obtained. It might be worth trying to cross species with semi-persistent indumentum on the upper leaf surface to try to increase this trait. I would suggest using *R. tsariense*, *R. yakusimanum*, *R. eximium* and *R. chaetomallum*, using of course only those forms that have this character pronounced. Often young foliage of these species is particularly handsome.

BREEDING FOR SCENT

Scent is also recessive. In the elepidotes, only a few large species have a strong scent, so there would be difficulty in transferring it to dwarfs in any strength.

In the lepidotes, again it is mostly the larger species of the Maddenii series plus *R. edgeworthii* which give off the strongest scent, but a few dwarf scented hybrids of this type do now exist, and it should be possible to improve on these for habit and hardiness also.

Some of the paler-coloured large-flowered Malesians have a fine scent, so there is scope here too.

FLOWERING YOUNG

With elepidotes this is a great problem, and many hybrids which are still in nurserymen's lists today take ages to flower. I feel that with a species that is slow to flower there is a different outlook. Species are such interesting plants, often with magnificent foliage. Hybrids are there to give a show. Luckily most dwarf hybrids do flower young. By young, I mean four years or less from a cutting.

Only a few elepidote species fall into this category and yet many hybrids do. There is no doubt that hybridization can lead to freer flower production. Species that help to produce this desired goal are *R. caucasicum*, *R. griersonianum* and *R. ponticum*, plus a few others. Nearly all dwarf lepidote hybrids flower very early in their lives.

HARDINESS

Hardiness is a relative term and is used by most people when referring to their own local conditions.

In north-east America and the continent of Europe, only a very few species can be considered hardy and one or more of these have to be used in the production of a hardy hybrid. In the elepidotes, the North American *R. catawbiense* and *R. maximum* are the most useful, with other members of the Ponticum series such as *R. smirnowii* and *R. yakusimanum*. D. Leach has been raising very promising hybrids by using *R. catawbiense* var. *album* 'Glass'.

In the lepidotes, again the native American species are invaluable, notably *R. carolinianum*, with the exotic *R. mucronulatum*, *R. keiskei* and *R. racemosum* proving useful. In north-east America, it is rare to get a really hardy hybrid using a definitely tender species as one parent in the first generation. Further crossing may bring increased hardiness. In Britain, we could make use of *R. carolinianum*, crossing it with very tender species, especially to improve bud hardiness. Unfortunately, in most cases when used as a seed parent, apomixy results and the Americans and myself have proved that it is not readily compatible with many desirable species. 'Dora Amateis' (*R. carolinianum* × *R. ciliatum*) is a fine breakthrough, but nobody has crossed *R. carolinianum* with the larger Maddeniis to date. Sad to say, *R.* 'Dora Amateis' is sterile so cannot be used for further hybridization.

D. Hobbie has done very valuable preliminary crossing in Germany, largely using *R. forrestii* var. *repens* and *R. williamsianum* with hardy hybrids. It is a pity that he released so many inferior seedlings. Some named clones though, especially reds, are excellent. Taken a stage further, first-class dwarf hybrids with good trusses should appear. Work to this effect is being carried out in the Netherlands.

Dr C. Phetteplace, past president of the American Rhododendron Society, believes that any choice varieties, however tender, should be experimented with.

A new discovery is that reduction in the water content of the stem increases hardiness. See p. 44.

BREEDING FOR FROST-HARDY FLOWERS AND BUDS

This factor seems to be completely neglected. It is not by any means easy to know what species will stand up to several degrees of frost when in flower, because a large number flower after the danger of frost is over. In Britain, where we get frosty spells well after the flowering season has begun nearly every year, this point should be seriously studied. Of the earlier species, I have noticed that *R. dauricum* can stand about 8–10 °F of frost ($-4 \cdot 5$–$5 \cdot 5$ °C) for one or two days and then succumbs. Likewise, some of the Lapponicum series can stand several degrees. These include *R. parvifolium*, *R. intricatum*, *R. microleucum* and *R. hippophaeoides*. On the other hand, nearly all of the early red-flowered species and hybrids are turned to pulp after a night of 3–4 °F of frost ($-1 \cdot 5$–$2 \cdot 25$ °C). *R. moupinense* can usually stand 6–7 °F ($-3 \cdot 25$–4 °C) under a tree but *R. ciliatum* only 2–3 °F. Hybrids containing an easily frosted species like *R. ciliatum* such as *R.* 'Praecox' and *R.* 'Cilpinense' can stand little more than *R. ciliatum* itself. I suggest crossing *R. dauricum* with some of the tough Lapponicums.

My own hybrid *R.* 'Ptarmigan' (*R. microleucum* × *R. leucaspis*) is nearer the tender *R. leucaspis* in flower hardiness, but a more recent cross of mine, *R. carolinianum* var. *album* × *R. leucaspis* can definitely stand 1–2 °F more frost than *R. leucaspis* itself, which points to flower as well as plant hardiness in *R. carolinianum*.

To turn to the elepidotes, *R*. 'Elisabeth Hobbie' has much more frost-resistant flowers than most reds, including its parent *R. forrestii* var. *repens*. This shows promising hardiness in *R*. 'Essex Scarlet', the seed parent. Unfortunately the parentage of *R*. 'Essex Scarlet' is not apparently known.

Many species and hybrids are notoriously bud-tender, although the plant itself may survive quite well. Guilty of this crime are many of the Maddenii and Boothii series and their hybrids. However, it is hard to get these to cross with the tough Lapponicum and Carolinianum series, but there are examples such as *R*. 'Yellow Hammer', so we should persevere with this line of breeding. Those species like *R. pemakoense*, which are bud hardy while still dormant, become very susceptible once the buds start to swell. These should be crossed with later flowering varieties. I find some siblings of *R. pemakoense* × *R. davidsonianum* slightly more bud hardy than *R. pemakoense* itself. Use should be made of late species like *R. ferrugineum*, *R. nitens* and *R. viridescens*.

BREEDING FOR LATE GROWTH

This is another overlooked characteristic. Many perfectly winter-hardy species in east Scotland start into growth at the first hint of mild weather. Particularly bad for this are the few species from north-east Asia where presumably they have to grow as soon as the warm weather comes in order to complete their growth in time. Among these are *R. dauricum*, *R. parvifolium* and *R. chrysanthum*. The two former species have the unusual ability of being able to set flower buds after their first growth is frosted. Bear this early growth in mind when breeding with these three and other similar species, and use late growers to compensate. Early frosted growth usually leads, not only to no flowers, but to bark-split which can kill or severely damage plants of all sizes (see *pp*. 275–6).

LONG DISTANCE CROSSING

As explained in Chapter 5, the genus *Rhododendron* is divided into several more or less distantly related groups. These groups show a natural incompatibility with each other. Many people have been attempting to make wide crosses between lepidotes and elepidotes, deciduous azaleas with elepidote rhododendrons and Malesian species with other groups. On the whole the results have been

disappointing so far. In most cases, even if seed is set and it germin-
ates, the seedlings die in infancy or have badly chlorotic foliage.
Personally, I feel that there is abundant scope for all with the more
compatible species, but I can see the great challenge this type of
breeding has. Even using the various tricks of the trade (see *p.* 250)
to produce fertile seed, it is very hard indeed to get a good garden
plant this way.

Apart from the well-known *R.* 'Grierdal' and the various so-
called azaleodendrons, there are the quite successful *R. racemosum* ×
Obtusum azalea hybrids, recently raised in the Netherlands, and a
cross of C. Ingram's, 'John Marchand' (*R. moupinense* × *R. sperabile*),
which seems to be authentic. A. C. Martin of California has raised
several lepidote–elepidote crosses which show the characteristic
rimless scales of *R.* 'Grierdal'. Also a few similar crosses have been
raised and successfully flowered at Boskoop Research Station, the
Netherlands.

Little result has been had to date with the Malesian species but it
should be possible to cross these with the apparently closely related
Vaccinioides series. Hybrids with *R. kawakamii* from Taiwan, which
is possibly hardy, have so far failed. If anyone does make this breakthrough, it might lead to a few hardy or half-hardy hybrids with the
alpines from Borneo and New Guinea. A very interesting New Zealand hybrid, *R. virgatum* × *R. lochae*, is said to be mid-way between its
parents.

OBTUSUM AZALEAS. The unfortunate RHS *International Rhododendron Register* is inundated with a surfeit of names of hybrids in
this group. Much valuable work has been done in raising these cultivars in Japan, Europe and America. It is in the USA that the naming
spree has largely taken place and that country is still churning out
registered names. On checking through the American Rhododendron
Society's Bulletins, I find no less than twenty-seven named clones of
R. 'Helen Close' × *R.* 'Purple Splendour', nearly all of the unpopular
purple hues. Personally, I feel that no clones should be named until
they have proved themselves to be of garden value and an improvement on existing varieties. While it is within an individual's rights to
name so many clones of one cross, public condemnation of this
practice should put a stop to it.

There is now a tremendous wealth of varieties for warm climates
but there is still ample scope for raising more hybrids for cold summer
areas like Scotland where we cannot flower the vast majority. The

late dwarf red *R. nakaharai* seems promising, as does crossing the hardy *R. kaempferi* group with the Satsuki and Hirado hybrids.

The flowers of some varieties tend to be unstable and can produce streaks and different coloured flowers, as do certain camellias. Many hybrids are double or semi-double and while I am not a great admirer of most double flowers, I feel we could do with more hardy varieties of this type.

LEPIDOTES

Blue lepidotes. Much has been done but several varieties have a chlorotic tendency. Room for improvement yet, maybe using the best forms of *R. scintillans.*

Yellow lepidotes. My own favourite line. There is still scope for improved and hardier hybrids using *R. burmanicum*, *R. chrysodoron*, etc., combined with *R. chryseum* and perhaps *R. carolinianum.* Crossing the deciduous members of the Trichocladum series with evergreen species usually leads to scanty, poor semi-deciduous foliage.

Pink lepidotes. So far, I have found clear pinks elusive but there is a great future in using such species as *R. cephalanthum* var. *crebreflorum*, *R. trichostomum*, *R. racemosum*, certain forms of *R. calostrotum*, *R. carolinianum*, *R. tephropeplum* and *R. charitopes.*

White lepidotes. To cross the white Maddenii series with *R. carolinianum* var. *album* presents a challenge. White albino forms of *R. dauricum*, *R. microleucum*, *R. racemosum*, *R. virgatum*, *R. trichostomum* and others seem to give great hopes of excellent dwarf whites. It has been proved possible to breed whites from pale forms of a species.

Red lepidotes. Little room for manoeuvre here. Only *R. spinuliferum*, *R. kongboense*, *R. cinnabarinum* var. *roylei*, *R. calostrotum* 'Gigha', *R. moupinense* deep rose and *R. campylogynum* var. *cremastum* near-red form, are anywhere near true reds.

Pastel-shaded lepidotes. There are endless possibilities of crossing different colours together, some of which might bring startling results, although the majority will produce muddy tones.

Orange lepidotes. This shade appears to be elusive in dwarfs. *R. concatenans* is about the only hope.

Purple and violet lepidotes. Very neglected, but there are many promising combinations available, using such species as *R. baileyi*, *R. lepidotum*, *R. rupicola*, *R. russatum*, *R. pseudoyanthinum*, some forms of *R. campylogynum* and so on.

Hybridizing at Home

Many keen gardeners consider that the operation of hybridizing is beyond their capabilities. In a few words it can be shown how really simple the whole process is. All that is needed is to apply some pollen of the desired male parent on to the stigma of the female or seed-bearing parent. In most cases pollen readily exudes from the anthers when the flowers are opening or shortly after.

The only precaution I take to discourage bees and flies from carrying out pollinating themselves is to remove the corolla and stamens carefully down to their base, either with my fingers or scissors. This must be done shortly *before* the flower bud opens; avoid touching the stigma in case any pollen should adhere. In multi-flowered trusses, do not keep more than six flowers per truss for pollinating. Label all trusses so treated.

Some stigmas, although immature, may be developed enough for the pollen to germinate, grow down the style and fertilize the ovules. But it is usually better to wait a few days until the stigma is ripe and in a sticky condition before attempting pollination. I always pollinate 2–3 times over a period of about a week so as to give every chance of success. Apply plenty of pollen each time.

SOURCE OF POLLEN

I have found that the majority of species are self-sterile, that is they will not set seed with their own pollen. So, for the seed production of species, it is advisable to collect pollen off a different clone (another plant of the same clone will *not* do).

Pollen still attached to the anthers, if dry will, remain viable for a considerable period when stored in small envelopes. It can be collected in other gardens or even posted from abroad this way.

When hybridizing, occasions arise when a desired cross includes two plants with normally flower at different times of the year. It is quite simple to bridge the gap by storing pollen for several months, which is much easier than forcing the later flowerer in heat. Small gelatine capsules, available at any chemist, make excellent stamen containers. Pick the stamens when dry, if possible when the pollen is just about to burst from the anther, and put them into an opened capsule. Replace the lid and label carefully. Take a glass bottle or test-tube, half fill it with calcium chloride (from any chemist) as a desiccant, put in a layer of cotton wool and place the capsules on top.

Then replace the stopper, which should be as airtight as possible. Store in a cool cupboard. Under refrigeration at 0 °F (−17 °C), pollen will keep for years. It should be pre-dried in a freezer before putting it into the jar with the desiccant. It may be thawed and re-frozen several times, but warm before using.

Young rooted cuttings often flower indoors their first spring and can be used as pollen or seed parents. Grafted shoots with flower buds are a great aid to the hybridizer. Pollinate 2–3 flowers. Very good capsules usually set.

It has become apparent that the seed parent carries the greatest say in the progeny. If there is a choice of seed parents, the plant with the less desirable characters should be used as the pollen parent.

Mention has been made in the first section of this chapter on the different divisions of this genus is divided into and the fact that these can not easily be bridged. Another not so obvious obstacle is caused by polyploidy. Almost all elepidotes are the normal diploids (2n = 26) so there is no problem here. Amongst the lepidotes there are, as well as many diploids, tetraploids, hexaploids, the rare octoploid and even a dodecaploid (2n = 156) (see RHS-RYB, 1950, 78–96).

I have found that diploids are hard to cross with any polyploids, and the late O. C. A. Slocock bore out this statement. The different polyploids seem to cross quite easily amongst themselves. This divides the lepidotes into two groups, diploids and polyploids.

There are various ways of attempting to overcome the reluctance to set seed on widely related varieties. If the difference is in the chromosome count, it may be possible to turn a diploid into a polyploid with the use of colchicine or by other methods. So far only limited success has been achieved. My own efforts on treating small seedlings met with complete failure. Dr August Kehr of Beltsville, Maryland, USA, has raised a tetraploid *R. carolinianum* which should be a tremendous breakthrough for hybridizing. It has been named 'Epoch'. He succeeded by treating the seed but has also failed with treated seedlings.

Other tricks of the trade are to pollinate as many flowers as possible, or to use mixed pollen off two or more different varieties. Another way is to apply the desired pollen and then add mixed compatible pollen two days after. Yet more ideas are to pollinate before the stigma is fully developed; cut off half the style and pollinate the stump; and to apply naphthaline acetamide, 1 per cent in lanoline, on to the corolla stump or the ovary. I have only just begun to test these tricks so cannot vouch for their success.

Most of the resulting seedlings of long distance crosses will be sterile. If the chromosomes can be doubled, sterile seedlings often become fertile. This happens widely in other genera so it will probably work with rhododendrons.

Incompatibility is often the cause of a failure to set seed or of death in infancy. Work is being carried on in the Netherlands to counteract this trait by applying embryologic breeding methods of the germ.

I find myself that with dwarf lepidotes I get about one cross in ten to give a good batch of seedlings. Where there are only a few seeds, they usually germinate poorly and then die in infancy. Most fail to set any seed at all. I have yet to get any good results when the germination is poor. Even in some cases of good germination, the majority of the seedlings may have curious narrow, striped or twisted foliage. Most elepidote crosses produce good seed.

THE RESULTS

Speeding up flowering can be accomplished by various methods also. These are grafting a seedling on to itself, taking a cutting off the top of a small seedling which usually outgrows its parent, restricting the flow of sap to a branch, giving a heavy dose of phosphates, and possibly spraying with cycocel or other chemicals.

To be quite frank, any dwarf hybrid seedling which takes more than ten years to flower naturally from seed is not going to be worth anything these days. It could though, possibly show valuable characters for future hybridizing. Hybrids between two species invariably produce a relatively uniform batch of siblings. Therefore for the F1 inter-specific crosses, there is not much point in raising hundreds of seedlings. But if a further generation is made, by back crossing on to one parent, selfing, crossing two siblings or crossing with another species or hybrid, a much greater variation is to be expected. This often gives the whole range from near each of the original species involved to many combinations between them. Grow as many seedlings as possible in the F2 or subsequent generations as a tremendous variation in garden value may emerge. A very large percentage will be utterly valueless and it may be possible to discard a high proportion in a juvenile state because of poor vigour or foliage. M. Adams-Acton once wrote 'Success in hybridization depends upon being unafraid of a bonfire!'

Colours often lead to surprises. The white azalea *R.* 'Mucronatum' gives an almost complete set of purple seedlings. Red crossed red occasionally produces a yellow. So do not always consider a mistake has occurred if the result is not quite what was expected.

Never judge a seedling by its first effort at flowering, because the first flower buds are often not properly developed. Also, a badly shaped seedling does not necessarily give untidy plants when grown from cuttings, nor does the best and most vigorous seedling necessarily have the finest flowers. When first evaluating one's own progeny, it is all too easy to look at them through rosy spectacles. Names have to be given to clones nowadays, and not to a group (grex) of siblings. With a cross between two species, one often selects and propagates the wrong one. Never name a plant unless friends genuinely agree that it is worthy of an award. Rudolph Henny of Oregon, USA, flowered 30,000 seedlings. He kept 300 and destroyed the rest.

For anyone wanting furher information on hybridizing, I recommend D. Leach's *Rhododendrons of the World*.

9 *Propagation*

The innovations of polythene, electric soil warming cables, 'hormone' rooting substances and so on, have enabled the amateur to propagate much more easily.

If it is desired to reproduce a rhododendron exactly like its parent, some means of vegetative propagation must be applied. This can be divided into three main groups; cuttings, layering and grafting. In the future, a fourth, meristematic progagation, may be added.

When it is not necessary to reproduce the facsimile of an existing plant, seed may be resorted to.

Vegetative Propagation

CUTTINGS

Success with producing plants from cuttings somehow gives rather more satisfaction than from layering. The harder they are to root, the more of a kick can be had out of it when roots appear and a nice healthy plant results. Grafting need only be resorted to when cuttings are next to impossible to root and when layering is out of the question.

The production of young rhododendron plants from cuttings is really not very difficult provided a few simple basic rules are observed. Whatever method is used, be it a heated or cold frame, intermittent mist or pots covered with polythene and so on, the following points hold good. Stagnant conditions must never be allowed to develop in the rooting medium and if water has to be applied frequently, excellent drainage is essential. The rooting medium must always be kept moist but not sodden. The air around the portion of the cutting above soil level must be kept near 100 per cent humidity or the foliage must remain wet. Except in mist, direct sunlight should not reach the foliage but the maximum light possible is needed. This encourages the production of carbohydrates in the cuttings which in turn improves rooting. All frames and other containers should be thoroughly cleaned before use. The rooting medium should be completely replaced with every fresh batch of cuttings and it even helps to put unrooted ones back into a fresh mixture. Always harden off rooted cuttings slowly and carefully.

Propagating facilities

If a new venture of cutting propagation is to be started from scratch, thought should be given to the quantity to be handled and what varieties will be attempted. If only a very few are required for a small garden, it is foolish to go to the trouble and expense of installing a mist unit or a thermostatically controlled frame or pit. A few cuttings can be successfully rooted in sweet jars, a box with a wire cage covered with polythene, pots or pans enclosed in polythene bags or a cold frame. If plans are made to propagate a fair number of plants over several years, it is worth getting something a little more sophisticated.

Small mist units can be acquired which are controlled by electronic 'leaves' or solar controls which turn themselves on when the surface of the 'leaf' dries out or by sunlight. Other mist units are operated manually or by a time switch; these are not suitable for Britain. The idea is to keep the surface of the foliage wet but allow as little run-off as possible. If the mist is on too much, the rooting medium will become flooded, which causes a rapid deterioration of the peat.

Heated frames are usually warmed by plastic-coated cables set at intervals of a few inches, and are set in sand just below the rooting medium. An alternative to this is bare wire or wire mesh, also heated by electricity but with the voltage much reduced by a transformer to make it safe. Plastic-coated cables are commonly used under mist units. These heating wires are thermostatically controlled by a rod-like thermostat in the soil. The optimum temperature for the more difficult varieties is about 75 °F (24 °C) but many easier kinds do not need so much heat. If the rooting is slow, the temperature can be lowered from 75 °F (24 °C) to 60–65 °F (15·5–18·25 °C) after 3–4 months. Many will root well with no artificial heat at all.

These heated frames should be as airtight as possible to maintain the saturated humidity around the cuttings and to save watering. It has now been proved that it is quite unnecessary to lift the cover and dry it off. The condensation that forms on the lid drips back on to the cuttings and is in fact beneficial. Either polythene or glass may be used singly or better still a layer of polythene and glass giving a double covering to improve the fit on the top. This should be level so that the condensation drips back evenly over the cuttings inside. If polythene is used, it should be kept absolutely taut. Overlapping polythene on the lid when damped sticks to the sides when pressed against them, and good airtight conditions can be achieved.

These frames can be in a greenhouse or an outhouse or cellar. In the former they must be carefully shaded from direct sunlight. In the latter two, artificial light is necessary as mentioned for seedlings on pages 263–4. The amount of water needed depends on the airtightness of the frame and how much sunlight reaches it. Under ideal conditions, a thorough watering is only necessary every week or two.

Cold outdoor frames suit most dwarfs very well and are little bother to look after. Ideally, they should be designed in such a way that all direct sunlight is excluded, but as much light as possible reaches the foliage. G. G. Nearing, a pioneer of rhododendron culture in east USA, invented the 'Nearing' frame. This has a hood and sides, with white-painted insides for maximum light reflection. It has to be modified to suit the sun, depending on latitude, and it is important to place it facing exactly due north. In cold climates, the base of the frame should be buried in the ground.

Whether indoors or out, a frame has to be a certain depth to give room for plenty of drainage, 3–4 inches (7·5–10 centimetres) of rooting medium and head room for the cuttings. Drainage, as mentioned earlier, is all-important. It can be provided either by a metal or concrete base full of holes, covering an air space or by different grades of clinker, stones, broken bricks or gravel. Start at the base with a large grade, finishing with fine gravel in which the electric cable can be buried if present. Never place the cable in peat as it can overheat there. Really airtight frames or boxes do not need elaborate drainage because water is seldom applied.

The rooting medium

The best rooting medium is a fifty-fifty mixture of sphagnum peat and sharp sand or fine gravel. The latter must be salt-free. Other media are pure peat, perlite, peat and perlite or one third shredded foam plastic (styrofoam) with one third peat and one third sand or 40 per cent polystyrene pebbles, 40 per cent perlite, 10 per cent peat and 10 per cent ground mica. Only use the best grade of coarse sphagnum peat. Shredded pine bark may be used instead of peat and gives good results. The medium can either be put straight into the frame or mist bench or into boxes, pots or pans. Cuttings often root well around the edge of a pot. Gently level out the rooting mixture but do not firm, as this harms the aeration so necessary for success. The smaller the type of cutting to root, the finer the medium should be, although I never use fine sand. I use peat put through a half-inch riddle for everything and prefer gravel about $\frac{1}{8}$–$\frac{1}{4}$ inch (3–6 millimetres) for the larger varieties and $\frac{1}{16}$–$\frac{1}{8}$ inch (1·5–3 millimetres) for the small dwarfs. The medium should be at least 3 inches (7·6 centimetres) deep. Cover the surface with a thin layer of gravel which helps to check the growth of moss and algae, and make the surface as level as possible.

The peat, after a few months, looses its texture and breaks down into a soggy mess with no air pockets. Hence the need for renewing the medium. For improved aeration, holes can be bored around the base of a frame. Extra oxygen fed into the medium improves rooting.

Taking and making cuttings

When to take: cuttings vary enormously in their ability to root. This variation is further emphasized by the time when they are taken and even from year to year. Francis Hanger once wrote that the larger the leaf, the earlier the cutting should be taken, starting in June and finishing in December. This sounds like a good theory but in practice it is nonsense. Many large varieties, not included here, do not make their growth until August and these cuttings are not ready to take until September or even October. Also, while the easiest dwarf lepidotes may root all right taken in December or even later, these and many more difficult ones will root splendidly when made in July.

Nearly all rhododendron cuttings root best if taken in a half-ripe condition. A half-ripe cutting is one which will bend a little but will break if bent double.

Many dwarf lepidotes make two growth flushes a season, especially as juvenile plants. I find that cuttings off the first flush taken in July root far easier than those from the second, taken in October or later. For the best results under Scottish conditions, Obtusum azaleas should be taken in July, dwarf lepidotes in July or August with a few in September and elepidotes mostly in August. A few Sanguineum types ripen very early and are best in July. It is a fact that dwarfs, coming from high alpine regions with short summer seasons, ripen their wood early, but our prolonged growing season does encourage many of the lepidotes to make second growth. Some growers in America, where summers are hotter, succeed better with cuttings taken between September and November or even March.

Cuttings root better if they have growth rather than flower buds. In many cases with the dwarf lepidotes it is impossible to find any shoots without flower buds on established plants. As the majority of these root easily it does not really matter. With larger varieties such as the Neriiflorum, Ponticum and Taliense series, it should be possible to avoid flower buds. It is often said that these should be removed. With some difficulty, this can be done on the larger varieties but too much damage is liable to be done on the smaller dwarf lepidotes. Thin short side-shoots are best but really poor weak growth should be avoided.

Always collect cuttings when turgid, that is *not* at the end of a hot day. Polythene bags are an absolute boon for holding cuttings and checking evaporation. Do not prepare and insert into the propagating medium when the sun is blazing down.

Preparation of cuttings

Only young shoots of the current year's growth should be used. Older wood may root but it is never so desirable. The old myth of the necessity of a heel of old wood has now died. In many cases the presence of a heel is actually detrimental to rooting. With many dwarf lepidote cuttings that are very short and small, there is no harm in having the base of the cutting at the joint of old and young wood.

I like to trim or carefully pull off all leaves on the part of the cutting to be inserted into the medium, as close to the stem as possible without damaging it. If the leaves are buried they are liable to rot, and this may spread to the whole cutting and neighbours too. Trim off with a sharp knife or razor blade or bend back and pull off with the finger with small cuttings or sever with the thumb nail.

Never make the cuttings too long. For a real dwarf, 1–1½ inches (2·5–3·8 centimetres) is ample and for the larger Neriiflorum series, not over 3 inches (7·6 centimetres). As a rule, about a third to a half of the length of the cutting should be buried, although Leach suggests burying 2 inches (5 centimetres) of a 2½ inch (6·3 centimetre) cutting, right up to the terminal cluster of leaves.

Make the base as clean and as straight a cut as possible, just above a node if available. Most of these dwarfs can now be inserted

s

straight into the medium. If they can be pushed in, well and good; if not, make a small hole with a label, knitting needle, nail or thin dibber. Do not firm, but water in well. With mist no watering-in is needed.

For the larger more difficult cutting, 'wounding' and 'hormone' treatment can be given to encourage rooting. To obtain the best root system, cut a slice down each side of a cutting, just through the bark into the wood below the cambium layer. It is now recommended not to slice right to the base. The wound should be between $\frac{1}{2}$ and 1 inch long (1·3–2·5 centimetres). If the leaves are long, no harm is done by removing about half, cutting cleanly straight across the leaf blade. With the larger leaved varieties, only 3 or 4 leaves need be left on.

Rooting 'hormones'

Various 'hormones' are available in powder or liquid form, usually based on indolebutyric acid. For varieties hard to root, a stronger mixture than is normally available in Britain, is needed. There are three different methods of application. The simplest, but perhaps the least effective, is with a powder form. The others are a quick dip liquid solution and a long soak for twelve or eighteen hours in a weaker solution. The powder should be about 1·6 per cent indolebutyric acid in talc for difficult varieties. In America the liquid sold under the name of 'Jiffy Gro' is quite strong enough and usually has to be diluted. It is said that this, sprayed on the foliage of slow-to-root cuttings, gives quite promising results. Read all instructions carefully and keep liquid rooting substances in a refrigerator as they may deteriorate under normal temperatures.

Fungicides

A fungicide is a great help in stopping the rotting of cuttings of all varieties. I previously used Captan, sometimes mixed into the medium or on the stems which were dipped into the powder. I now use a new general purpose fungicide, Benlate (Benomyl Dupont), for use with cuttings or seedlings. It is partially systemic and can be used for dipping cuttings in or for spraying. It is still expensive but is said to be much better than Captan. 5 per cent in talc is the recommended strength, or one level dessert spoon to a gallon (4·55 litres), and it is available in Britain.

Rooted cuttings

Most cuttings will root within six months in heat and should be potted, boxed or placed in peat benches as soon as they are well rooted. Place back into a closed frame, under mist or a sheet of polythene and harden off, gradually allowing in a little air or less frequent mist spray. This hardening off should be started after one week in winter but must be done more slowly at warmer times of the year. Completion of hardening off should be done in 3 to 5 weeks. Any cuttings not rooted after six months should be re-wounded and placed in a fresh medium. Do not pot up cuttings that only have a few small roots present. As a guide the root ball should be almost equal to the leaf spread. Roots are often very delicately attached and may come from only one point. These need extremely careful handling.

Cuttings in cold outdoor frames should not be disturbed until late spring or summer, regardless of when the roots are formed. These cold frames should only be watered enough to keep the medium moist, provided the sun does not shine on the leaves. In this case frequent watering is needed. In winter very little watering is necessary at all. Cover the frames with layers of hessian or old jute sacks during severe frost.

Never pull out cuttings in the early stages to see if rooting has started, as this will seriously check root development. Later, a gentle pull, without actually removing the cutting, will indicate whether roots are formed or not.

Dwarf lepidotes rooted indoors can be potted singly but they prefer to be put in flats or boxes. The composts mentioned on pages 264–5 for seedlings are also suitable for rooted cuttings. Some varieties, notably the Neriiflorum series, if rooted in heat, find it hard to break their dormant buds. When well rooted and semi-hardened off, transfer into a cold frame and plunge the pots in peat. Cover well in frosty weather. The cooling period encourages growth.

Leaf-bud cuttings

These are not generally recommended. They give a smaller percentage take and are often hard to break away from what is normally an axillary bud. Do not bury the bud as it will rot. These can be useful if material is scarce.

Air rooting

A novel way of rooting cuttings is in air with 100 per cent humidity. There must be a box with mist overhead and water underneath which is heated with an element. A thermostat is set in the air space above the water. This is covered with black polythene and the cuttings are pushed through this into the air space below. Root formation can be watched without disturbance.

LAYERING

This is really quite a simple operation. If just one or two young plants are required, select a few thin outer branches which can be pulled down to the soil-level. If the soil underneath is on the dry side and lacking in organic matter, dig out a little trench and add some leafmould and peat. Do not attempt to root branches that are thick or old. They will be harder to root and much more difficult to establish once removed from the parent plant.

Bend the shoot to be rooted into a U shape, using a peg at the bottom, and if necessary, a stake to hold the shoot upright. After the soil is filled in again over the U bend, a stone may be placed there. This helps to conserve moisture as well as keeping the shoot from springing up at any time. In a damp climate it is possible to layer into a box, making removal after rooting easier and avoiding disturbance to the roots of the parent plant. Too many layers made around an established bush may damage the root system considerably.

Layers vary enormously in the time they take to root. Generally the drier the soil the slower they will be. Under ideal conditions sufficient roots may be formed in one year, in others it may take as much as four to five years. This is especially so with subjects hard to root from cuttings such as the Taliense series, sub-series Roxieanum. Rooting can sometimes be speeded up by slitting the stem above and giving it a little twist, taking care not to break it.

Another method of layering, especially suitable for a straggly drawn specimen, is to lay the shrub on its side, carefully replanting the root ball at an angle and spreading out as many shoots as possible with the tips bent upwards. Cover up with a good friable soil mixture, leaving only the bent tips of the branches above ground-level. Do not heap up the soil too much as it will dry out easily.

When well rooted, most people sever the stem connecting the

layer to the old plant some weeks before lifting. This is to avoid the double check of severance and lifting at the one time. I have not always found this desirable if the soil where the layer is rooted is dry or impoverished or if it is heavily overhung. Prompt removal to good conditions in a moist, shaded nursery bed may save the layer from dying off. Never plant out any layers directly into their final positions. Always leave them for a year or two in a nursery. Rooted layers are best moved in early spring but the autumn is generally satisfactory. Aerial layering for dwarfs is not recommended.

GRAFTING

Use grafting only if all else fails. Only the larger, hard to root semi-dwarfs are likely to be tried. I do not recommend the use of *R. ponticum* as the under-stock, especially for slow growers. In warm climates, *R. ponticum* is highly susceptible to root rot and there is always the threat of suckers. Seedlings closely related to the scion are often ideal.

As grafting is of such minor importance in the propagation of dwarfs, I shall not explain here how to carry out the various different types of grafting. Information is readily available in any good book on propagation.

The standard practice is to graft in a heated greenhouse in January or February on to stocks established in pots and brought into the house some weeks earlier to get the sap running. I use a saddle graft and put the whole pot into a polythene bag with the top kept off the leaves with wire hoops. Tie the top and place on the greenhouse floor out of sunlight. Like all rhododendron grafts, these need very careful and slow hardening off after they are well callused.

Late summer grafting is now becoming more popular, using half hard wood. This can be done out of doors using polythene bags or indoors in a frame or in polythene bags again. If outdoors, wrap the union in clean sphagnum.

An innovation is to graft on to a cutting before it is rooted, using a side graft. Naturally, the cutting used as the stock must be near to the thickness of the scion, and be a very easily rooted variety. One difficulty using this method is in getting the scion to break into growth. Grafting can also be done on to already rooted cuttings.

A variation of this practice is to graft an easily rooted variety on to the top of a difficult subject. The root forming auxins pass down into the cuttings underneath assisting them to root.

Seed

COLLECTION AND SELECTION OF SEED

Far too many people in the past have sown open pollinated seed. In the majority of cases, this has been hybridized by insects, leading to much disappointment. Growing rhododendrons from seed is usually a long-term business although many dwarfs will flower in 3 to 4 years, and some even in one year from seed.

Most dwarfs are easily grown from cuttings, or if these are hard to root, from layers. But for those doing hybridizing, sowing wild collected seed, trying to produce a better or hardier strain of a species or just sowing seed for the fun of it, make sure the source of the seed is reliable. To be sure of the seed of a cultivated species coming true, it must be the only one in flower at the time, too distantly related to be compatible with any other, or hand-pollinated (see Chapter 8).

Collect the seed when the capsules are turning brown or black, or when a sign of splitting can be seen. Most dwarfs ripen their seed earlier than the larger varieties. *R. pumilum* is the earliest I know, being ready about August. The majority ripen in October and November and some, such as *R. chryseum*, do not mature until December. Some people now sow seeds from green capsules, opened in gentle heat, in August, with good results, but at present the old way is still recommended.

Either store straight away in envelopes or put into open containers such as old cups or tins to dry off in a sunny window. Some capsules open naturally, while others need prizing open by hand. Take care not to get much broken capsule and chaff among the seed, as this encourages mould to develop on the seed bed. The seed is best cleaned by using a series of sieves with various mesh sizes. Most alpine species will go straight through a $\frac{1}{32}$ inch sieve, while the larger elepidotes will barely go through a $\frac{1}{16}$ inch. Store in small envelopes or folded paper, and keep in an airtight tin in a cool dry place. If collected fresh, most seed (except Malesian which loses viability after a few weeks) will keep for 2 to 3 years. Under carefully refrigerated conditions, it will remain viable for many years.

SOWING

If a frame with bottom heat is available, plus artificial light, seed may be sown as soon as it is ripe or later if desired. If the seedlings can be kept growing, the longer the season, the larger they will grow before the following winter.

Seed may be sown in pans, either earthenware or plastic, or wooden or plastic trays. Do not sow more than one variety per container because time of germination may vary. Avoid small earthenware pans, as they dry out so quickly. Always use perfectly clean sterilized or disinfected containers to help guard against disease problems. Fill the bottom third with clean broken crocks and/or gravel.

Various sowing media are used with success. I normally use peat put through a ¼ inch (6 millimetre) riddle plus 25 per cent of fresh or dried sphagnum, mixed together. Sphagnum is almost sterile and has mild antibiotic properties which give protection against disease. It contains a perfect moisture balance, once soaked, and gives ideal acid conditions. For the more difficult dwarfs, I cover the surface of the sowing medium with ½ inch (1·3 centimetre) of finely sieved or milled sphagnum. Pure peat or sphagnum or peat mixed with silver sand are also recommended. A percentage of rotten wood may be used with good results, but it should be sterilized because of various fauna such as millipedes.

Fill the container level with the top and gently firm, finishing with as level a surface as possible. Soak in non-alkaline water from the base until saturated, then allow to drain off. Sowing can now take place.

Sow the seed very thinly, especially the small alpine type. Overcrowding encourages botrytis (grey mould) which can rapidly destroy a whole pan of seedlings. Use clean labels, writing on the name, source of seed and date. Never cover the seed. Put in a closed frame, set if possible at about 70 °F (21 °C) and cover with a thin layer of paper, hessian or cheese-cloth to shade. Germination takes place at this temperature after 12 to 20 days, although some may occasionally take longer.

Gradually open the frame when the cotyledons are developing and allow more light, but no direct sunlight. When most of the cotyledons are opened, the pans may be put out on an open bench or can be plunged in sand, old ashes or peat. Keep the temperature at a minimum of 50 °F (10 °C). I cover the seedlings with a sheet of clean polythene for a week or two, turning over if heavy condensation forms. Keep the polythene from touching the leaves.

Either an 18-hour or a full 24-hour lighting can be given by supplementing the daylight in the morning and evening or by growing entirely under artificial light. At present, the best combination for the latter is one Grolux tube to one warm white and one cool white but more perfect lighting may become available soon. In the green-house, I just use warm white tubes controlled by time clocks. The settings are changed according to the time of year to give a total of 18 hours' light. Much quicker growth can be achieved with constant or intermittent light using a fuller spectrum and more heat plus feeding.

During this early period, no watering whatsoever is needed. Cover with a single sheet of newspaper in sunshine. Keep a careful watch for botrytis and pests such as aphids, slugs and mice. Any signs of mould should be carefully removed and a little Captan or Benlate applied in that area. Do not apply Captan initially as it may inhibit germination. Some people soak the pans in a weak solution of potassium permanganate.

The polythene can be removed when the cotyledons are fully developed, but paper should still be used during sunny weather. Better still, use some shield to keep off the sun's rays. Dilute feeding can start once the first true leaves appear, either by soaking or by an overhead syringing applied every two weeks. Syringing with rain or soft water can now be done regularly in a heated greenhouse. When the peat starts to shrink, soak the pans. Drying out may be tested by lifting the pans to test their weight. If a growth of algae appears, cover the surface with a sprinkling of fine sand from a sieve. Some varieties appreciate a little peat through a sieve after germination, to aid in their establishment.

PRICKING OUT

Pricking out can be done whenever the seedlings are large enough to handle, by gently holding the leaves. If the seed has been sown very thinly, the seedlings may be left untouched for a year but some growth will be lost. Space evenly apart in rows in boxes or trays which should be from 2 to 4 inches (5–10 centimetres) deep. These boxes, flats or trays can be any size that is easily handled. Good drainage at the base is essential. This can be provided by wire mesh, narrow wooden slats or wider ones with plenty of small holes bored in them. Always treat wooden boxes with preservative and re-treat after a year or two. After pricking out, place under the mist or in shade or on the floor, or cover with polythene for a few days. Watch out for botrytis all the time and increase heat or ventilation if it appears.

Various media can be used for pricking out. I use 25 per cent beech or oak leafmould, 25 per cent fine gravel, 50 per cent peat put through a $\frac{1}{2}$ inch (1·3 centimetre) riddle, plus 1 ounce of fritted trace elements,

3 ounces of superphosphate, 1½ ounces of potassium sulphate, 1 ounce of ammonium sulphate or another form of nitrogen and 1½ ounce of magnesium sulphate (Epsom salts) per 3 bushels.

Many other equally good composts may be tried, either with a good sandy loam, or soil-less. Some people add a proportion of sphagnum moss or sterilized rotted wood. Certain growers in the east USA advocate sprinkling finely sieved short-growing woodland mosses on the surface of boxes or flats to give the seedlings natural conditions to grow in. This helps to avoid disease troubles. Strong growing mosses, liverworts and ferns must be removed, as they may choke out the seedlings. Overhead feeding helps to speed up growth, applying once a fortnight with syringe or watering-can. There are many suitable preparations on the market. The best include trace elements. Do not feed nitrogen-shy varieties (see Chapter 5).

Seedlings can also be pricked out into outdoor frames during the warmer months of the year or into small pots. The trouble with the latter is that they dry out easily. There is less difficulty over this if the pots are packed close together or if square peat or polythene pots are used. F. P. Knight, past director of Wisley Garden, Surrey, is of the opinion that rhododendron seedlings like company, and hate to be transferred singly into pots. In many cases this theory seems to hold good.

Epiphytic, Malesian or Vaccinioides species or hybrids usually grow best in pure sphagnum or sphagnum plus leafmould, peat and/ or gravel. The growing sphagnum gives the semi-natural conditions which are ideal for these plants.

SOWING SEED WITH NO GREENHOUSE

For those with no heated frames or greenhouse, excellent results can be obtained by using clear plastic food containers with a clear lid, or preserving jars or small aquaria covered with glass. Holes may be made in the bases of the plastic containers. Otherwise there are no drainage holes, so great care must be taken not to over-water. Sowing is best done early in the year.

Place a layer of gravel in the base of the container, then fill with any of the media previously mentioned. Leave plenty of room at the top of containers for growth to develop. Keep the covers on until cotyledons are formed or the first true leaves appear. Open them up gradually over several days or the seedlings will collapse. Again no watering is necessary until the cover is removed. Be careful not to let the seedlings become weak and spindly due to lack of light. Place by a north window or use artificial light, but avoid direct sunlight. Pricking out may be done at the same stages as mentioned earlier.

SOWING OUTSIDE

If there is no hurry over the growth of seedlings, seed can be sown in a cold frame in April. An interesting alternative for surplus seed if available is to use a shaded mossy bank or rotten tree stump as a seed bed. Again, it is better to avoid positions that receive direct sunlight.

Growing On of Young Plants

Many young plants are lost during the stage from greenhouse or frame to becoming established out of doors. Just as a rooted cutting or seedling, when first transferred from propagating bench or seed pan, needs careful attention, so does the same plant when first venturing outside. The precautions taken all depend on the climate and the varieties involved.

All exceptionally small plants and any of doubtful hardiness should spend their second winter in a greenhouse, cold frame or lath house. For these, a soil mixture similar to that used for pricking out or potting can be used; or for a greenhouse bed plenty of peat, leaf-mould or pine needles should be well forked in. Lath houses are made of slatted wood or metal, usually with a 50 per cent air space between the slats. These structures give about a 5 °F protection against frost as well as shade and shelter from wind. They are very popular in America and are even used for growing on a collection of the more tender or difficult varieties.

In east Scotland I do all my planting-out in May and June into nursery beds. Even those two year old plants wintered under cover are not put out until the danger of frost is over, because they invariably start into growth earlier. All plants in pots and boxes are first cooled off indoors with all the ventilators left open night and day for a week or two. Then they are set outside in a semi-shaded position for another ten to fifteen days before finally being planted into the nursery.

All root balls are made thoroughly damp before planting. The beds are either hand forked if small or rotovated with 2 to 4 inches (5–10 centimetres) of peat and leafmould plus a little slow-acting fertilizer and all are well mixed into the existing soil. These beds are watered overhead a day before planting if at all dry, The plants are put in with trowels with about $\frac{1}{2}$ inch (1·3 centimetres) of soil over the root ball and are well watered in immediately. In our cool climate it is not necessary to shade these plants except for a few of the more difficult and shade-loving varieties. On no account is the soil allowed to dry out. If it does, the sprinklers are put on for two to four hours, giving the beds a good soaking.

Where only a handful of young stock is concerned, similar modified treatment can be given. In warmer climates it is usually essential to apply shade for the first season at least. This can be done by fixing bamboo slats, snow fencing, thin hessian, etc. on overhead wires attached to posts. Beds can be mulched to retain moisture and shelter fencing erected if shelter from wind is lacking.

Naturally, careful weeding should be carried out where necessary. Hoeing is better avoided, but if done, only hoe very shallowly.

Very small plants are liable to be thrown out of the ground by frost during their first winter. These should be replanted and gently firmed up.

Many dwarfs need no pinching to produce a good habit, but most Obtusum azaleas and rhododendrons such as 'Yellow Hammer' benefit from constant pinching, both indoors and after planting out. Certain rhododendrons can be over-pinched, resulting in weak stems which bend down with the weight of flowers, leaving a hollow centre.

Cuttings rooted in cold frames can be transferred to other cold frames which will need shading until established, after which the lights can be removed to be replaced for the winter. Allow plenty of head-room, as shoots touching the glass or other coverings are easily frosted. Leave a little aeration all winter.

Young grafts are shaded in a lath house or similar position for their first season, and so are recently lifted layers.

MYCORRHIZA

Root hairs are normally lacking in rhododendrons which instead have a mycorrhizal association which is a form of symbiotic partnership of fungi and roots. Not much is known about how the partnership works and whether it is to the mutual advantage of both parties. In a sterile medium of sand or sphagnum, rhododendrons will produce root hairs, and provided adequate nutrients are present, will grow happily. As soon as normal soil conditions are introduced, the root hairs disappear and the mycorrhiza take over.

10 *Pests, Diseases and Disorders*

Pests

Rhododendrons are remarkably free of trouble caused by pests compared with most other cultivated plants. There are in fact quite a number of insects which *can* cause damage, but this is so rarely severe that only the most common will be mentioned here. Apparently in America insects can be more of a bugbear than in Britain where it is uncommon for anyone to carry out a regular programme of insecticide spraying or dusting. My advice is never to start spraying unless it is absolutely necessary. It is only adding pollution to our already vastly over-exploited world, and once spraying starts, the balance of the prey and predator relationship is upset and all the more spraying will have to be done. Always follow all instructions on the containers carefully.

Pests can be divided into two categories: vertebrates and invertebrates. To be quite frank, here at Glendoick the vertebrates are by far the most annoying. Roe deer eat the leaves and shoots and rub off bark, hares and rabbits nibble shoots and eat bark, and moles loosen up and even throw out newly planted dwarfs. Titmice ruin flowers by pecking for nectar, especially red flowers, and man tramples about on beds consolidating the soil. Even mice can strip leaves off cuttings and dogs urinate on and burn out portions of a plant which may actually die. For effective exclusion, deer need a 6 foot 6 inch (1·98 metre) to 8 foot (2·44 metres) fence and rabbits and hares 3 feet 6 inches (1·067 metres). Rabbits are especially fond of Obtusum azaleas and the Saluenense series and the 'blue' hybrids. Feeding tits on nuts and fat helps to keep them occupied.

INSECT PESTS

Along with fungus diseases, insect pests are more liable to attack unhealthy plants and ones growing under unsuitable conditions. In

America all-purpose sprays are often used by nurserymen to deal with insect and fungus attacks. Again I wish to stress that unless this is found to be absolutely necessary, it is bad practice. Likewise, persistent insecticides of the organochlorine group (such as DDT and aldrin), where not already banned, should only be used if there is no alternative available. Unfortunately, truly systemic insecticides are still highly poisonous but may in future be the answer.

Weevils

Various species of weevil can cause damage. The adults chew notches out of the edges of the leaves and the larvae which live in the soil, girdle the roots or the stem below ground-level. While the leaf damage is rarely more than unsightly, the larvae can cause unhealthy foliage and wilting in severe attacks. This latter trouble is uncommon in Britain.

The most usual species are the vine, clay-coloured and strawberry weevils but two species of 'woods' weevil are now becoming serious pests in America. The latter are resistant to aldrin and dieldrin, and their increase is probably due to the control of the other previously more prevalent species by these insecticides. Dr Phetteplace, past president of the American Rhododendron Society, reckons that weevils are the most serious and widespread insect pests of rhododendrons.

These woods weevils tend to eat a bigger proportion of a leaf than the others and have a wide variety of alternative food plants. Also eggs hatch at almost any time of the year. This habit together with their resistance to insecticides make them very hard to control. One desperate measure to save a plant is to lift it, wash off all soil (plus larvae) and replant in clean ground.

The other weevils are difficult to control too. The adults may be poisoned with baits containing a proprietary poison (depending on local availability) or the larvae may be killed by using a soil insecticide. The best are still the nasty poisonous aldrin, dieldrin and BHC. Adults can be sprayed in June to August with malathion or diazinon by drenching the soil or mulch. The latter is quite effective on woods weevil adults.

Aphids

These are usually only troublesome indoors on young seedlings and rooted cuttings, especially Obtusum azaleas, and young or older

Malesian varieties. They distort young growth and, if numerous, weaken the plants. Spray, fumigate or dust with malathion.

Thrips

These also can be annoying indoors on foliage, especially under hot dry conditions, and are also bad in certain districts outdoors such as the Auckland area of New Zealand. They rasp away the tissues and suck the juices. Treat as for aphids.

Rhododendron and azalea whitefly

These feed on the leaf underside, causing yellowing and mottling. A black sooty mould may form on the honeydew secretion which is unsightly. The azalea whitefly chiefly attack *R.* 'Mucronatum' and its allies but not Kurumes. The rhododendron whitefly is usually found on varieties free of scales, indumentum and without a thick epidermis. Control with malathion or diazinon in early autumn.

Caterpillars

Various species can be troublesome in woodland conditions, especially on soft woolly young foliage as found in the Neriiflorum and Taliense series. Usually they are not plentiful enough to cause severe damage. They are easily spotted by the eaten foliage and are commonly found in a rolled-up portion of the leaf. Control is easiest by hand picking and killing the individuals.

Red spider mites

Again these are generally severe indoors only, especially on azaleas. The leaves get a whitish or grey appearance and minute webs are formed. They can be bad out of doors in very hot dry weather. Azaleas in south USA may be badly attacked. These mites can be discouraged by shade and moisture. Spray with malathion or diazinon, or use predator mites.

Asiatic beetles

The various species of Asiatic beetles are found in the eastern USA only. These cause very similar damage to the weevils, both to leaves and roots. The leaves, which are attacked from June to August, can be sprayed with malathion. The larvae may be controlled with chlordane sprayed on to the soil.

Various other insects may cause damage in isolated cases, especially in warm areas like south-eastern USA.

Diseases

Rhododendrons grown under suitable conditions suffer very few ills; in fact there can hardly be any more trouble-free plants. Unfortunately the majority of people attempting to grow these plants do not live in districts where anything like an ideal climate or soil occurs. More and more places are now being considered as possible rhododendron areas, due to improved methods of culture and new varieties.

It would appear that the further from perfection a region is, the more liable rhododendrons are to attacks from disease. In Britain we rarely treat our rhododendrons against diseases and generally get away with it. In America, with much greater extremes of climate and often thoroughly unsuitable soil, diseases can prove disastrous and in a few areas special remedies have to be taken for any success at all.

ROOT ROT (PHYTOPHTHORA WILT)

This is probably caused by three species of *Phytophthora*. It is perhaps the most important disease in America and it is said to occur under certain conditions in the Netherlands and New Zealand, and in containers in Britain. It is worst at high temperatures, over 80 °F (26·75 °C), and in moist situations, especially if the drainage is poor. It can occur at all stages from a cutting to mature specimens. A very low pH seems to control the trouble but this is obviously impractical. Plants that show symptoms in high temperatures and humidity never recover.

The disease starts by attacking the young roots and gradually the whole root system dies. Leaves may turn a dull yellowish-green and then the affected plant soon wilts permanently and dies.

This disease has spread in recent years and is encouraged by container growing where higher temperatures reach the roots than normal and moisture is more difficult to control. In California, alpine varieties are very susceptible. Eelworms often let in the disease to the roots and it is spread in soil-water.

Control

Adequate drainage and avoidance of over-watering in high temperatures are all-important. Promising materials for control are Dexon (Bayer & Co, Germany) and Terrazole (Olin Mathieson Co). Read instructions carefully. The pathogens themselves are difficult to identify, being microscopic. The cell sap has to be examined.

STEM AND TIP BLIGHT (PHYTOPHTHORA CACTORUM)

In this case the stems are attacked first rather than the roots. The stems shrivel and the leaves become discoloured and wilt which can spread and kill a whole bush.

Control

Good drainage and sanitation are essential, as are properly balanced soil minerals. Prune off and burn affected branches and allow more light and air movement. Various sprays can be used effectively after flowering.

Another wilt and blight disease has appeared in the USA, caused by various species of *Cylindrocladium* which moves around with shipments of azaleas. It is a real killer of azaleas at temperatures over 70 °F. It differs from Phytophthora in that black fungus bodies form on the undersides of leaves which are absent in the latter.

HONEY FUNGUS (ARMILLARIA MELLEA)

This fungus is common in Britain and other countries and normally lives on dead plant tissues. Unfortunately it frequently becomes a pathogen. In Britain gardeners from all over the country complain of substantial losses. In many west of Scotland and south-west England gardens, one or more rhododendrons plus other shrubs, trees and even herbaceous plants are lost every year. Susceptible plants are those which have suffered damage to the roots through bad drainage or wind-shake. This damage may not be noticeable from the general appearance of the plant. Some may die off branch by branch while others suddenly collapse, shortly after showing unhealthy foliage symptoms such as leaf-drop and chlorosis.

Tree stumps are the usual source of infection. Long brown or black bootlace-like strands wander about in the soil from the stumps and may attach themselves to a rhododendron root; if the plant is unhealthy they may eventually kill it.

Armillaria rarely acts as a pathogen in America although it occurs quite widely. It may perhaps be a different species from that we suffer from in Europe.

Control

Removal of stumps and roots is the best cure, plus good drainage and healthy plants. Unfortunately, the removal of stumps and roots may be impracticable, as are the other suggested remedies of renewing the soil or sterilizing it with 2 per cent formalin. A possible help is refined creosote, sold in Britain under the trade name 'Armillatox'. Fibrous-rooted shrubs like rhododendrons are damaged by it, but the trunks of larger specimens may be carefully treated if infected near the base. Areas well away from trees are unlikely to be affected.

PETAL BLIGHT (OVULINIA AZALEAE AND OTHER ORGANISMS)

This is quite a serious disease which has become more widespread in recent years. It damages the flowers only, chiefly Obtusum azaleas, but also occasionally rhododendrons and deciduous azaleas. It starts in damp weather as little brown spots on the flowers and these rapidly spread, turning the whole flower to pulp which sticks on the branches and remains very unsightly. Three different fungi are involved, causing similar symptoms, but these have not been accurately identified in Britain.

Control

Methods of control are similar for all three pathogens. Avoid over-head watering when plants are in flower. If the trouble has started or is expected, the bushes may be sprayed with Zineb two or three times a week. Copper-lime dust, dusted over all buds, is moderately effective. Bordeaux mixture 2–2–50 is more successful but needs many applications. The new American fungicide Benlate (Benomyl) is partly systemic and should be applied once a week in spring. Covering the beds with several inches of mulch may stop the production of spores from the resting structures in the ground.

GALLS

These are common on many Obtusum azaleas, the Ferrugineum

T

series and its hybrids. They appear as ugly green, pink or reddish swellings on leaves, stems or even flowers, and later turn white when sporing. In a light attack, hand-pick and burn. If severe, spraying may be necessary. This nuisance is worst in wet climates. Apply Zineb, Ferbam, Bordeaux mixture, Captan or Benlate.

RUSTS

Several species of rusts attack different groups of rhododendrons and often have alternative hosts on other shrubs and trees, especially *Picea* and *Ledum*. They are not commonly met, but can be serious on susceptible hosts. In Britain, these alternative hosts rarely grow in close proximity to rhododendrons, so rarely bother the latter. They usually appear as orange powder on the leaf undersides.

Control

Either burn affected plants or destroy the leaves and spray or dust the rest of the bush with a locally recommended fungicide. Benlate is effective.

BUD BLAST

This disease does not seem to have been getting any more troublesome in recent years. Flower buds die and black spore-producing bristles appear, also on the capsules. *R. caucasicum* and some of its hybrids are susceptible. It is probably spread by a leaf hopper.

Control

If very serious, spray against the leaf hopper. Normally collection and burning of dead buds gives an adequate control. Spraying may be done with a fungicide after flowering.

LEAF SPOT

While various pathogens may cause leaf spots, these commonly result from too much shade and moisture or poor root conditions. They are most common on old neglected collections or after a very wet summer, and can be serious in eastern America, where spraying may be necessary with Captan or Zineb.

BOTRYTIS (GREY MOULD)

A mould common on young seedlings which was discussed on *p.* 264.

LICHEN

This might be classed as a disease although it is in fact a symbiotic association of a fungus of single-celled algae. It is particularly troublesome in wet districts, especially on azaleas lacking in vigour. Liberal top dressings (see Chapter 4) to increase growth, and cutting out old wood, are a great help. Unfortunately fungicidal sprays are liable to damage the leaves of evergreen varieties. Use carbolic soap and a nail brush if only a bush or two is affected.

NATURALLY OCCURRING DISEASES

Dwarf rhododendrons are remarkably free of endemic diseases and pests but the following have been recorded from various parts of the world: galls on leaves and shoots of *R. ferrugineum* and *R. hirsutum* in the Alps of Europe; *R. lepidotum* with rust in Nepal; *R. primuliflorum* with leaves attacked by fungus; seed capsules destroyed, especially *R. fragariflorum*; and indumentum on the leaf undersides in the Sanguineum sub-series with fungus which turns it a dark coffee colour. A few fungi also attack bigger species.

Natural Injury and Malnutrition

As mentioned in Chapter 2, frost is one of the major hazards most rhododendron growers have to contend with. Young growth can be completely frosted, resulting in its withering away or falling off and necessitating new growth to be made from dormant buds. This growth is never as satisfactory as the primary and often leads to the failure to set flower buds. Many varieties grow early but by careful siting it can be possible to minimize the damage. Half-frosted growth often looks diseased, usually being distorted, puckered, one-sided or even partly chlorotic. This damage may come when the growth buds are just beginning to expand.

A sharp frost when the sap is flowing very often leads to bark-split which can affect a plant from ground-level up to second-year wood. When the bark starts to dry, it opens, peels back off the stem and leaves an ugly wound. If all the bark curls back, the plant or stem will die, and if not quite so severe, the stem may survive a year or two and heal up or die subsequently. Affected trunks or stems can be bound with tape but it is really too late to do this once the bark curls back. The base of the stem may be protected by wrapping with hessian or burlap until the frost danger is over. Fungus diseases may enter the wounds and cause bark, trunk or root decay.

Incorrect planting or failure to guard against wind-shake can lead to root damage and hence susceptibility from fungus attack. Too deep planting may cause chlorosis, lack of vigour and eventual death.

Chlorosis can occur for a variety of other reasons, such as inadequate drainage or an exceptionally wet season or, of course, from an imbalance of plant nutrients. It is very hard to diagnose the various deficiences and toxicities from the type of chlorosis present, but a rough guide may be a help. Add elements as recommended in soil analysis.

DEFICIENCIES

Nitrogen. Stunted growth, leaves dwarfed and a uniform light green. They shed early. Flowers are scarce and too small. Add as ammonium salts, not nitrates.

Phosphorus. Foliage darker than normal and growth retarded. Leaves may turn purplish or reddish-bronze and the lower leaves may turn brown and fall off. Add any form of phosphate.

Potassium. Dead areas may appear on older leaves, following orange mottling or yellowing of the margins. The tips or edges may curl and then drop off. Best applied as potassium sulphate.

Magnesium. Chlorosis between the veins, often nearly yellow. Present in chlorophyll. Add Mg sulphate (Epsom salts).

Iron. Severe interveinal chlorosis and young leaves initially yellow, the whole plant eventually becoming chlorotic. Add iron chelate. Other forms of iron are rarely available to the plants.

Calcium. Growth stunted, yellowish between veins on young leaves, and tip scorching, shrivelling and die-back. Add gypsum (calcium sulphate).

Trace elements. Various forms of chlorosis, lack of growth or distortion. Add fritted trace elements (see Chapter 4).

11 *Recommended Lists*

Species

EASY SPECIES

calostrotum, degronianum, ferrugineum, glaucophyllum, impeditum, keleticum, lepidostylum, microleucum, pemakoense, racemosum, scintillans, yakusimanum.

FOR FULL SUN IN NORTHERN AREAS (INCLUDING SCOTLAND)

campylogynum, camtschaticum, carolinianum, fastigiatum, intricatum, keleticum, kotschyi, lepidotum, racemosum, scintillans, trichostomum, williamsianum.

FOR SHADE

aperantum, chamae-thomsonii, chaetomallum, chrysanthum, citriniflorum, forrestii var. *repens, sanguineum.*

FOR THE CONNOISSEUR

baileyi, cephalanthum var. *crebreflorum, forrestii* var. *repens, kongboense, lowndesii, ludlowii, megeratum, parmulatum, pumilum, recurvoides, sargentianum, setosum.*

VERY LOW-GROWING OR PROSTRATE

campylogynum var. *myrtilloides, camtschaticum, cephalanthum* var. *crebreflorum, chrysanthum, forrestii* var. *repens, hanceanum* 'Nanum', *imperator, lowndesii, prostratum, proteoides, radicans.*

FOR FOLIAGE

campanulatum var. *aeruginosum, dasypetalum, fastigiatum, haematodes, lepidostylum, leucaspis, makinoi, metternichii, pseudochrysanthum, roxieanum* var. *oreonastes, tsariense, viridescens, wasonii, williamsianum, yakusimanum.*

FOR BEAUTY OF FLOWER

callimorphum, calostrotum 'Gigha', *cephalanthum* var. *crebreflorum, charitopes, forrestii* var. *repens* or *chamae-thomsonii, haematodes, leucaspis, moupinense, russatum, scintillans, trichostomum, williamsianum, yakusimanum.*

VERY HARDY SPECIES FOR WESTERN EUROPE

camtschaticum, carolinianum, caucasicum, chrysanthum, fastigiatum, ferrugineum or *hirsutum, hippophaeoides, keiskei, parvifolium, racemosum, yakusimanum.*

VERY HARDY SPECIES FOR NORTH-EASTERN USA

carolinianum, caucasicum, degronianum, hippophaeoides, keiskei, metternichii, racemosum, yakusimanum.

FOR MILD GARDENS

burmanicum, chrysodoron, ciliatum, edgeworthii, leucaspis, pendulum, sperabile, spiciferum, sulfureum, tephropeplum, valentinianum, virgatum.

EARLY-FLOWERING

beanianum, chamae-thomsonii, chrysanthum, ciliatum, leucaspis, moupinense, parvifolium, sulfureum.

LATE-FLOWERING

brachyanthum, campylogynum, dichroanthum, sanguineum ssp. *didymum, ferrugineum, nitens, santapauii* (tender), *trichostomum, viridescens.*

FREE-FLOWERING

calostrotum, campylogynum, chryseum, glaucophyllum, fletcherianum, hanceanum 'Nanum', *hypenanthum, impeditum, pemakoense, racemosum, scintillans, tephropeplum, trichostomum.*

ALKALINE SOIL WITH pH OVER 7 (SEE CHAPTER 4)

ciliatum, sanguineum ssp. *didymum, hippophaeoides, hirsutum, scyphocalyx, williamsianum.*

Hybrids

EARLY-FLOWERING

Bo-peep, Cilpinense, Talavera (Golden Oriole group), Praecox, Ptarmigan, Seta, Snow Lady, Tessa and Tessa Roza.

VERY COLD AREAS −10 °F (−23 °C) FOR WESTERN EUROPE

Bluette, Conemaugh, Cutie, Dora Amateis, Elizabeth Hobbie, Baden Baden, Ems, Lenape, Pink Twins, P. J. Mezzit, Purple Gem (like Ramapo, Wilsoni, Windbeam, Wynokie.

NORTH-EASTERN USA

Anna Baldsiefen, Canary, Conemaugh, Cunningham's Sulphur, Dora Amateis, Guyencourt hybrids (Lenape, Chesapeake, etc.), Jacksonii, Mary Fleming, Myrtifolium, Purple Gem, Ramapo, Wilsoni, Windbeam, Wynokie, *yakusimanum* hybrids.

DWARFS 1–3 ft. (30–91cm), hardy to 0 °F (−17¾ °C)

Carmen, Chikor, Curlew, (*hanceanum* × *keiskei*), Jenny, Pipit, Prostigiatum, Ptarmigan, Rose Elf, Sapphire, Sarled.

SEMI-DWARFS 3–5 ft. (91cm–1·52m), hardy to 0 °F (−17¾ °C)

Blue Diamond, Bowbells, Elizabeth, May Day, Moonstone, Olympic Lady, St Breward, Unique.

Obtusum Azaleas

SPECIES FOR COOL AREAS

kaempferi, kiusianum, nakaharai, poukhanense, tschonoskii.

SPECIES FOR MILD AREAS

indicum, macrosepalum, oldhamii, ripense, scabrum.

HYBRIDS FOR COLD AREAS

Chippewa, Delaware Valley White, Fedora, Favorite, Gaiety, John Cairns, Kure-no-yuki, Naomi, Vuyk's Scarlet, Willy.

Appendix A

Rhododendron Collectors

Space unfortunately does not permit a list of what plants each collector introduced into cultivation. The early, major and minor collectors are grouped separately, giving the dates they collected and where they went. Those who collected in and for their own countries are not mentioned.

EARLY COLLECTORS IN CHINA AND JAPAN

These people brought little into cultivation.

Captain R. Wellbank: 1808, South China, Azalea 'indica' (*R. simsii* varieties).

R. Brinsley: 1841, Hong Kong.

R. Fortune: 1844–5, 1848–51, 1853–6, South China, more Azalea 'indica' and nothing else except *R. fortunei*.

C. Maximowicz: 1859–64, Manchuria and Japan.

R. Oldham: 1861–4, Japan, Korean Archipelago and Taiwan, *R. oldhamii*.

J. M. Delavay: 1868?–95, Yunnan, seeds sent to France. Very extensive botanical collections.

P. G. Farges: 1892–1903, NE Szechwan. Sent few dwarf rhododendrons if any.

P. J. A. Soulié: 1866–1905, Szechwan–Tibet frontiers. Sent back few seeds.

MAJOR COLLECTORS

Sir J. J. Hooker: 1848–50, Sikkim, E. Nepal and Khasi Hills (Assam).

E. H. Wilson: 1900–11, W. Hupeh and W. Szechwan; 1914–19, Japan, Korea and Taiwan. Found and introduced many dwarf rhododendrons and azaleas into Britain and USA.

G. Forrest: 1910–32, NE. upper Burma, Yunnan, W. Szechwan and SE. Tibet. He introduced more dwarfs than anyone else. Seeds were widely distributed in Britain.

R. Farrer: 1914–15, Kansu; 1919–20, NE. upper Burma. Seed sent to Britain.

F. Kingdon Ward: 1911–54, Bhutan, NEFA, SE. Tibet, W. Szechwan, Yunnan, Burma, Nagaland, Manipur and Khasi Hills (Assam). Covered a greater area over a longer length of time than any other collectors and introduced almost as many dwarfs as Forrest. Seed well distributed in Britain and a little to America.

J. J. Rock: 1923–48, SE. Tibet, Yunnan and Kansu Covered rather similar ground to Forrest but introduced some new species and many fine forms into America and Britain.

Hon. H. D. McLaren: 1932–8 (using G. Forrest's collectors).

F. Ludlow and G. Sherriff: 1933–49, Kashmir, Bhutan and SE. Tibet. Explored passes in Himalayas thoroughly. A restricted distribution of seed to Britain. Several new species never established in cultivation.

MINOR COLLECTORS

W. Griffith: 1835–8 and 1838–42, Assam and Bhutan.

E. Madden: 1841–50, N. India.

T. J. Booth: 1849–50, W. NEFA.

J. E. T. Aitchison: 1879, Afghanistan.

E. E. Maire: 1905–16, Yunnan.

R. E. Cooper, 1913, Sikkim, seed?; 1914–16, Bhutan; 1924, Burma, seed?

K. A. H. Smith: 1921–34, Szechwan, SE Tibet (briefly). Introductions into Sweden.

F. M. Bailey: China, NEFA, 1911, NEFA, SE Tibet, 1913, 1927, Bhutan; 1936–7, Nepal Seed?

Hu (collector Yu): 1937, N. Yunnan and Szechwan.

A. N. Steward (with Chiao and Cheo): 1925, Kweichow; 1931, Hupeh.

N. L. Bor: 1938–41, India.

O. Polunin: 1949; Polunin, W. Sykes and J. Williams: 1952; Nepal. Mr & Mrs C. R. Stonor; 1954, Nepal.

J. D. A. Stainton, W. Sykes and J. Williams: 1954; J. D. A. Stainton: 1956; Nepal.

J. L. Creech: 1955, 1956 and 1961, Japan; 1967, Taiwan.

A. F. Serbin: 1959, Yakushima, Japan.

u

T. M. Spring-Smyth: 1961–2, Nepal.

J. L. Creech and F. de Vos: 1962, Nepal.

P. A. Cox and P. C. Hutchison: 1962, NE Turkey; 1965, Khasi Hills, NEFA and W. Bengal, India.

F. Doleshy: 1965– 67– 69–70–71, Japan.

A. D. Schilling: 1968, Nepal.

J. J. R. Patrick: 1969 onwards, Taiwan and Hong Kong.

I. Hedge and P. Wendelbo: 1969, E. Afghanistan.

M. Black: 1970, E. Nepal.

L. W. Beer, C. R. Lancaster and D. Morris: 1971, E. Nepal.

MALESIA

T. Lobb: 1845–54–55, Malacca, Java, Borneo, Sumatra and Celebes.

C. Curtis: 1884–1902, Malaya and Sumatra.

Division of Botany, Dept. of Forests, Lae, New Guinea: J. S. Womersley and staff. Plant material over many years, New Guinea.

C. R. Stonor: 1949, New Guinea.

N. E. G. Crutwell: 1952 onwards, New Guinea.

M. Rosendahl: 1955, New Guinea.

Mrs S. Collenette: 1960–2–3, Sabah.

H. Sleumer: 1960, Sumatra; 1961, W. New Guinea; 1963, Malaya and Thailand.

Australian National University: 1960 onwards.

P. J. B. Woods: 1962, Sarawak and Malaya; 1968, Java and New Guinea.

B. L. Burtt: 1962 with Woods, 1967 with A. Martin, Borneo.

C. D. Sayers and A. N. Millar: 1963, New Guinea.

G. A. C. Herklots, 1964, New Guinea.

A. C. Jermy (British Museum): 1964–5, 1967, New Guinea.

J. Comber: 1964, Sabah.

R. D. Hoogland: 1964, E. New Guinea. Material to Australia.

M. Black: 1965, New Guinea; 1968, Java, Malaya and New Guinea.

C. J. Giles: 1965, Sabah.

L. Searl: 1965 onwards New Guinea.

E. F. Allen: 1966, Sabah.

M. Sumner: 1967, New Guinea to America.

M. and W. R. Philipson: 1968, New Guinea to New Zealand.

H. F. Winters and J. J. Higgins: 1970, New Guinea and Indonesia.

D. Stanton: 1971, New Guinea.

Appendix B

Glossary

The definitions given here apply to use of terms in this book.

aberrant characteristics different from the type
appressed lying flat
auxin a growth-promoting substance occurring in plants in minute quantities
bullate blistered or puckered
calcareous limey or chalky
cambium the layer of actively dividing cells between the wood and bark of stems or roots
candelabroid inflorescence a truss with several tiers of flowers
chlorosis leaves partially or wholly pale green or yellow
chromosome rod-like objects in a cell-nucleus which hold hereditary characteristics. In multiples of 13 in rhododendrons
ciliate fringed with hairs
clone the vegetatively produced progeny of a single individual
conspecific of the same species
contiguous neighbouring parts in contact
cultivar the special name given to a cultivated variety to distinguish it from other varieties of the same genus or species
deflexed bent outwards
dolomitic magnesium limestone
elepidote without scales
embryologic the development of the embryo into a plant
epiphyte a plant growing on another plant without being parasitic
fastigiate having erect branches
floccose bearing soft wool
fritted trace elements trace elements held in a form of powdered glass, available to plants
glabrous hairless
glandular possessing glands
glaucous greyish-blue; covered with a bluish or grey bloom

grex all the seedlings of one cross in hybridizing

hormone growth-promoting substance

hose-in-hose a second corolla within the first

indumentum a woolly or hairy covering found on leaves, young shoots, etc.

lacerate scale torn or irregularly cleft scale

lath house a structure for protecting plants made of narrow strips of wood fixed on a framework

lepidote covered with small scurfy scales

meristematic propagation cell division from a growing tip used to form a complete new plant

monotypic a species forming a genus by itself

NEFA North East Frontier Agency of India

petaloid resembling petals

pH the measurement of acidity or alkalinity

plastered indumentum indumentum stuck down leaving a smooth finish

polyploid having more than the usual number of chromosomes

precocious flowering before the leaves appear

puberulous slightly hairy

pubescent clothed with soft hairs

racemose stalked flowers on an unbranched main stem

recessive an apparently suppressed character which may appear in subsequent generations

recurved curved backwards or downwards

reflexed abruptly bent backwards or downwards

rugose covered with wrinkles

scale small disc-like dots found on leaves, shoots and flower parts

self sterile infertile with its own pollen

serpentine a magnesium silicate rock

setose covered with bristles

sibling sister seedlings of one cross in hybridizing

spreading limb outward expanding petal lobes of a tubular flower

stoloniferous sending out suckers from the main plant

sub-series sub-divisions of the groups into which rhododendrons are classified

terminal at the tip of a shoot

vegetative any means of propagating other than by seed

Bibliography

Bartrum, D., *Rhododendrons and Azaleas*, Foyle, London, 1964

Berrisford, Judith, *Rhododendrons and Azaleas*, Faber & Faber, London, 1964

Bowers, C. G., *Rhododendrons and Azaleas*, Macmillan, New York, 1936

Bowers, C. G., *Winter Hardy Rhododendrons and Azaleas*, Massachusetts Horticultural Society, Boston, 1954

Clarke, J. Harold (ed.), *Rhododendrons 1956*, American Rhododendron Society, Portland, Oregon, 1956

Clarke, J. Harold, *Getting Started with Rhododendrons and Azaleas*, Doubleday, New York, 1960

Clarke, J. Harold, (ed.), *Rhododendrons in Your Garden*, American Rhododendron Society, Portland, Oregon, 1961

Clarke, J. Harold (ed.), *Rhododendron Information*, American Rhododendron Society, Sherwood, Oregon, 1967

Cooper, R. E., 'Rhododendrons in Bhutan', American Rhododendron Society *Quarterly Bulletin*, April 1955

Cowan, J. M., *The Rhododendron Leaf*, Oliver and Boyd, Edinburgh, 1951

Cox, E. H. M., *Rhododendrons for Amateurs*, Country Life, London, 1924

Cox, E. H. M., *Farrer's Last Journey*, Dulau, London, 1926

Cox, E. H. M. and Cox, P. A., *Modern Rhododendrons*, Nelson, London, 1956

Forrest, G., 'Rhododendrons in China', *Gardeners Chronicle*, LI, 1323, 1912

Grootendorst, H. J., *Rhododendrons en Azaleas*, Nereniging voor Boskoope Culturen, Boskoop, 1954

Hooker, J. D., *Rhododendrons of the Sikkim Himalayas*, Reeve, London, 1849

Hume, H. H., *Azaleas, Kinds and Culture*, Macmillan, New York, 1949

Ingram, C., 'Dwarf Rhododendrons', *Rhododendron and Camellia Year Book*, Royal Horticultural Society, London, 1969

Kingdon Ward, F., *Rhododendrons for Everyone*, Gardeners Chronicle, London, 1926

Kingdon Ward, F., 'Rhododendrons in Burma, Assam and Tibet', *Rhododendron Year Book*, Royal Horticultural Society, 1947

Kingdon Ward, F., 'Rhododendrons in the Wild', *Rhododendron Year Book*, Royal Horticultural Society, 1949

Kingdon Ward, F., *Rhododendrons*, Latimer House, London, 1949

Kingdon Ward, F., 'Address at Society Meeting', *Rhododendron Society Notes*, III, 3, 1927

Kingdon Ward, F., *Burma's Icy Mountains*, Jonathan Cape, London, 1949

Kingdon Ward, F., *Plant Hunter's Paradise*, Jonathan Cape, London, 1937

Kingdon Ward, F., *Plant Hunting on the Edge of the World*, Victor Gollancz, London, 1930

Kingdon Ward, F., *The Riddle of the Tsangpo Gorges*, Edward Arnold, London, 1926

Kingdon Ward, F., *The Romance of Plant Hunting*, Edward Arnold, London, 1924

Krussman, J., *Rhododendrons*, Ward Lock, London, 1971

Leach, D. G., *Rhododendrons of the World*, Allen & Unwin, London, 1962

Lee, F. P., *The Azalea Handbook*, American Horticultural Society, Washington DC, 1952

Lee, F. P., *The Azalea Book*, Van Nostrand, London, 1954

Leiser, A. T., '*Rhododendron occidentale* on Alkaline Soil', *Rhododendron and Camellia Year Book*, Royal Horticultural Society, London, 1957

Millais, J. G., *Rhododendrons Species and the Various Hybrids* (2 vols), Longmans, Green, London, 1917 and 1924

Royal Horticultural Society, *The International Rhododendron Register*, London, 1958

Royal Horticultural Society, *The Rhododendron Handbook*, Part One: Rhododendron Species, London, 1956, 1963, 1967

Royal Horticultural Society, *The Rhododendron Handbook*, Part Two: Rhododendron Hybrids, London, 1956, 1964, 1969

Sleumer, H., *An Account of Rhododendron in Malesia*, P. Noordhoff N. V. Groningen, Netherlands, 1966

Stevenson, J. B. (ed.), *The Species of Rhododendron*, The Rhododendron Society, London, 1930 and 1947

Street, F., *Hardy Rhododendrons*, Van Nostrand, London, 1954

Street, F., *Azaleas*, Cassell, London, 1959

Street, F., *Rhododendrons*, Cassell, London, 1965

University of Washington Arboretum Foundation, *Handbook of Rhododendrons*, Seattle, 1946

Urquhart, B. Leslie, *The Rhododendron* (2 vols), The Leslie Urquhart Press, Sharpthorne, Sussex, 1958 and 1962

Van Veen, Ted, *Rhododendrons in America*, Sweeney, Krist & Dimm, Portland, Oregon, 1970

Wakefield, G. R., *Rhododendrons for Every Garden*, Collingridge, London, 1965

Watson, W., *Rhododendrons and Azaleas*, T. C. & E. C. Jack, Edinburgh, 1911

Wilding, E. H., *Rhododendrons: their names and addresses*, Sifton Praed, London, 1923

Wilding, E. H., 'Contour, Climate and Distribution', *Rhododendron Society Notes*, ii, 5, London, 1923

Wilson, E. H. and Rehder, A., *A Monograph of Azaleas*, Arnold Arboretum, Cambridge, Mass., 1921

Periodicals and Year Books

American Rhododendron Society, *Quarterly Bulletin*, Portland, Oregon, 1947 onwards

Australian Rhododendron Society, *Quarterly Journal*, Olinda, Victoria, 1959–61

Australian Rhododendron Society, *The Rhododendron* (Quarterly Journal), Olinda, Victoria, 1962 onwards

Tacoma Rhododendron Society, *Rhododendron* (successor to *Bulletin*), Tacoma, 1951–69

American Rhododendron Society, *Year Books*, Portland, Oregon, 1945–9

German Rhododendron Society, *Rhododendron und immergrune Laubgeholze Jahrbuch*, Rhododendron-Gesellschaft, Bremen, 1937–42, 1953 onwards

Rhododendron Association, *Year Books*, London, 1929–39

Royal Horticultural Society, *Rhododendron Year Books*, London, 1946–53

Royal Horticultural Society, *Rhododendron and Camellia Year Books*, 1954–71

Royal Horticultural Society, *Rhododendrons*, 1972

General Index

Aberconway, the late Lord, 52
Aitchison, J. E. T., 281
Allen, E. F., 282
alpine house, 39
aphids, 269
Armillaria mellea, 68, 132, 272–273
Asiatic beetles, 270–271
atmospheric pollution, 26
awards, 74

Bailey, F. M., 281
bark-split, 246, 275–276
Beer, L. W., 282
Berrisford, Judith, 59
Black, M., 188, 189, 282
blue lepidotes, hybridizing, 248
B – Nine, 37
bogs and marshes, 22
Booth, T. J., 281
Bor, N. L., 281
Boskoop Research Station, 247
botrytis, 263, 264, 274
Brinsley, R., 280
Brodick, 176
bud blast, 274
Burtt, B. L., 282

Caerhays, 231
caterpillars, 270
chlorosis, 57, 60, 276
clay soils, 52
climatic conditions in Britain, 46
  Europe, 47
  Australia, 47
  New Zealand, 47–48
  Africa, 48
  North America, 48–49
  South America, 49
  Asia, 49–50
colchicine, 250
cold frames, 255
Collenette, Mrs. S., 282
Comber, J., 282

continental climates, 40–42
Cooper, R. E., 20, 282
Cox, E. H. M., 24, 25, 142
Cox, P. A., 282
Creech, J. L., 282
Crown Commissioners, 242
Crutwell, N. E. G., 282
Curtis, C., 282
cuttings, 253
  airrooting, 260
  leaf-bud, 259
  preparation of, 257–258
  rooted, 259
  when to take, 256–257
  wounding of, 258
Cylindrocladium, 272

Davidian, H. H., 109
deadheading, 63–64
deficiencies, 276
Delavay, J. M., 280
diseases and pests in the wild, 25, 275
Doleshy, F., 151–152, 153, 282
drainage, 27
drought, 22–23, 62–63
drought and heat resistent hybrids, 243

Edinburgh Royal Botanic Garden, 100, 141, 190
elepidotes, dwarf, 241
epiphytes, 23–24, 27

Farges, P. G., 280
Farrer, R., 15, 25, 77, 105, 281
fatty acid esters, 37
fertilizers, 56–60
flowering young, breeding for, 244
flower shapes, 72
Forrest, G., 13, 14, 21, 22, 23, 32, 63, 281
Fortune, R., 280

frost damage, 275–276
frost-hardy flowers and buds, breeding for, 245
frost pockets, 27
fungicides, 258

galls, 273
Giles, C. J., 282
Gigha, 184
Glenarn, 131
Glendoick, 32, 33, 43, 88, 100, 102, 152, 194, 268
grafting, 261
grey-mould, 263, 264, 274
Griffith, W., 281
ground-covers, 68
gypsum, 51–52

Hanger, F., 39, 256
hanging baskets, 39
hardiness, breeding for, 244–246
hares, 268
Harrison, Mrs. R., 32
heated frames, 254
Hedge, I., 179, 282
Henny, R., 252
Herklots, G. A. C., 282
Higgins, J. J., 282
Hobbie, D., 245
Hoogland, R. D., 282
Hooker, Sir J. J., 280
'hormones' for rooting, 258
Hu, 281
Hutchison, P. C., 282
hybrids, elepidote orange, 211–212
  pink, 205–208
  red, 200–205
  white, 212–213
  yellow, 209–210
hybrids, lepidote blue, 213–215

Index of Rhododendrons

Note: Main page references appear in italic type